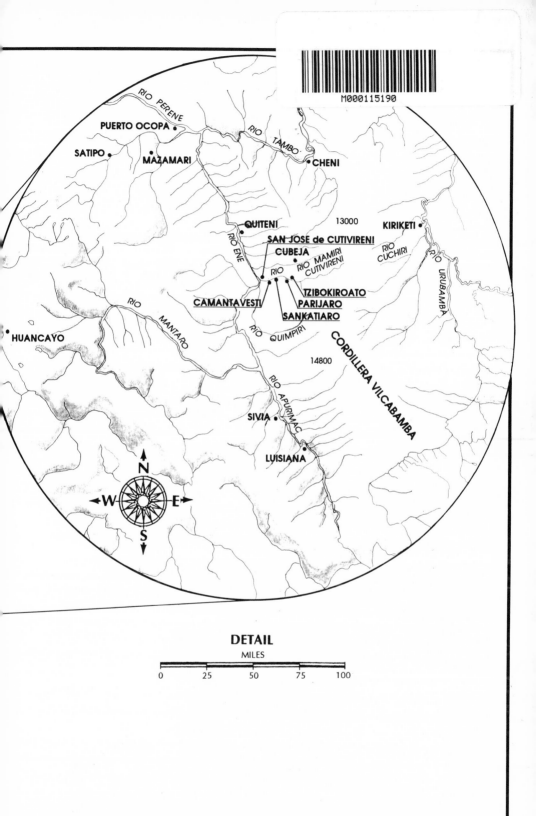

M000115190

DETAIL

MILES

0   25   50   75   100

Warriors in Eden

Other Books by
William and Marilyn Hoffer

Caught in the Act

Midnight Express

Every Other Man

Saved

Volcano

The Book of Granville

Not Without My Daughter

Mort! Mort! Mort!

Freefall

Cop Hunter

Victor Six

Adams v. Texas

Inside Out

The Senator

Betrayal

My Feudal Lord

Warriors in Eden

Friar Mariano Gagnon, O.F.M.,
with
William and Marilyn Hoffer

William Morrow and Company, Inc.
New York

It is the policy of William Morrow and Company, Inc., and it's imprints and affiliates, recognizing the importance of preserving what has been written, to print the books we publish on acid-free paper, and we exert our best efforts to that end.

Library of Congress Cataloging-in-Publication Data

Gagnon, Mariano.
    Warriors in Eden / Mariano Gagnon, with William and Marilyn Hoffer.
        p.   cm.
    Includes index.
    ISBN 0-688-11796-1
    1. Ashaninca Indians—Missions.   2. Ashaninca Indians—Social conditions.
3. Ashaninca Indians—Government relations. 4. Franciscans—Missions—Peru—Cutivireni River Region.   5. Sendero Luminoso (Guerilla group).   6. Cocaine industry—Peru—Cutivireni River Region. 7. Cutivireni River Region (Peru)—Social conditions.   8. Cutivireni River Region (Peru)—Politics and government.
    I. Hoffer, William. II. Hoffer, Marilyn Mona. III. Title.
    F3430.1.A83G34 1993
    266'.0089'983—dc20   92-41180
                                                                                                        CIP

Printed in the United States of America

First Edition

1 2 3 4 5 6 7 8 9 10

BOOK DESIGN BY WILLIAM MCCARTHY

In memory of Mario and Roy

ACKNOWLEDGMENTS

I wish to express my deepest gratitude to all those who contributed their resources and energies to the mission of San José de Cutivireni: to the legion of benefactors in Peru and elsewhere who, over the years, were not only generous with their financial support but with their moral support as well. I shall respect the wishes of many of them to remain anonymous.

I offer my recognition to the many dedicated people who, with a tender combination of love and perspiration, developed and sustained the mission: to the late Bishop Buenaventura León de Uriarte, who was instrumental in attracting me to Peru and whose missionary zeal continued to inspire me once I was there; to the late Bishop Luis Máestu, who had the vision and courage to publicly acknowledge his intention to ordain a native Ashaninka to sacred orders; and to the late Brother Pío Medina, whom I envied for his faith in the power of prayer.

My deep appreciation goes to Father Mario Brown, who helped lay the cornerstone of the mission of Cutivireni; to Father Tomás Martín, who knew how to forgive my shortcomings and whose friendship I cherish; to Father Teodorico Castillo, whose generosity and Franciscan poverty are a tribute to Peruvian missionaries and an inspiration to all of us; and to the nuns who labored at Cuti with unquestioned dedication.

My admiration and high esteem are extended to Doris Bourque, who initiated and for several years administered the medical clinic, a fine example of the lay missionary movement; to Michel Saenz, an impetuous and courageous Frenchman who became the big brother of the Ashaninka; to all the bush pilots who were a vital part of our lifeline, particularly Wayman Luy, who for many years flew and administered, under adverse circumstances, the mission plane, *Paz y Bien;* and to Armando Velarde Torres, the hero of this story.

To all of these individuals I say, *Que Dios se lo pague.* ("May God repay you.")

Numerous persons have contributed to the production of this book, and I must single out some for special mention: thanks to Father Flavian Walsh, vice provincial of the Franciscans of Holy Name Province, New York, for assisting my readjustment and offering numerous options; to Father Anselm Moons and Father Charles Finnegan of Franciscan Mission Service, for their comments on the manuscript, and for their personal hospitality; thanks to Jean Souza for her development of a comprehensible map; thanks to Pam Bernstein and Mel Berger of the William Morris Agency for their encouragement and guidance; thanks to our editor, Harvey Ginsberg, for the work of his sharp and talented pencil.

CONTENTS

*T*he vast, fertile valley in central Peru takes its name from the muddy Ene (pronounced "IN-ee") River that flows south to north. The valley lies between the towering Andes to the west and the nearly as formidable Vilcabamba Range to the east.

It is some of the earth's most pristine land. The numerous tributaries of the Ene flow east and west, feeding down from the highlands, eroding the soil, and creating intricate patterns in the topography. The headwaters of the Amazon are often found descending limestone cliffs in stunning cascades as they work their way toward the distant Brazilian border. Springs and rivers disappear underground and, just as suddenly, reappear. This inland side of Peru is subject to monsoonlike rains throughout the summer months of January, February, and March, which, at lower altitudes, create a natural greenhouse. The land is rife with timber and an exotic array of plant life. Banks of exquisite miniature orchids cling to the ground and to the bark of trees in the foothills and lowlands. The soil is hospitable to oranges, mangoes, bananas, pineapple, coconut, papaya, and avocados.

For centuries, the Ashaninka (pronounced "ah-SHA-nin-ka") tribe lived here in exquisite solitude. But by the latter decades of the twentieth century, the world was encroaching. The Ashaninka needed health care and job training and an introduction to modern economic realities. Most of all, they needed education. It was

11

for these purposes that with the assistance of numerous dedicated colleagues I cultivated a mission compound at the juncture of the Ene and Cutivireni rivers. The Ashaninka name their small settlements after the nearest river; thus, our mission was called Cutivireni, or Cuti, for short.

Cuti grew into a peaceful, thriving community. At the time that I began my work there, in 1969, I believed that the Ashaninka had at least thirty years in which to accomplish a transition into "civilized" society, but I was wrong.

I did not foresee the encroachment of the "narcos."

I did not predict the arrival of the terrorists.

The Ashaninka had only begun to learn about twentieth-century culture when it forced itself upon them in the form of government-sponsored settlers who gradually usurped more and more of their land. Before long, some of the settlers began to cultivate the coca plant, an activity that brought an influx of fortune seekers who sought to process the coca leaves into cocaine and ship it out of the rain forest to Colombia and points north. One of the more important narco facilities was located on an island in the Ene River, south of Cuti.

For a time, the narcos and the Ashaninka managed to coexist. Then the terrorists began to arrive.

Their leader was a charismatic revolutionary named Abimael Guzmán, a professor of philosophy at the University of San Cristóbal de Huamanga. In 1969, Guzmán and his fellow professors conducted a strike in protest of the high cost of tuition, which limited educational opportunities to the elite and perpetuated the harsh class system. After this, Guzmán went underground and spent some time defining and refining his theories, which ultimately developed into the most brutal and virulent form of communism. He recruited a cadre of intelligentsia who moved into teaching posts at various institutions throughout the country and quietly spread a gospel of bloody revolution.

Peru has always been controlled by an elitist society. In ancient days, the Incas conquered the land and forced the indigenous tribes to labor in slave conditions. The Spaniards picked up this theme when they invaded and manipulated Christian philosophy in an attempt to justify the exploitation of the "heathens." Even after Peru gained its independence from Spain, it retained a feudal style of government.

Today, although it displays the trappings of a democracy, Peru is still dominated by a social and political elite with strong ties to U.S. investment interests. The vast majority of the Peruvian population is composed of the remnants of the slaves who are today counted as free but remain in servitude to extreme poverty. This was fertile ground wherein Guzmán's vicious philosophies took root and grew.

In 1978, Guzmán resurfaced as the leader of the Communist Party of Peru for the Shining Path of José Carlos Mariátegui (the founder of Peru's first Communist party), commonly known as Sendero Luminoso. The terrorist group launched a People's War committed to the destruction of nearly every facet of Peruvian society to enable them to build a new order.

The movement grew strongest in the five *departamentos* that make up the mountainous spine of Peru. The Ene River valley, with its severe but central geography, was a natural lair. In this remote region, the terrorists established an alliance of convenience with the narcos. The terrorists offered protection; the narcos offered money. They shared a matrix of informants who had infiltrated the military, political, educational, and social systems.

The center of operations in the area, Sendero's Pentagon, was rumored to be in a maze of caves in an area called Ucherauto, near the Quimpiri River. The location was strategic. Peruvian military forces could clamp the headquarters into a vise with a three-pronged attack emanating from the Guardia Civil base in the town of Mazamari to the north, from the army base at Huancayo to the west, and from the naval base at Luisiana to the south. But Sendero had a lifeline to the east. If pressed, the terrorists could disappear into the roadless, poorly mapped terrain of the rain forest, where the rivers worked their way toward the treacherous Vilcabamba Range and beyond—to Brazil and the Amazon.

To utilize this option, Sendero's forces would have to move

north from the Quimpiri to a point where the Cutivireni merged with the Ene. From here, they would turn directly eastward, toward the haven of the rain forest, to flee along the one logical escape route—the Cutivireni River.

Only three things stood in their way: our mission, the Ashaninka, and me.

PART ONE

The People

When I arrived in 1969, the Ene River valley was an unspoiled land of peace and natural prosperity. I planned to take my time and study the area carefully before I established a presence among the Ashaninka tribe.

After twenty-one years in Peru (eight as a student and thirteen as a small-town padre), I had finally persuaded Bishop Buenaventura León de Uriarte, of the Vicariate of San Ramón, to allow me to attempt to set up a new mission for the Ashaninka. His permission was granted with reluctance, for he found it difficult to understand why I would bother with a handful of Indians when there were multitudes of other Peruvians who also had critical needs.

I grew up in New Hampshire, of French-Canadian stock mixed with Indian blood. I was told that my father's mother was a full-blooded Iroquois. Perhaps it was this latter influence of my heritage that ultimately drew me to the Ashaninka. Even today I do not fully comprehend my motivation. All I know is that for as long as I can remember I had been driven by an insatiable curiosity regarding Native Americans.

My mother always spoke highly about the Indians who lived near her rural Michigan home. She reminisced about how, when she was small, her mother would bake bread and set a loaf on an outside windowsill. Unseen, the Indians would take the bread and leave in its place a portion of venison, or some other form of barter. I found the silent ritual fascinating.

In fact, I found everything about Indians fascinating. As I had grown toward manhood I realized that I wanted, somehow, to work with Native Americans—the more primitive, the better—and when I heard about missionary opportunities in Peru, I made up my mind to pursue an adventurous life in the South American jungle. As a side benefit, I discovered that I had a certain affection for Saint Francis.

My decision to enter a Franciscan seminary in Peru was impetuous and selfish. I was only eighteen years old. But the rewards that came to me over the years are proof that God does, indeed, work in mysterious ways.

Perhaps the bishop understood that. Or perhaps my persistence wore him down.

Whatever the reason, I had his blessing when I embarked upon a week-long journey from Lima to a remote location in the Ene River valley, San José de Cutivireni, where I knew that an old Franciscan brother was laboring to help the Ashaninka. I left the coastal capital city of Lima and by stages made my way across the Andes to Huancayo, Ayacucho, San Francisco, and finally to a mission in Sívia. There, I hired a boat, a motor, and two Quechua men. "Can you take me to see Brother Pío?" I asked.

"*Si, padre,*" one of the guides replied. Every Quechua in the valley knew about Brother Pío's tiny mission, located at the point where the Ene and Cutivireni rivers intersected.

The Quechua are of Indian stock themselves, perhaps the most numerous subclass of a group of Peruvians also known as Serranos ("People of the Altitude"). They have been exploited for centuries, first by the Incas, then by the Spaniards, and, today, by anyone with an iota of power in Peru. The only people to whom the Quechua feel superior are the indigenous tribes of the rain forest.

It was the midst of the dry season. The Ene, which rages at times, was low and sluggish. On several occasions, the depth was insufficient for our large dugout canoe, known as a *casco,* and we had to hike along the riverbank, hauling the boat and our gear with us.

As we walked we were bombarded by *manta blanca* ("white cloud") insects that assaulted seemingly by the billions, biting fiercely at the exposed skin of our faces, necks, arms, and legs.

It was late afternoon when we finally reached the juncture of the Ene and the Cutivireni. We grounded the dugout on the shore and began to unload my meager store of supplies.

I glanced up and saw that a group of about a dozen men and boys had appeared, silently slipping from the edge of the forest. Some were dressed in cloth robes, in various hues of gray and brown, with contrasting vertical stripes. Others were bare-chested and clad only in shorts. A few had their faces painted with bright red pigment in a variety of designs composed of both straight and whorled lines. Each man and boy held a bow and arrow, tipped with iron-hard chontawood.

They stared at me, the gringo, with quiet wonder, but their eyes settled more warily upon my Quechua guides. The Quechua and the natives of this region suffered from a mutual distrust.

Nearly everyone in Peru calls these people Campas, and over the years, the term took on derogatory overtones. The epithet *Es un Campa* ("You are a Campa") had come to describe one who is uneducated, undesirable, and even savage: A Campa paints his face; a Campa is lazy—he does nothing but hunt and fish and eats *imoqui* (large, wormlike creatures found in the rotting wood of palm trees); you cannot communicate with a Campa, for few speak even a smattering of Spanish or Quechua. Sometimes, the even more derisive term *chuncho*—a difficult-to-translate word that implies dirt, filth, and scum—was applied.

But they refer to themselves as the Ashaninka, which means, simply, "the People."

The faces of this group on the riverbank reflected the delicate, light-tanned beauty of Polynesian stock, and, I supposed, their ancestry traced to the west, far across the Pacific Ocean. But it was not the Ashaninka past that concerned me; I was interested in their present and their future.

Now I was here, among them. What was I to do? What was I to say? I could not speak their language, nor could they speak mine. I requested simply, "Pío?"

The Ashaninka indicated their understanding, and motioned for me to follow them.

We entered the rain forest and immediately began a rapid, upward jaunt along a barely discernible path. At forty years of age, I considered myself to be in reasonably good shape, but I labored to keep up with the Ashaninka. These men and boys *flowed* along the forest floor, their bare feet easily handling the rocky terrain as I slipped and slid behind them, even though I was wearing comfortable, heavy-soled sneakers. The fabric of my shorts and T-shirt caught constantly on branches and briars, but the Ashaninka did not seem to be encumbered by their full-length robes.

There was a young man in the group, perhaps in his late teens or early twenties, who took a special interest in my presence. He tried out a few halting words of Spanish and seemed pleased to note understanding in my face.

We walked for ten or fifteen minutes before we emerged into a small clearing, where a few thatch-roofed huts with floors of hard-caked dirt composed the mission of San José de Cutivireni—Cuti, for short.

I had met Brother Pío Medina a few times over the years at meetings in Lima conducted by the province, which directed the work of all Franciscans in Peru. Pío received almost no support from either the Province or the Vicariate of San Ramón, which governed Church activities throughout central Peru. Instead, what resources Pío had scraped together came from the generosity of private donors in Lima. I had heard that he prayed daily for an American missionary to come to Cutivireni, because he believed that a gringo would have more access to money than a Peruvian padre. Pío was of Quechuan descent, in his seventies, dark-haired, short, and stocky. He greeted me with deference and enthusiasm, for he believed that I was the answer to his prayers. I did not have the heart to tell him, at the moment, that I had not yet decided to establish a base at Cuti, or that Bishop Uriarte had warned, "Don't ask me for any money."

Pío showed me around Cuti's primitive facilities, explaining that the huts were built by Ashaninka and were similar to the natives' own houses. One served as a chapel, one was a combination schoolhouse and dormitory for the few girls who studied here, and a third was where Pío and the boy students lived. The single amenity in Pio's hut was a *tushpa*, a wooden platform with shallow sides, filled with hardened clay and stones, that served as a cookstove. The staple of Pío's diet was peanuts, which he stored in a fifty-five-gallon drum and ate—raw, boiled, baked, or mashed. His bed was a pallet covered with mosquito netting.

Pío showed me where he and a few of the Ashaninka had begun work on an airstrip. They had cleared about sixty feet of land, felling huge trees with axes and digging and burning away at the stumps. There was much more work to do on the airstrip, and it was a critical venture if Cuti was ever to have access to the outside world.

Pío's subservient manner was typical of a mere brother's relationship to a padre, a hangover from the past when the brothers were regarded as little more than pious servants to the more exalted priest. But much lay below Brother Pío's servile exterior. He was, I thought, very proud of his humility. I was somewhat uncomfortable in this anachronistic role, and I pointed out to him that I had much to learn. For a time, I wished to merely observe.

Before four o'clock every morning, Pío rose from his slumbers and journeyed to the hut that served as a chapel, where he knelt before a crude altar and commenced the prayers that encompassed the bulk of his day. In the school, Pío taught the boys, and a young woman teacher (who doubled as Pío's cook and laundress) instructed the girls. Students left their families to journey here, sometimes from great distances. Even in this remote corner of the world, there was an understanding that education was vital to survival in an uncertain future. Pío taught the students a bit of Spanish, but much of their time was spent on the catechism, and he led them in interminable repetitions of the Rosary.

The old brother's philosophies left no room for compromise. If you were not baptized as a Roman Catholic, you were doomed to hell. As a Quechua, Pío was subject to the prevalent prejudices, but he rose above them. He recognized that each of the Ashaninka was endowed with a mortal soul that was in need of salvation. His solemn quest was to prevent the Ashaninka from falling into the clutches of one or another of the various groups of Protestant missionaries who "competed" for the souls of the natives. The bishop had granted him the authority to baptize, and he did so with a vengeance. At Cuti, if you wanted a new machete, all you had to do was allow Pío to baptize one of your children.

From the moment of my arrival, I was uncomfortably aware that Pío and I were at cross purposes. Pío's total quest was to convert the natives to Catholicism; mine was more complex. I wanted to delay, for as long as possible, the inevitable encroachment of civilization. But at the same time, I wanted to prepare the Ashaninka, through education, to cope with the coming changes, and I wanted to sensitize the rest of the world to their existence and their vulnerability. Perhaps most important, I simply wanted to be with them.

Before I decided on a permanent location for my work, I wanted to conduct a census of the Ashaninka population. I was in the midst of this task when a Peruvian military commander asked if I would conduct a service for his troops to celebrate the Feast of Santa Rosa. The site was Mazamari, east of Satipo, and the only way I could get there was to walk. I conducted the requested service at the training base of a paratroop unit of the elite Guardia Civil, known as the Sinchis, and developed an immediate affinity for the troops. Seeing this, the commander asked if I would be willing to give a series of lectures. I accepted the invitation on the spot, for I reasoned that the Sinchis might be willing and able to provide help in the future to the new mission.

The paratroops listened politely to my lectures, even though they were toughened soldiers and I was a tenderfoot padre. Then one day at breakfast a Sinchi officer—a man with the intriguing name of Captain Cheyenne, who fancied himself a tough guy— asked me sarcastically, "Would you jump?"

"Why wouldn't I jump?" I responded, even as I chided myself: Mariano, what are you doing? You are forty years old.

Captain Cheyenne called out to a couple of his troops, "Set up the tower."

The training tower was situated at the bank of the Mazamari River, positioned in such a way that it seemed to overlook a gigantic void. From the top, trussed into a harness, I could see nothing, and had to accept by faith alone that there was earth somewhere below. Captain Cheyenne eyed me skeptically, which only strengthened my determination. I gritted my teeth and stepped into the void. A rush of air hit me, followed by the jarring but comforting strain of straps against my shoulder. The shock drove the air from my lungs. Almost instantly the jump was over, and I found myself dangling in air, with my feet just off the ground. I felt like a worm hanging from the end of a fishhook. Finally, I released myself from the harness and rolled to the turf.

One of the Sinchis chided, "Sure is tougher than handing out little holy pictures, isn't it Padre?"

"How was that?" Captain Cheyenne asked.

You're not going to get the best of me, I vowed. Aloud I said, "Wonderful. Let's do it again."

After several jumps off the training tower, Captain Cheyenne, with a new measure of respect in his voice, asked, "Why don't you join our crew? We have no chaplain."

"Yeah," I agreed with a nod.

Before long, Captain Cheyenne had secured permission for me to be enrolled in the full training course; now I was to be both a padre and a paratrooper.

Months of intense effort passed. My aching muscles long remembered the innumerable practice jumps and the prebreakfast runs that were several miles long. Near the end of my training, Bishop Uriarte came for a look. Old and ill, reeking to high heaven as a result of a colostomy bag, he watched as my harness was tethered to a Jeep and I was dragged along the ground. When I had extricated myself and inventoried my bruises, the bishop grinned and asked, "Gringo, are you sure you want to go through this?" I could tell that he was proud of me; he was even more pleased when I told him that three fourths of the Sinchis were receiving the Eucharist on Sundays. I laughingly suggested that Sinchi training be added to the seminary curriculum.

At least twenty thousand Ashaninka were scattered throughout the region. Many had fled from the highlands to elude the steady encroachment of the Quechua settlers from the north, the west, and the south. My census showed that the area in and around Brother Pío's mission at Cutivireni was now the centerpoint of the Ashaninka population, and I agreed to Pío's pleas to settle there.

As soon as I arrived to take up residence, Pío introduced me to the family who lived nearby.

I recognized some of the faces I had initially encountered on the riverbank, and one of them was the young man who had attempted to communicate with me in Spanish. He said that his name was Pepe García. I was delighted to see the children at play, swatting away at a featherlike toy in a game that resembled badminton. I joined their game and quickly became friends with the youngsters.

Over the course of several weeks, Pepe and I made several forays into the jungle. If we were going to build more facilities for Cuti, I wanted to study other nearby sites. I agreed with Pío that completion of the airstrip was a top priority, and I liked the area near the site. For one thing, it was far enough from the river to be a comfortable distance from the *manta blanca* plague.

Pepe's Spanish was minimal, yet he had a natural facility for understanding the nuances of my voice inflections and gestures. We communicated well, and soon Pepe agreed to lead me across the swift currents of the Cutivireni River to meet some of the families who lived on the south bank.

One of our first excursions was to the home of Martín, the shaman, or medicine man. We crossed the Cuti just east of the juncture with the Ene and then moved farther east, following the riverbank. Our progress was impeded at times by fortresslike formations of immense boulders that forced us to detour into the jungle's interior. To me, there seemed to be no path through the forest, but Pepe showed me spots where others had bent twigs to signal the way.

I was panting heavily by the time Pepe stopped and pointed through a gap in the opening between trunks of huge, white-barked trees to a clearing ahead. A handful of crude huts was visible. Off to one side was a cultivated patch of yucca plants.

Following Pepe, I edged over to an invisible boundary. We stood there silently, with our backs turned toward the huts and our arms folded, waiting for the appearance of Martín.

After a time I was aware of a quiet approach from the direction of the huts. From behind us, a voice said, *"Aviro?"* ("Do you exist?")

"Narobe" ("I do"), Pepe replied.

"What did you come here for?" Martín asked.

That was a deep question. I was in the early stages of a quest that could not be explained in a few words; on the other hand, the Ashaninka seemed to have a highly functional intelligence network, and Martín had probably heard about me already. Pepe simply announced that we were here for a visit.

Martín appeared to be in his mid-twenties. He was quite tall for an Ashaninka, with a muscular body, chiseled features, and intelligent eyes. He invited us to follow him. We turned and walked toward an empty hut within the small compound that was reserved for visits.

Soon after we entered the hut, a woman appeared, bearing a large, shallow half-gourd filled with a drink known as *piarinsti,* a fermented brew produced from the yucca root. She did not enter the hut but waited for Martín to step outside and accept the gourd. He returned to us, poured a portion of the liquid into a smaller gourd, and passed it to Pepe, who presented it to me. I sipped the tart, cool liquid and returned the bowl to Pepe. In turn, he drank and returned the *piarinsti* to Martín. Our host drank last. The significance of this ritual was clear; it was the Ashaninka variation on the classic scriptural theme: "The last shall be first."

Following the *piarinsti,* roasted monkey was served in a common dish. I watched Pepe and Martín carefully so that I could observe the proper etiquette, and I realized that each person was supposed to scoop a portion from the gourd and pass it on to another.

Wheat is not grown in the Ene River valley; the natives do not know what bread is. There are no grapes; wine is a foreign substance. Yet this stylized method of sharing a meal with others struck me as genuine communion, perhaps in its purest form.

We sat there for some time, sipping *piarinsti* and talking.

Pepe and Martín chatted in their rapid, expressive tongue. Occasionally a word or two of Spanish filtered through, but most of the conversation was beyond my comprehension. Yet both of them appeared to understand me completely.

I tried to answer Martín's question: "What did you come here for?" Indeed, what was a gringo priest doing here in their world? I had come to evangelize, and what I found was a true gospel living absent of all the paraphernalia of twentieth-century accumulation that has overshadowed the true meaning of gospel teaching— Christianity in its purest form. In the words of Pope Paul VI, to evangelize meant "liberation from everything that oppresses human beings." Yet I wondered: How does that goal translate to reality in such an environment?

Pepe tried his best to explain my reasons for being there, repeating what I had told him in several conversations. It was inevitable that change would encroach upon Ashaninka life. In the short term, I hoped to slow the pace of that change. The Ashaninka lived in harmony with the land, and I wanted to be around to help them cope with pressures that would surely come and that they would just as surely fail to comprehend.

Martín was perceptive. Despite his isolation, he knew that I was right. He had been as far as Satipo, the nearest encroachment of what we called civilization. He had seen the wonders available there—shiny-bladed steel machetes that made quick work of the bark on a yucca root; pots and pans that were far more durable than gourds; axes that could easily fell the hard-wooded chonta tree; short-wave radios that could broadcast strange dialogues from faraway places; bolts of cloth; hard candies and Chiclets for the children; and that most wonderful of hunting tools, the 16-gauge shotgun.

Martín had also noted that Satipo was populated largely by Quechuas. What he had difficulty in understanding was the inevitable fact that the Quechuas would continue to encroach upon Ashaninka territory.

If change was coming, and *if* I hoped to prepare the Ashaninka for it, how would I accomplish this?

Pepe communicated my answer in a word that Martín understood: education.

CHAPTER TWO

I told Brother Pío that I was going to the Summer Institute of Linguistics, located at Lake Yarinacocha near Pucallpa, in the northeastern portion of the country, not far from the Brazilian border. My purpose was to recruit a teacher. The institute, affiliated with the Wycliffe Bible Translators, had been established more than twenty years earlier and, in my opinion, offered the most effective educational program to aid the Indian populations of Peru. It had studied over sixty native language groups and hundreds of dialects in an attempt to bring education and Christian teaching to the various tribes. The institute enrolled natives from numerous areas of the country, taught them Spanish, schooled them in trades, and sent them back home to teach others. Bill Kindberg, a faculty member of the institute, had translated the entire New Testament into the phonetic language of the Ashaninka.

Brother Pío's response to my suggestion was "No! They are Protestants!"

"The terms *Protestant* and the *devil* are *not* synonymous," I responded.

But to Brother Pío, they were. For years, the people of the Summer Institute had been trying to establish a presence at Cuti, but Pío would have none of it. Now, he dropped to his wrinkled old knees and wept like a baby. "You are Satan personified if you ally with the Protestants," he announced.

Ignoring Pío, I journeyed to Pucallpa and invited the institute to provide us with a teacher. They responded by sending a full-blooded Ashaninka named Miguel and his wife, Natasha.

It was gratifying to see how many of the Ashaninka wished to take advantage of the opportunity. Our school was quickly filled with students, including many adults. Pío accepted their presence grudgingly.

I enjoyed the company of the children immensely. As with children all over the world, one of their main activities was to emulate the adults. I could sit and watch for hours as they painstakingly painted their faces, fashioning intricate designs from the oily, brilliant red achiote berry and an equally vivid black pigment produced from an assortment of roots. They stored the dye in small vials of hollow bamboo reeds and applied it with care, using small twigs as paintbrushes and glancing into bits of mirrors somehow acquired from the outside world. An Ashaninka could tell if another was happy or sad, belligerent or flirtatious, simply by noting the design and colors of the face painting. I decided that this custom was not much different from the way we adorn ourselves in so-called civilized society.

As soon as they could walk and talk, boys hunted birds with tiny bows and arrows, and the girls helped their mothers process the yucca root. Young boys chopped firewood; young girls carried huge baskets full of yucca on their backs, held in place by straps across their foreheads. An Ashaninka parent rarely had to administer discipline; childhood disobedience seldom occurred. They were happy youngsters; their laughter, when they romped naked in the forest rivers, was shrill, sharp, free—and angelic.

The boys and I loved to spar, shuffling our feet in the dirt and raining mock blows upon one another. Often, in the clearing around the mission, I enjoyed the clamorous excitement of their *fútbol* games; throw a soccer ball in amidst a group of Ashaninka boys, and they will amuse themselves for hours.

One morning a young fellow arrived and announced that he was going to school. I knew him from some of my visits across the river, and I said, "That is great, Justín."

I followed him into the schoolhouse hut and watched him march up to Miguel. "What is your name?" Miguel asked.

"Carbólico," the youngster replied.

I was confused. I was *sure* that this was Justín.

Miguel laughed at my consternation and explained that the Ashaninka guard their identity closely, for if an enemy learned one's personal name, he could tell it to the shaman, who might cast a harmful spell. This presented the Ashaninka with a unique problem, for in Peru, everyone is required to provide a Christian name and the surnames of both parents for all documents. Without such documents, one could not enroll in school, vote—or even purchase a bus ticket. The Ashaninka were not about to reveal their true names to a government official, so they simply adopted "civilized" names that they heard elsewhere: Juan, Pedro, Natasha, Greenwood, Taylor, Johnson. Such identities were transitory, and would be changed at whim.

Brother Pío theorized that Justín had heard, somewhere, of carbolic soap and decided that he liked the name. "Tomorrow he might be Hermano or Gertrude," Pío said with a chuckle. "Out here"—he waved his hand toward the jungle—"we even have a Hitler and a Stalin."

I did not foresee a mission in the traditional sense, one that would evolve into a town with all the amenities and all the problems that accompany them. My long-term goal was to persuade the government of Peru to preserve the area around Cuti as a national park, immune from further settlement. Thus protected, it would retain its unblemished beauty and remain safe from those who would disrupt the natural harmonies of life in the valley. (Parque Nacional de Cutivireni—Plan Piloto para América Latina, an idea that I had appropriated from the Pan American Union, suggested that Cuti could be used as a model program for all of South America.) One critic scoffed, "What do you want to do—create a zoo for the Ashaninka?" I explained my concept: The mission itself would not be part of the public lands. In the surrounding jungle, the Ashaninka could live their lives as they always had. Those who chose to could come to the mission to learn language skills and a trade. They would have options.

I wrote scores of letters to various government ministries and, over time, built a base of support. Money trickled in for education and health care.

But more help came from the private sector. Brother Pío told me about the Pardo family in Lima, who had provided considerable support for the early work at Cuti. Like most of Peru's upper class, the Pardos could trace their genealogy back almost to the time of the conquistadores, both in Peru and Mexico. At one time, the family firm was one of the country's largest producers of sugarcane and also owned a number of subsidiary companies, including newspapers and textile mills. The businesses were managed by a group of family members, most of whom had been educated in England by the Benedictines.

My first chance to meet the family was when Juan Pardo and his wife Mari came for a visit, bringing along their friends Graham and Nancy Curtis; British-born Graham was a broker for Lloyds of London in Lima. Brother Pío asked if I would take a *casco* to meet our guests upriver at an experimental farm in Pichari, run by the Benedictines.

I was impressed. The Pardos were leaders in Peru's tiny elite society, and the Curtises were prominent in the business world, yet they fit right into the simple austerity of jungle life. Mari, accustomed to being waited on by a retinue of servants, cooked dinner over a hot fire that spewed smoke in her face; Nancy pitched in eagerly. They uttered no words of complaint about the giant cockroaches that lived in the thatching of our houses, and all four of our guests used the primitive outhouse facilities without flinching.

The visit was the beginning of a deep and lasting friendship. From then on, whenever I journeyed to Lima, I visited the Pardos and Curtises. They, in turn, introduced me to other members of their social set, who, over the course of many years, helped finance many of our mission activities.

To the Ashaninka, I stressed the point that Cuti was not my

mission but *our* mission, and anything we accomplished, we would do together. I told them that I had friends in Lima who were willing to donate money; that money was not mine, but *ours.*

Through discussions with Pepe, Martín, and others, we decided that the first priority was to complete the airstrip that Pío had started so that we might ferry in supplies from the outside world. The process took about a year. Using hand axes and push-pull saws and the strong backs of the natives, we felled the trees, burned the enormous stumps, and filled in the holes with dirt and rocks, which we then tamped down. Each small section of the airstrip required an inordinate amount of labor—but labor was our major asset.

Working on the airstrip was backbreaking toil and torturously slow, and I finally decided to journey to Mazamari to ask my friends at the Sinchi base to assist us. There, I was able to convince about twenty of them to return to the mission with me, and we decided to go in by parachute.

As the Sinchis' old DC-3 circled over the partially completed airstrip at an altitude of little more than a thousand feet, the always-curious Ashaninka heard the roar of the engine and gathered, looking skyward. One by one, the Sinchis and I jumped from the plane and began our descent. When the Ashaninka saw me spiral to the earth, drop, roll, and gather my fatigue-patterned parachute, many of them fell to their knees, holding their sides, laughing in delight and surprise. The middle-aged padre, who was a lackluster hunter and a barely adequate fisherman, had garnered a bit of machismo respect.

The Sinchis were a great help to us. They used dynamite to extract huge tree roots that protruded from the surface of the airstrip, and they added their own strong backs to our assortment of workers.

When the airstrip was finally finished, we registered it in Lima. Government officials came out to measure it to make sure that it met their bureaucratic requirements. Then they pronounced that it legally belonged to the government of Peru—although the cost of its upkeep would be our responsibility.

We did not care about the ownership, for we had our link to the outside world. Now we could fly in food, medicine, blankets, radios, and construction supplies from Satipo and even faraway Lima—not to mention cigarettes and an occasional bottle of Scotch.

During this same period, several Ashaninka families moved closer, building their huts in a small cluster at the far end of the airstrip; gradually the settlement took on the appearance of a small town. Martín ministered as best he could to the medical needs of the natives, using traditional herbal remedies; one treatment consisted of playfully blowing tobacco smoke on the head of the sufferer.

Ashaninka culture does not generally require the presence of a strong leader, but each tiny settlement is more or less under the direction of one man, and at Cuti, that gradually became Pepe's role; I thought of him as the mayor, and, indeed, he was entrusted with the responsibility of keeping the paperwork that the government required, such as birth certificates and voter-registration rolls. Neither he nor any of his people knew what the papers signified, nor did they care, but I thought Pepe comprehended when I told him that he had to keep the papers in a safe place.

The daily routine of the Ashaninka was clearly defined. The men hunted and fished and carried the news from family to family. They hunted only for survival, and they often had to cover vast distances in search of their prey. The men considered themselves to be the providers and patriarchs, but the women were the ones who held the society together. When a man and woman married, the man was generally drawn in as a part of the woman's family.

The Ashaninka cultivated yucca much as they bred children. Yucca was the staple of the diet, the staff of life. It was the man who cleared the land—at least two acres per family—and it was the man who thrust the yucca shoots into the ground. But it was the woman who weeded, nurtured, cultivated, and harvested.

Yucca root, when baked, fried, or boiled, is highly nutritious, as evidenced by the wiry but muscular stature of the young men and their preference for plump-fleshed women. Yucca was most prized as the primary ingredient of *piarinsti,* and making the brew was a daily ritual. Women sat next to baskets piled high with yucca root. With razor-sharp knives and machetes, they slashed along the lengths of roots and peeled off the bark. They chopped the roots into small pieces and pitched them into pots of water sitting over open wood fires. Once boiled, the yucca was mashed and worked into a paste. Women and girls chewed mouthfuls of this mixture, like cud, and spat them back into the pot. The brew was then allowed to ferment. As they worked, the women gossiped about the latest (usually imaginary) love triangle. The natives drank gallons of *piarinsti* every day, and this promoted an abandoned, exaggerated laughter, which at times continued until the wee hours of the morning.

During my occasional trips to Satipo, I boarded at the Franciscan parish house, located on the north side of the town's central plaza. Satipo was a conduit between Lima and the primitive rain forest. In the shops surrounding the plaza, salt, sugar, axes, flashlights, shotguns, transistor radios, and other cherished goods were swapped for the commerce of the jungle: cacao beans, coffee, oranges, bananas, beautiful, lush papayas, and lumber.

At the parish, I could always count on a friendly greeting from Soledad, a lovely young Ashaninka woman who had lived with and worked for the nuns in Satipo since she was a child. Her name meant "Solitary" or "Alone one." On one of my visits, Soledad was nowhere to be found. When I asked about her, the nuns related the story in hushed, seemingly reluctant tones. Soledad was pregnant, they announced, and despite her years of diligent service, they had been forced to ask her to leave. They told me that the father was Rigoberto. I knew him. He was a reed-slim, high-strung, somewhat restless young Ashaninka man.

The nuns assumed that I would agree with their action. With lowered eyes they muttered, "What would people have said? What would people have thought?"

I raged, "You kicked her out on the streets at the time when she needs you the most!"

I took my anger to the streets of Satipo and was able to locate Soledad. Her sad eyes suddenly brightened when I told her that we would welcome her at Cuti.

Soledad moved back to the jungle and became my housekeeper and cook. In time, she gave birth to a beautiful baby girl.

Matías Miranda left the Franciscan settlement upriver at Sívia to join us at Cuti. He was a genial young man, quiet and intelligent. With a detached grin on his face, he puffed on a cigarette held from underneath, in the European manner, as he listened to me tell a group of Ashaninka, "Don't ever be ashamed of your customs. You received them from God. You should be proud of them. Tasorensi does not want you to change; He only wants to love you." The Ashaninka have no external liturgy, but they very much believe in God, whom they call either Tasorensi or Pava. To me, the image of Tasorensi, the white-tailed hummingbird, was far more beautiful than the melancholy dove of classic Christian tradition. Matías told me in passable Spanish that he understood and appreciated my words.

Matías's young wife, Olga, came to work at the mission, helping wherever she was needed, handling basic tasks of cleaning and cooking, working side by side with Soledad. Her broad, open smile was warm and friendly, and her wide-set eyes held a mischievous glint. Shining black hair hung past her shoulders, framing a face that epitomized the beauty of the lightly bronzed Ashaninka. I enjoyed teasing Olga, frequently imploring her to run off to Cubeja and marry me. Cubeja was a particularly foreboding terrain that Pepe had told me about, higher up in the mountains. From Cuti, one could see Cubeja and its majestic waterfalls, and I had developed a minor obsession about visiting it. Pío warned me, "Nobody has been able to penetrate that jungle. It is dangerous." He said that the journey, even for the hardy Ashaninka, involved a full week's trek across precipitous cliffs.

When I teased Olga, she returned the banter. "You are no good for me," she countered. "Matías hunts and brings home the fish, the monkey, the tapir, and the boar. You—you are good for nothing." Still, she could never hold back a giggle as she served the whole baked yucca root. When a woman presented the yucca root to a man, it was an agreement to marriage; the Ashaninka recognized it as an oversized phallic symbol.

One day Matías, during the height of passion, abandoned his usual temperate behavior and bit deeply into Olga's nipple. She retaliated by smashing him over the head with the butt of a shotgun, then ran to Brother Pío for treatment of her wounds. A few minutes later I walked in to find that Pío had attached a wad of cotton to a two-foot stick, dipped it into iodine, and was attempting to swab the wound at long distance. With his head turned away, he jabbed in the direction of the bare breast.

I could not resist teasing the pious old man. "Pío, what do you think you are treating there, a bomb?" I chided. "Here is your opportunity. Make the best of it. This could be your last chance—make the most of it. I promise you, it will not explode!"

Almost all the Ashaninka had been pushed into the Ene River valley by encroaching civilization. Most came from the various nearby river regions, but others were born and raised higher in the mountains, where life was harsh; they tended to be more aggressive. Such was the case with old Gregorio and his extended, rambunctious clan.

They had lived in a region called the Gran Pajonal, northeast of Satipo, a treeless plateau centered in a wedge of land between the Tambo and Perené rivers, and we shared similar feelings about the two other Franciscan missions in central Peru, ostensibly serving the Ashaninka. Gregorio and I, in our separate ways, had found them disappointing. Gregorio had been born and raised near the mission at Obenteni in the Gran Pajonal. At the time that the mission was established, the Gran Pajonal was the center of Ashaninka culture, but the missionaries had brought about radical change. The plateau was abundant with natural grasses, and the good brothers of Obenteni reasoned that cattle would flourish there. Considering the Ashaninka to be relatively worthless, the missionaries had encouraged the migration of "good Catholic" Quechua settlers, who established their herds and requisitioned portions of the land. Some Ashaninka were employed—or coerced—as cheap labor, but most gradually migrated, following the Ene south toward more isolated regions. The mission at Obenteni flourished—producing, for example, Peru's finest coffee—but it no longer served the Ashaninka.

Gregorio's clan had moved near the second, newer mission at Puerto Ocopa, midway between Satipo and Obenteni. Originally founded as a refuge for abandoned Ashaninka children, the mission was now under the direction of Father Teodorico Castillo, a man of extraordinary energy and dedication who almost never allowed himself a respite from his work. Father Castillo, who truly loved and respected the Ashaninka, was committed to the belief that the Ashaninka had to assimilate into modern society—the sooner the better. While this sounded like a realistic approach, I could not help but wonder: Do we have to be so realistic? Do the Ashaninka *have* to change overnight? Must we arbitrarily impose our culture upon them? Why can't we just accept them, and love them as one more variation in God's glorious world?

Father Castillo was a good man, and he meant well when he contended, "There is no choice. Is it fair to give them false hope? Must we prolong the agony? The Western culture will take over. It is inevitable."

I was overcome by the complexity of the issue. It is a simple thing to provide an Ashaninka with a manufactured shirt, but then, how was he supposed to keep it clean? The traditional, loose-flowing *cushma* did not gather dirt and grime like a shirt; one could clean it by pounding it against a rock on the riverbank. But a shirt needed to be laundered, and for that, one needed soap. And what happened when a button was ripped loose? One needed a needle and thread, and the ability to sew. Each tiny advance brought with it additional problems. Many of the Ashaninka at Puerto Ocopa were out of their element and, to me, appeared disoriented.

After a series of altercations with the rigid Father Castillo, Gregorio and his family appeared at Cuti and provided a fascinating study in the Ashaninka's struggle between the past and the present. Gregorio was older than I, but he could hike barefoot along the mountain trails with the agility and energy of a youngster. Puffing calmly on his pipe, he regarded the world through the knowing eyes of experience. I affectionately called his wife La Vieja, "the Old Lady."

He had five sons and five daughters. One son was in Lima, but Nicolás, Teodoro, Juan, and Pablo came with him to Cuti. Of the sons, Nicolás was at once the most tempestuous and promising. Father Castillo's mission, despite operating with very limited resources, had sent him (and several other Ashaninka) to trade school, in Huancayo and Lima. Nicolás was clearly proud of his educational status, and advertised it by a preference for store-bought shorts and T-shirts instead of the traditional *cushma*. He enjoyed flashing his wristwatch. Most of the Ashaninka played *fútbol* barefoot, but Nicolás wore cleated shoes. The strict Catholic education had done little to suppress his colorful vocabulary, and he taught me many useful swearwords, in both Spanish and Ashaninka.

Of the daughters, I grew closest to Cecilia, the most levelheaded and articulate of the bunch; and I kept a watchful eye on her sister Claudia, an attractive young woman, high-strung and full of intrigue, who came up only to my shoulders in height.

They were a fiery group, but I grew to like them immensely, and they served to remind me that the Ashaninka are no different from the rest of us. They, too, are subject to the seven capital sins.

Shortly after the family's arrival, Claudia's husband, Alejandro, died of tuberculosis, leaving his widow in what, to an Ashaninka woman, is a desperate limbo. Who would hunt and fish for her? Who would plant the yucca?

My first hint of Claudia's plight came during a visit to Father Castillo's mission at Puerto Ocopa. The nuns drew me aside and asked, in excited whispers, if I knew what was going on between Claudia and Pedro.

Pedro, a Quechua from Satipo, was a talented mechanic who had come to work with us. The Ashaninka could tolerate the presence of a Quechua in their midst, especially if he pulled his weight and worked for the good of the community, as Pedro did—but it was rare for them to socialize.

The nuns' question puzzled me on two levels. As far as I knew, there was nothing going on between Pedro and Claudia. But even more perplexing was the efficiency of the mysterious long-distance rumor mill. I assured the inquisitive sisters that their concern was ill founded, but they were insistent. "They are having an affair," one of them declared. Their tongue-clucking curiosity did not surprise me. Perhaps the celibate life-style helps to create the tittering ambivalence that so often accompanies matters relating to the flesh.

When I returned to Cuti, I asked Pedro if the accusation was true. He denied it, and I had no reason to doubt him. I let the matter drop.

But that very evening Pedro came to me in panic and confessed that he was, indeed, involved with Claudia. Now the rumor had spread through Cuti and Claudia's father, Gregorio, had threatened to kill him. Trembling with fear, Pedro asked if he could take refuge in my house. Somewhat confused, I let him in. In matters of sexual dalliance, the Ashaninka blame the woman, not the man, considering the female to be responsible for the decision to acquiesce. So why was Gregorio angry with Pedro? Perhaps he was upset that his daughter had taken up with a Quechua, but was there more to it?

Almost before I knew what was happening, Gregorio and several of his sons surrounded my house, demanding that I turn over Pedro. This is trouble! I thought. I immediately got on the radio to Satipo and arranged for an airplane to evacuate the frightened young man. Then I grabbed my pistol and went outside to face Gregorio.

"Cool down," I demanded, making sure that Gregorio took note of the gun at my side. He began to protest, but I shouted him down. "I'm going to count to ten," I warned. "Then I'm going to start shooting." The group dispersed, but I knew that they were very angry with me.

By the next morning, Gregorio was calmer, but he was still argumentative. He confronted me, claiming that I had no right to turn his daughter over to Pedro.

"I did no such thing," I told him. "Who told you that?"

"Claudia told me," Gregorio insisted.

Now I had a better understanding of Gregorio's wrath. He was upset not only with Pedro but with me! I knew that I had to straighten out this mess quickly. I sent for Claudia, and under the stern eye of her father, she reluctantly admitted that she had lied about my involvement. "I was scared," she said.

Gregorio took his daughter off to settle their differences, and I tried to center my attention on the morning mass. Ironically, this was December 8, the Feast of the Immaculate Conception.

No sooner had I finished saying the mass when another irate father called Cristóbal appeared, with fire in his eyes and a bow and arrow in his hands. "Pedro has been sleeping with my daughter," he accused.

I grabbed the weapon from him and was about to speak when I heard the welcome sound of the airplane that I had summoned the day before. With dispatch, I whisked Pedro to the airstrip and sent him and his libido back to Satipo. A Spanish expression flashed through my mind: If your shorts were made of metal, they'd always be ringing.

The Pardos offered to provide the mission with a new Ford tractor, which was disassembled and shipped to Cuti on about fifteen separate flights. The toughest task was to transport the tires, which had to be squeezed out of shape in order to fit into a Cessna 206. Juan and Mari Pardo came along for the delivery, bringing a mechanic named Salazar to reassemble the parts.

The Ashaninka—especially Matías—watched this procedure with intense curiosity. In their own way, the Ashaninka were very clever with machinery. They could not decipher the pictures and diagrams in an instruction manual, but if they had the opportunity to watch a mechanic at work, they could copy the procedure immediately.

I was extremely grateful for the gift of the tractor, but on a daily basis, I did not wish to give the Ashaninka anything; I wanted them to learn the concept of earning it. I declared that there was plenty of work around the mission, and that anyone could ask for a paying job and get it. Our wages were not grand, but they were fair—comparable to what a laborer could earn in Satipo. Nicolás took advantage of my offer and proved to be an excellent carpenter, when he chose to work, but I could only count on that for a couple of days; if I pleaded with him, I might keep him on the job for a full week. Then he disappeared into the jungle to hunt and fish, and I would not see him again for weeks.

***

One day a boy about twelve years old appeared at the mission and announced that his family had moved into the area so that he could go to school. He was a scrawny kid, but dressed neatly in shirt and pants. Something was obviously wrong with his right eye; the iris was injured, its color blurring into the white background. When I asked about it, he shrugged and told me he had had an accident with a machete many years ago. He had no vision in the eye. He was called Roy.

Roy was nearly a full-blooded Ashaninka, but there was a trace of Quechua on his father's side. His parents lived quite far from the mission, so he took up residence with us. Ashaninka children frequently strike out on their own at an early age, but Roy's story was particularly poignant. I had learned from Father Castillo that, to the Ashaninka, loss of a body part is one of life's worst tragedies. Without an eye, Roy was considered less than a man. His ability to hunt was diminished. Other Ashaninka tended to shun him, not out of malice but because of the Ashaninka view of reality and practicality. Why bother with a man who has one eye when there are so many who are whole? Roy had come to regard the world, through his one eye, as a bleak and lonely place. Education was clearly his best opportunity to improve his lot, and at the mission we were able to offer him acceptance and a measure of dignity.

I hired Roy as a sort of houseboy, and he performed his work conscientiously. He also quickly distinguished himself as one of our better students. All of the natives possessed a knack for retaining detail, and Roy proved to be one of the best. He was able to recall minutiae at will.

Roy's father, Ponce, helped me to understand the Ashaninka concept of ownership. On one occasion he arrived at the mission to present me with a *motelo,* a land turtle. This was a large one, more than a foot in diameter, and as I looked forward to a delicious stew of meat mixed with green bananas, I asked Ponce, "How much do I owe you?"

He was perplexed. "Nothing," he replied. "I found it in the jungle."

I came to understand: Anything that comes from the jungle is provided by Tasorensi, so how could anyone own it? A man's battered machete was his own; a woman's tin cup was her own. But the notion of possession extended only to man-made objects. What came from the land was to be shared by all.

Gradually I realized that, to the Ashaninka, working for money was a means to a specific end—to buy something tangible. But no self-respecting Ashaninka man would work a paying job in order to sustain his family. Food came from the jungle—one hunted for food, or fished for it, or harvested it. If you could not feed your family by tapping the resources of the jungle, then what kind of man were you? Nature provided lumber for building and thatching for roofs. Working for money was merely a way to secure luxuries.

This was why Nicolás chose to work at the mission for only a few days at a time. A wage was unimportant compared to the gifts that Tasorensi provided in the jungle.

Miguel, our first teacher, decided to relocate to be closer to the family of his wife, Natasha. Before he left, he recommended a young man by the name of Mario Zumáeta as his replacement, and Mario's arrival proved to be one of the mission's greatest blessings. He was from the Atalaya area and, like Miguel, had received his training at the Summer Institute. His blood was a mixture of Ashaninka and Shipibo. Shipibo mothers tie boards across the foreheads of their babies in order to produce what they consider to be an attractive flattened brow, and behind Mario's level forehead was a sharp mind and a photographic memory. He was of medium height, strong, and athletic, a handsome specimen of a native man who was equally comfortable hunting with a bow or scrawling Spanish phrases onto a blackboard.

In Peru, a teacher is provided with a single tome, titled *The Encyclopedia,* containing the entire curriculum: Spanish, arithmetic, literature, history, and science. Because of budget limitations, many classrooms had only one copy of *The Encyclopedia,* and the teacher read from it as the students copied the words verbatim. Mario went far beyond this. During math class, for example, he stood at the blackboard, detailing the basics of addition, subtraction, multiplication, and division; in turn, each student came up

41

front and worked the numbers. Exhibiting incredible patience, Mario did not stop until he was sure that the student had grasped the concept.

He enjoyed the children's sense of play and incorporated it into his teaching. One of his favorite lessons was to re-create the solar system in the classroom. One child was the sun, another, the moon. Others were the various planets. Mario sent them into their proper orbits, and the classroom spun with laughter.

Roy wanted to become a teacher, and he studied Mario's techniques. With a flashlight and a papaya, he illustrated the action of the sunlight on various parts of the earth.

More than any of the others, Mario understood why I was here, and he, too, wanted to help his people adjust to what were, at the time, only vaguely definable threats. He developed into a valued friend.

After a few years at the mission, Mario married Gregorio's daughter Cecilia, and they were eventually blessed with a beautiful baby girl whom they called Yaní. Mario developed a symbiotic relationship with his brother-in-law Nicolás. His calm demeanor and Nicolás's fiery spirit complemented one another. And the two were clearly our best *fútbol* players.

Some of the Ashaninka tried their hand at growing cacao—the chocolate plant—and shipped the beans to Satipo for sale. Over time, more and more natives adopted simple farming techniques, and finally they had a cash crop.

The government of Peru, as part of a general program of earthquake relief, provided us with an entire medical clinic. The prefabricated structure was flown in on a military transport plane and assembled by government workers.

A community was taking shape, and I surveyed the land carefully, seeking to build future structures closer to water; I envisioned hydroelectric power.

One day, as I was swimming in the Mamiri River with some of the natives, I glanced up and saw, high on the far bank, a cluster of trees, lush with bright pink blossoms. "Why don't we go up there?" I suggested. We scaled the steep slope of the riverbank to find a

42

plateau that appeared perfect for building additional facilities. From here, there was a spectacular view of Cubeja and its cascading waterfalls. "This is it!" I declared.

The natives cleared the land, and we erected a huge building that we subdivided into a mechanical workshop, a generator storage room, and a lumber mill. We also constructed a guesthouse, a mission house, a sort of barracks for workers, a new school, and another building that served as a sort of town hall.

Finally we established a cooperative store, where the Ashaninka could bring in their cacao crops and receive a fair price. We exchanged the cacao for cash rather than credit, for I wanted the Ashaninka to learn how to deal with money. They also brought in a few handmade items, such as *cushmas* and necklaces made of monkey teeth, for export to Satipo. In older times—and still in the most remote areas—the *cushma* was made from the bark of a special tree—called *kiriniroki* or *potoo*—that could be worked into a coarse fiber. But the Ashaninka in and around Cuti had learned the wonders of modern cloth. An Ashaninka man would only wear a *cushma* that was handmade by his wife—or perhaps his mother. A woman harvested cotton from tall jungle stalks, fashioned it into thread, wove it on rustic looms into a long rectangular cloth, and dyed it in a traditional dark, vertical stripe pattern. The final touch was to cut a V neck in the middle. To dress, the man merely pulled the V neck over his head. A man was also expected to provide *cushmas* for his wife and daughters, but he would never make them himself. Somehow, he had to earn enough money to order the cloth from Satipo. He then presented this to his wife for completion. A woman's *cushma* featured a long slit across the shoulders, providing easy access for breast-feeding. We soon discovered a market in handmade *cushmas*, which we exported to Lima, where they had become popular.

I used the store as a teaching device; frequently I purposely shortchanged a native to see if he would notice. If he did not, I shouted at him as he turned to leave, "*Caramba!* Count your money. You must learn to protect yourself." This was a difficult and long struggle, for the Ashaninka were simply too trusting.

The progress of the cooperative made recurrent trips to Satipo necessary, and I developed a relationship with several bush pilots whom I could contact by shortwave radio. One or another of them was generally available whenever I needed to get into town.

It was in Satipo that I met Fortunato Cárdenas. He was of Quechua extraction, strong as an ox, a mason by trade, and in need of a job. Since he claimed to be an expert in construction, I decided to give him a try, and he accepted my job offer with a beaming grin and a firm handshake. At Cuti, Fortunato quickly developed a respect for the native way of life. He may have been a Quechua, but he was extremely loyal to the needs of our mission and of the Ashaninka in general.

As the mission grew and prospered, more and more Ashaninka settled nearby, on the other side of the airstrip. Under Pepe's direction, the community took on aspects of a town, laid out in small blocks of houses.

Matías's brother-in-law, Capitán, was one of the key builders. The mission had sent him to carpentry school in Huancayo, and now he used his skills in the developing town. He was one of the taller Ashaninka and walked with a stiff-backed aristocratic gait that belied his meek and gentle personality. In Capitán, I saw a flash of affection uncommon in the nondemonstrative Ashaninka. He married one of the most beautiful women in town, and when God blessed the union with a baby girl, Capitán could be seen, on occasion, cradling her lovingly in his arms. This is not the way with an Ashaninka father, but on Capitán it played well.

Each morning I walked to the settlement and strolled among the people. Quite often, Capitán's wife presented me with a gift—a bunch of green bananas or a papaya.

The Ashaninka were enthralled by the corrugated aluminum sheeting that we used as roofing on the mission buildings. To them, it became a visible sign of progress to replace the thatching on their huts with this sturdy imported material. Before long, the cooperative was doing a respectable business, trading two-by-six-foot panels of roofing material in exchange for cacao crops. About forty sheets were necessary to complete the roof of one hut; the mission supplied twenty, but the natives had to purchase the remainder. I watched them develop, very slowly, a sense of pride in ownership.

Periodically I made the mistake of attempting to train them toward serious farming and husbandry. A herd of cows was a complete failure, for the Ashaninka were afraid of the large animals, and to complicate matters, the cattle were attacked by plagues of vampire bats. The calves were especially vulnerable. Once, I brought in a few pigs so that the natives could learn to raise them as a reliable source of food. But the Ashaninka were not good at the necessary tasks. One has to raise corn to feed the hogs, and one has to see to their regular, if minimal, needs. To the Ashaninka, it made much more sense to shoot the wild boar that Tasorensi had already provided.

We were more successful when we brought in a supply of chickens. They flourished in this environment—for some reason, there was a lack of disease and parasites—and we soon had eggs in overabundance. The schoolchildren often began their day with a breakfast of hard-boiled eggs served by Mario. On holidays, we could cook a feast featuring twenty-five or thirty birds. Following this success, we obtained a few ducks, and they thrived also. But I learned quickly that I did not care much for the eggs, and the ducks adopted the annoying habit of wandering about the compound, leaving their droppings at the precise points where I was sure to step on them.

Through the years, I saw the Ashaninka develop a healthy sense of pride in what they could accomplish. Their children gained an education. Each family had an acre or two of cacao under cultivation. Their huts were covered with aluminum roofing. A few of the men had shotguns. Most of the women wore store-bought panties; the men loved jockey shorts. In sum, they had been introduced in a careful fashion to a handful of the conveniences of modern life. They had accepted and rejected others and managed, so far, to retain their unique identity.

But our progress did not come without a price. On the negative side, I could see that the Ashaninka were slowly learning certain unfortunate traits, such as envy and greed. On occasion, there was even an incidence of petty theft—behavior previously unknown here.

Extraordinary pressures were coming to bear on our mission, and the Ashaninka were caught between competing philosophies. I confronted this dilemma when I arranged for Roy to become the first Ashaninka ever to be fitted with a glass eye. One of our benefactors agreed to help, and Roy and I flew to Lima for an appointment with a Dr. Gonzalez, recommended as one of the best available eye surgeons.

During the trip I stopped to visit my provincial, the elected head of our province of Franciscans. When I told him why I was in town, he had to restrain himself from laughing out loud. "Why do you want to get him a glass eye?" he asked. "This is so ridiculous. You say you don't want to change the natives, yet you want to spend money on a glass eye for a boy who lives in the jungle?"

I explained how critical it could be to Roy's future. The glass eye would improve his appearance greatly, and he would no longer be, to the Ashaninka, visibly less than a man.

The provincial listened with a dubious expression on his face, which seemed to say: crazy gringo.

The chapel was to be the crowning glory of Cuti: Fortunato and Roy fashioned a beautiful altar out of an inverted tree root, flattening and polishing the top to a high sheen. It was magnificent in its simplicity.

Some of my colleagues viewed theology mainly as an intellectual discipline; the primary task was to convince the nonbeliever of the truth of the Christian faith. In my view, the purpose of theology was to respond to the conditions in which human beings live. I never imposed my own religious customs on the Ashaninka; as far as I was concerned, they shared my beliefs already. I never invited them to church; they came anyway. I never proclaimed that they had to be baptized, but Pío had paved the way long ago with his well-meant bribes. I did not coerce them into receiving communion, but they did so, willingly.

One day I said to Mario, "I think I'll wear a *cushma* at service." The native robe was in some ways similar to my floor-length alb.

What did it matter that an alb was always white and a *cushma* is dark, usually brown? On the following Sunday I selected one of the *cushmas* from our store, donned it, and placed my stole on top of it.

I was surprised when, not long after that, Cecilia and Mario appeared at my house, bearing gifts. Cecilia gave me a *cushma* that she had made herself. Smiling at her side, Mario then gave me a beautiful neckpiece made of multicolored stones. In the center, held by two short lengths of twine, was a beaded square pendant, about three inches across. The background was composed of white, violet, and blue stones. The foreground, in bright red stones, was the shape of the cross.

Practically every morning, at about six o'clock, I could count on finding Mario at the altar, waiting for the communion wafer. After he received the Host, he stepped back to his place, pulled the wafer from his mouth, broke off a small piece, and gave it to his daughter Yaní.

This was consistent with the Ashaninka's basic concepts. What did it matter that the Church had established certain rules and traditions? Tasorensi had provided a world full of blessings, which were freely available to every man, woman, and child. Sharing the bounty was a natural inclination.

Such behavior came naturally and was beyond discussion. In fact, the Ashaninka did not spend much time thinking about Tasorensi, because God is good. The one you have to worry about is the devil.

PART TWO

The Poison

CHAPTER THREE

The first Quechua settlers arrived in the Cuti area in the late 1970s, coming down from the Andes in search of more fertile ground. There were only a few, but I knew that they were harbingers.

President Fernando Belaúnde Terry of Peru promoted the idea of opening the country's vast inland areas to the populations of the mountain towns. In theory the plan had merit but it was implemented with inadequate preparation and absolutely no concern for the natives. I reasoned that before you bring an avalanche of people to the rain forest, you must first prepare the people who are already there. The Ashaninka lived off the land and therefore needed vast areas to support them. How could you take away those lands until you first trained the natives to survive in a more restricted area? To do otherwise was to forment a classic breeding ground for tension.

For a variety of reasons, the Ashaninka had little regard for the settlers. They considered the Quechua to be unclean. Most Ashaninka bathe several times daily in the swift rivers of the rain forest; the only odor they carried was an aura of smoke embedded in their *cushmas,* from the fires in their huts. In contrast, the Quechua, accustomed to the frigid climate of the altitude, seldom bathed. Almost all Quechua chew the coca leaf, which produces a constant spittle, and the women's long skirts frequently smelled of urine. But the primary reason that the Ashaninka disliked the

51

Quechua was that historically, when the two had come together, the Ashaninka got the short end of any available stick. The more aggressive and wily Quechua had repeatedly exploited the natives, treating them like chattel, placing them in slavelike working conditions and then refusing to pay them an agreed-upon wage.

The Ashaninka concept of land ownership was tenuous, but they understood that when a man builds a hut in a given spot, the surrounding area within a kilometer or so is his, until he chooses to go elsewhere. Thus, an Ashaninka was uncomprehending and vulnerable to a slyly smiling Quechua who might ply him with *agua ardiente* ("firewater"), then offer him an ax and a machete in return for signing or placing an inked finger on a piece of paper.

"Don't sign anything!" I warned. "Don't touch their papers!" But the natives simply could not conceive that a piece of paper could supersede natural law, or that a sign or a fence could keep anyone off of God's freely given property.

As the leader of the community at Cuti, Pepe had to file and maintain whatever paperwork the government gave him, such as birth certificates, reports concerning the ownership and maintenance of the airstrip, and, as time passed, an increasing number of rulings regarding land ownership. One of the most important of these was a government declaration delineating the limits of the Quechua's legal encroachment. This was a mere line drawn on a map (reminiscent of when Pope Alexander VI, in his Treaty of Tordesillas, scratched a line that divided South America between the Spaniards and the Portuguese). As additional settlers moved into the area, I decided that it was necessary for me to study that document carefully, so I asked Rigoberto to fetch it from Pepe. Rigoberto had finally settled in at Cuti. He and Soledad now had three daughters, and I hoped that he had found happiness.

Rigoberto returned from his errand with a report that Pepe had "no papers."

"What do you mean?" I asked.

"No papers," Rigoberto repeated with a shrug.

I headed for Pepe's house to investigate and learned that he had burned all of the documents.

"Burned them? Why did you burn them?" I asked, bewildered.

8-32" plants
mid to late
bouquets.

☼

ants)
17%!

Russian Sage

A delicate cloud of long-lasting violet-blue flowers appears in
late summer when others are fading. Silvery foliage. Grows 3-5'
tall, spreads 2½-5'. Perfect for borders, large rock gardens.
Great for cutting and drying. *Perovskia atriplicifolia*   ☼-◑

N12914 Russian Sage (top quality potted plants)
3 for $7.99   **6** for **$13.99**   **12** for **$24.99**   *SAVE 22%!*

arden

nials on this
top quality
fessionally
ctive use of
ons.

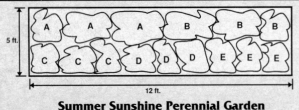

Summer Sunshine Perennial Garden

A - Russian Sage   D - Golden Marguerite
Wonder of Staffa

"What do I need with these papers?" Pepe responded. "I can't read."

The Ashaninka are a fierce people when necessary, but their first instinct is to flee from trouble. Thus, in the beginning, those who lived closest to the encroaching settlers simply moved their huts across to the south shore of the Cutivireni, farther into the rain forest. They did not seem to realize that other settlers would follow and eventually squeeze them into oblivion.

I could see from my maps that the Ene River valley might be the last stand for the Ashaninka. The only other possibility lay far to the east, across the nearly impenetrable Vilcabamba Range, in the region of the Urubamba River, and the Machiguenga tribe, cousins to the Ashaninka, already lived there.

One day I spotted a large metal sign that the Quechua settlers had placed on the far bank of the Ene, announcing a land boundary. Nearly three yards wide, it read: COOPERATIVA DE SANTO DOMINGO. In a fiery mood, I went in a canoe with Matías and a group of other natives across the river, and the Ashaninka watched as I tore the offending sign down and smashed it to bits.

On occasion I lectured the natives, advising them to resist the encroachment. I told them that they had every right to defend their land. My private thoughts were more vivid. To myself I thought: Maybe you should put an arrow up a settler's ass.

The one thing that the Ashaninka had in common with the settlers was a passion for *fútbol*. At first I thought that the activity was good, clean fun. But it soon grew too serious, especially when the opposing groups began to place side wagers on the outcome of the games. The sums appeared paltry, and yet they could be the equivalent of a week's wages, or more. And I knew that the settlers could manipulate debt to their advantage. I warned Mario and Nicolás, "If you get mixed up in this *fútbol* with the settlers, you are going to lose your land."

A few of the settlers sought to establish trade with the natives. They set up stores of their own and offered the Ashaninka a higher price for their cacao beans than the mission cooperative could pay. I was immediately suspicious, for the cooperative was careful to pay the going rate, established in Satipo, and I could not understand how the settlers could afford to overbid. I asked Mario to investigate, and he posed as a customer, reporting back to me that some of the settlers had weighted their scales, or used other tricks to bamboozle the natives. One of their favorite gimmicks was to pay in small bills, so that the wad appeared to be a great sum. Mario and I tried to explain these devious activities, but the Ashaninka had a difficult time grasping them. They could not conceive of lying; you could tell an Ashaninka two conflicting stories, and he would believe both of them.

The Quechua, in their dealings with the natives, were no different from other elements of Peruvian society, which suffers from a distinct lack of ethical principles. Wages are minimal throughout the country. There is only a small middle class; a great gulf exists between the rich and the poor. In such an economic climate, slyness becomes a necessity, subterfuge a virtue. What is wrong is to get caught.

It was inevitable that President Belaúnde's grand scheme to parcel out land would be abused. Some of the settlers, after they had blazed fields out of the rain forest, destroying thousands of acres of virgin lumber—ostensibly to plant crops of cacao and bananas—used some of their land to grow coca. I found this regrettable, but understandable. Coca is the oldest stimulant known to man, and chewing the dried leaf has sustained the people of the Andes since prehistoric times. Vessels containing coca leaves have been unearthed from burial sites in Peru dating back to 2100 B.C.

The Incas considered the plant divine, brought from heaven by the legendary founder of their dynasty, Manco Capac. Inca social and religious life revolved around coca. The right to chew it was a sovereign gift bestowed upon priests, doctors, warriors, scholars, and relay runners who traveled 150 miles a day. It was said that if coca was the last thing a dying man tasted, he went to heaven.

Even today, coca is the gift that some Peruvian Indians give to the parents of a prospective bride, to be placed under the cornerstone of a new house. It is also an abundant source of vitamins. Millions of Peruvians routinely chew coca leaves, and millions more drink *mate de coca* ("coca tea"), which is sold in every outdoor market. Growing coca is not illegal in Peru. Like all of God's gifts, if you use it correctly, it can be beneficial. You can walk into the finest hotels in the mountain cities and order brewed coca to combat the penetrating headache caused by what Peruvians call *serroche* ("altitude sickness").

But coca has long had its opponents. In 1567 the Council of Lima (established by Spain) described the drug as "a worthless object, fitted for the misuse and superstition of the Indians." Over seventy ordinances concerning its use were issued by Francisco de Toledo, the fifth Spanish viceroy. The prevailing attitude, however, was that coca was a relatively harmless opiate. A Jesuit missionary, Father de Acosta, proclaimed: "I think it works and gives force and courage to the Indians, for we see the effects which cannot be attributed to imagination, so as to go some days without meat, but only a handful of coca . . ." At times, the conquistadores paid Indian mine workers in coca leaves, and the Church even collected tithes from them in coca.

Today, the majority of Quechua are addicted to the mild high of the coca leaf, and Peruvians have difficulty understanding how cocaine, the principal alkaloid of coca, is used in the United States and elsewhere to destroy people. They do not comprehend why it is illegal to sell the leaves, or the processed paste, to anyone other than a licensed government official.

Such ambivalence allows drug traffickers to thrive. If a Quechua has a cash crop of coca leaves to sell, he sees nothing wrong in peddling it to the highest bidder. Peru is the world's largest grower of coca.

As the coca trade in the Ene River valley grew to be an ever more thriving business, it placed the mission in increasing jeopardy. The settlers sold their crops to a few mysterious and sinister characters—some Peruvian, some Colombian—who took up periodic residence in the area; at the mission, we referred to them as narcos or amigos, but they were not our friends. On the other hand, they were not our enemies either. They had their business, and we had ours. So long as the two worlds did not clash, I felt there was little I could or should do to intervene.

The Ashaninka trusted me, but as time passed I could sense trouble in the air. More and more, we heard the eerie whine of high-speed-motorboat engines plying the heretofore quiet waters of the Ene, heading between the settlers' town and locations far down the Ene and Tambo rivers.

During a hunt on the banks of the Mamiri, natives discovered a suspicious-looking area. They reported this news to me, and some of them accompanied me on an inspection tour. We took a boat to the site, which was beautifully camouflaged both from the river and from the air.

What we found appeared to be a makeshift coca-processing laboratory, consisting of little more than three holes in the ground. Off to one side was a supply of heavy plastic sheeting. Studying the arrangement, I surmised that the settlers lined these holes with plastic, filled them with coca leaves, added a chemical such as kerosene or an acid, and mashed the leaves into coca paste, which was much easier to transport than the leaves.

I decided to gather what evidence I could. I scraped a residue of coca paste onto one of the plastic sheets and folded it into a manageable rectangle. Back at the mission, I stored it safely until my next trip out of the jungle.

Discussing this find with the natives, I was enraged to learn that some of the amigos had offered the Ashaninka coca seeds and pledged to buy the crop at prices well above the official government rate.

On this point, I had to be firm.

I told the people, "If I ever see one coca plant on your land, I will leave. You choose. Do you want to plant coca or do you want me to stay?"

Later, when I was able to show my evidence to an officer at the military base in Mazamari, he raised his hands in a gesture that communicated that he had heard it all before and gave me the same advice I had given to the Ashaninka. "Don't get involved," he warned. "Forget about it."

"Divine Providence" persuaded my bishop to assign four nuns to Cuti. I would have preferred a swarm of *manta blanca.*

Sister Carmen, a gentle woman of Basque heritage, took over operation of the community store and did an excellent job.

Sister Candelaria was an aged Quechua woman with a disposition cold as ice, but she liked the Ashaninka very much and they responded to her. She taught the women basic needlework and improved the curriculum of our school.

Sister Yolanda was a young woman from Requena, a northern village in the Iquitos area of Peru. She had a touch of Indian blood in her veins, which helped her to develop an affinity with the natives. Her task was to teach catechism courses to the children.

Sister Primitiva, the nominal superior of the group, was an attractive woman in her forties who marched into the clinic and assumed it as her private domain. She provided competent health treatment for the natives, yet for some unfathomable reason, the clinic always seemed to be in a state of disorder. She was obsessed with the idea of piety, and demanded the same of her three companions. She saw sin in everything, accusing me of a trinity of, admittedly accurate, trespasses: smoking, drinking, and cussing. I once muttered to a shocked Brother Pío, "If this is the bride of Christ, then I don't much care for His taste in women."

Sister Primitiva was rankled by Sister Yolanda's friendship with the natives. The elder nun complained to me that too many of the natives sought the company of Sister Yolanda, rather than hers. "I'm the superior," she reminded me.

I explained that I had no control over whom the natives spoke to, and I attempted to point out that because Sister Yolanda was much younger—and part Indian—the natives found her more approachable.

My words did not appease Sister Primitiva, and I foresaw trouble. Soon, Sister Primitiva began taking time away from her work at the clinic to monitor Sister Yolanda's catechism classes, and grumbled that the young nun tended to stray from some of the more rigid Church doctrines.

One day, as Sister Yolanda prepared to leave for Camantavesti on a field trip with some of the catechism students, Sister Primitiva made a point of saying to her, in my presence, "Be careful about your vow of chastity!" Sister Yolanda's face reddened.

"That was uncalled for," I reprimanded, but Sister Primitiva marched off without a word, knowing that she did not have to please me.

I never investigated the details, but before long, Sister Yolanda was transferred from Cuti.

It was Sister Primitiva who declared, unilaterally, that she was going to open the clinic to the settlers. She was blissfully unaware of the tension that would create.

"Keep the settlers away from me," I muttered. "Very far." The clinic had been established for the Ashaninka, not the Quechua. Sister Primitiva simply did not understand the sense of betrayal that the natives would feel.

Before long, she was badgering me to make pastoral visits to the Quechua. "If I cross the river and go to the settlers, the Indians will be offended," I said. "Again, it would seem like betrayal."

"The Quechua are Catholic," Sister Primitiva argued. This was true. Although few of the Quechua were highly devoted, their heritage was Catholic.

I pointed out that the settlers were welcome to come to the mission for mass. I never refused the sacraments, but I did nothing to encourage the Quechua's presence.

In her holy indignation, Sister Primitiva took her complaint to the new bishop of the Vicariate of San Ramón, Luis Máestu, who quickly called me on the carpet. "The settlers are Christian people," he reminded me. "You must go visit them."

"With all due respect, Bishop, I cannot do that," I replied.

He glowered and asked why.

"If I cross the river to go visit the settlers, the natives will never accept it. They will think that the padre is abandoning them."

The bishop thought this over but instructed, "The settlers are entitled to receive the sacraments."

"I promise you, I have never denied them the sacraments," I assured him. "If they come to mass at the mission, they are welcome."

The naturalness of the natives, particularly in sexual issues, dominated the nuns' thoughts. They had a difficult time accepting the pure simplicity of the Ashaninka. A breast-feeding mother or a bare-bottomed child made them uncomfortable. More than once I saw the nuns admonish the youngsters to cover themselves or give the women a "tsk . . . tsk" if they allowed a nipple to flash into view. This was especially true when a visitor, such as my friend François, a bush pilot from Satipo, was present.

After a while, I could take no more of this nonsense. Following mass one day I made a speech to all of the nuns. My gaze lingered for a moment on Sister Primitiva. "François is coming today, and I know what you are going to do," I said. "You're going to tell the women to cover their breasts and warn the little girls not to show their private parts. You are teaching them shame. They don't need shame." The sisters were sullen and silent. Sister Primitiva's eyes accused: Yes, François is bringing in supplies for the people, but he is also bringing Scotch and American cigarettes for you. "Okay," I continued, "if I see you doing that today, I will go out to the plane completely naked. You choose."

We had no more lessons in shame.

If the natural, open behavior of the Ashaninka confounded the nuns, the sisters' very existence was a curiosity to the natives. They were single women, so the Ashaninka considered them to be marriageable. "No, no, no!" Sister Primitiva explained far and wide. "We are the brides of Christ."

A few of the Ashaninka men lived in perfect harmony with two or three wives, and this was a situation that the nuns found intolerable. Roy complained to me one day that the nuns wanted to ban his two younger sisters from our school. Since Roy's father had two wives, the sisters had decided to make an example of him by shunning his children. Roy asked with genuine confusion, "Why can Christ have all these wives and my father can have only one?"

That's a very good question, I decided, and took delight in

referring him to Sister Primitiva for the answer.

A friend in Lima had given me a little plastic friar. When you pushed down on the doll's shiny bald head, an erect portion of anatomy parted his vestment. I had seen Sister Primitiva eyeing this delightful little toy, but she never remarked about it in my presence. One afternoon, when I spotted her marching toward the kitchen, I placed the friar on the table and sequestered myself behind a partition, out of her view.

Sister Primitiva entered what she thought was an empty room. She glanced to the left, then to the right, to assure herself that she was alone. Then she walked over to the table, picked up the statue and flipped it upside down.

"Aha!" I yelled, jumping from my hiding place. "You want to see his *pájaro* ["little bird"]!"

She ran from the room, hands aflutter, shaking her head and screaming.

Gregorio and his family had a penchant for intrigue and confrontation. Once again they put the entire village in an uproar; Gregorio's sons, Nicolás and Teodoro, had assaulted Pepe.

"Nicolás is a *pig,*" Sister Primitiva complained. She said he had used the most abusive language she could imagine.

Pepe was furious and demanded a *reunión,* a meeting. At the *reunión,* several people suggested that it was time for Gregorio and his troublesome family to leave Cuti. Gregorio threatened angrily to ally himself with the settlers and launch a war, and I worried that he could and would do it.

Finally, Pepe asked me what I thought. "I'm not the mayor," I said. "I just have a mission here. But it seems to me that the one who is really offended is Gregorio."

Several eyes looked at me in astonishment. Gregorio's face beamed as I praised him—quite excessively—for his contributions to the community. I chided his sons for embarrassing such an honorable man. Then I suggested a solution: Nicolás and Teodoro should buy an entire bolt of cheesecloth for Pepe as a reparation, and they should pledge that if they were the cause of future trouble, they would leave voluntarily.

The compromise was accepted by all parties. Pepe was happy with his cheesecloth. Gregorio and his family were pleased that they could stay. Only Sister Primitiva was furious.

The passing years brought visible signs of the settlers' profligate use of the rain forest. The roots of jungle trees are shallow. When you slash and burn, you expose a thin layer of topsoil with a clay base. The first rainy season is sufficient to wash away the topsoil, and you are left with hard, infertile land. Many of the Quechua saw their new fields disappear, and thus had to encroach further, destroying more of the forest. It was a vicious cycle that, if left to its own, was sure to push out the natives.

In my efforts to draw public attention to the tenuous existence of the Ashaninka, I enlisted the aid of the press. Through a series of newspaper and magazine articles, we attracted notice of the conflict over the Ashaninka territory, the final bastion of their culture. As a result, we hosted increasing numbers of visitors, including government officials. This brought criticism from some of my colleagues in the Church who viewed me as a publicity grabber, but if it helped the Ashaninka, I did not care.

Fighting back, some of the settlers denounced me to the Peruvian government, leveling the ridiculous charge that I utilized the Ashaninka as slave labor to work a secret gold mine and thus secure my fortune. I received several hostile letters, one from as far away as Survival International of London accusing me of encouraging the natives to give up their land to the settlers and of using religion as a cosmetic facade. More serious was the charge, leveled by others, that I trafficked in cocaine.

The nuns' insistence on ministering to the Quechua did not help. Sister Primitiva was determined to open our school to the Quechua children.

The tension made me ill.

One day, after riding my motorbike down to inspect some of our farmland, I felt unaccountably disoriented, and I decided that I had better go to the clinic for an examination. "My ears are buzzing," I complained to Sister Primitiva. "I'm having dizzy spells."

She checked my blood pressure, and her face registered alarm.

"What a fool you are," she declared with a scowl. "You smoke and you drink that *piarinsti,* and you have François fly in some Scotch, too. Don't you?"

Some things are too obvious to deny. On occasion, François was even able to ferry me in a supply of Chivas Regal, and he always brought American cigarettes.

Sister Primitiva lectured me for several minutes, until I pointed out that my blood pressure had never been a problem until she arrived at Cuti. Undaunted, she prophesied, "You will either have a heart attack and die, or you will have a stroke and be paralyzed."

"Oh, Sister," I said, "I much prefer the heart attack. I don't want to go through life with my *pájaro* paralyzed."

"Everything is funny to you," she scolded. "That is no way for a priest to talk."

CHAPTER FOUR

In 1978, former university professor Abimael Guzmán emerged from self-imposed political exile, to proclaim himself as the leader of Sendero Luminoso, the Shining Path. Its goal was to wipe out the old order in Peru and replace it with a People's Republic of the New Democracy, patterned after the Cultural Revolution of Mao Tse-Tung. Guzmán christened himself Presidente Gonzalo; his followers proclaimed him to be the Fourth (after Marx, Lenin, and Mao) Sword of the Revolution. Surprisingly, he directed his strongest rhetoric not at the right (he proclaimed that their conservative stand "sharpened the contradictions") but at rival groups on the left who, he said, diverted attention from the central task of the People's War. For example, he scorned the rival Túpac Amaru Revolution Movement as just another brand of "bourgeoisie revisionism" and labeled Che Guevara "a chorus girl."

Sendero resorted to such vicious tactics that the governments of China, the USSR, and even Cuba repudiated it. The Shining Path responded to that news by bombing the Chinese and Soviet embassies in Lima.*

Stripped of outside support, Sendero nevertheless continued to

---

*In her 1991 book, *Children of Cain,* Tina Rosenberg reported: "Sendero breaks all the rules of guerrilla warfare: It commits brutal massacres of the very people whose hearts and minds it is trying to win over, . . . 'Only through the violence of class war will the people take power,' Javier, a Senderista guerrilla told me. 'Fifty thousand people will have to die.' "

grow, using fear to win converts. Guzmán's strategy was not to make life better for the common Peruvian, but to make it *intolerable* in order to foster a revolutionary spirit.

Although it had a base of support in Lima, Sendero could not survive openly in the populous areas, so it sought out isolated havens. It established schools and rudimentary health clinics in remote areas, using these contacts with the people as opportunities to disseminate propaganda.

On the eve of national elections in 1980, Sendero launched its revolution. Protesting the legality and fairness of the election, the terrorists invaded the highland village of Chuschi and torched ballot boxes. The following morning, residents of Lima awoke to the sight of slaughtered dogs hanging in slings from lampposts.

For a time, few took Sendero's actions seriously. But the authorities began to notice when the rebels sent their women into villages to entice police officers. Those officers were found with their throats slit and their weapons stolen. More than one government official was found murdered, his eyes and tongue missing.

Sendero's strategy was to use violence to destroy any and all democratic institutions, to deter citizens from participating in any government functions, to destroy the economy, and to cripple any possible aid programs for the disadvantaged. Put simply, Sendero wanted to make life so miserable for everyone in Peru that they would overthrow the existing powers and create a void that Guzmán—Presidente Gonzalo—could fill.

On occasion, Sendero would raid an entire village and destroy the municipal buildings and banks. Rebel troops arrested those in authority, condemned them at public "People's Trials," and executed them on the spot, reserving its most brutal tactics for labor leaders and other liberals who were attempting to work for change within the system. One report told of a local official who was tied to a post in the center of town; every villager—man, woman, and child—was forced to slash a portion of flesh from the victim's living, writhing body until, after more than an hour, a merciful death ensued. Then the villagers were informed that they were now members of Sendero. Not surprisingly, they provided what money and supplies they could. No one dared to complain when a husband, son, or brother was marched off to fight for Sendero.

Often, the government response played into rebel hands. After a Sendero raid, villagers could expect a brutal counterattack from Peruvian troops, who moved in and subjected obvious sympathizers to torturous interrogation. The most vulnerable villager was the leader whom Sendero may have spared. Such episodes unfortunately proved some of Guzmán's key points and delivered more and more Peruvians into the Sendero camp.

Sendero infiltrated the ranks of the military, which was relatively easy, for the rebels had a natural constituency among the rank and file, who were drawn from the oppressed classes. In Peru, the military is a mirror of civilian society, and a few privileged officers impose total dominance upon the troops. These boys are often conscripted at whim, taken off the streets, thrown into trucks, and shipped to training camps without even being given an opportunity to say good-bye to their families. Their resentment shows, and an officer is forced to regard them much as a circus tamer views his caged lions and tigers. On occasion, I even encountered a few officers who were sympathetic to Sendero. Should any of them gain real power, it would be a simple matter to subvert the military to the Sendero regime.

At first I was only vaguely aware that the terrorists were gradually approaching Cutivireni, setting up operations on the west bank of the Ene. I naively hoped that they would leave us alone in our sanctuary—what were the Ashaninka to them? I did not realize that our mission lay directly in their vital escape path.

As the terrorists gained a foothold in the valley, they preached a false gospel to the Quechua settlers and found a willing audience. A portion of the settlers embraced the cause genuinely—no one could deny that the Quechua were among the world's most exploited people. Others were coerced into cooperating.

In the Ene, a strange and uneasy alliance grew between Sendero and the cocaine traffickers. Across the land, Sendero preached a stern morality, with proscriptions against adultery, homosexuality, alcoholism, and drug use. But in the Ene, the drug traffickers managed to coexist with the rebels. I could envision a time when members of the two factions would happily slit each other's throats; but for convenience's sake, both sides were willing to declare a truce. The drug traffickers dealt not only in cocaine but in significant amounts of cash, some of which was channeled to the revolutionary cause.

Sendero also whispered into Ashaninka ears, claiming that I had enslaved the Ashaninka, that I was the principal obstacle to their freedom, and that I must be stopped. They claimed that I was an agent of the United States and that if the Indians did not do something, sooner or later, the *yanquis* would take over all of Peru. This argument was underscored over time by the visible presence of agents of the U.S. Drug Enforcement Administration (DEA) and Green Beret support troops at Mazamari, where they were assigned to train and assist the Sinchis.

Mario came to me one day, visibly upset, and told me that he had seen a message painted on a stone by the riverbank. It was a message from Sendero, threatening to dismember the padre.

I saw the fear in Mario's eyes and tried to make light of the threat. I joked, "You should write on the stone that I would prefer a bullet."

In some of my sermons, I referred directly to Sendero. "We are both fighting for the same thing," I told the people. "We do have to have more justice in Peru. But we cannot accept the means that Sendero uses. We cannot use violence."

Peru needed a revolution, to be sure, but a true revolution based on the dignity of the Christian message: "You shall know the truth, and the truth shall make you free." A revolution that does not recognize the dignity of the human being is doomed to fail.

I warned anyone who would listen: "You cannot change the hearts of people with machine guns."

We attempted to take care of our own business, and I had a special idea I wanted to discuss when Bishop Máestu arrived on his yearly canonical visit. "It would certainly be helpful to our work if one of the natives could be ordained to holy orders," I said. "I have not spoken to him about it, but I am sure that Mario would be interested."

Bishop Máestu's face showed deep thought. He agreed that this would be a boost to the Ashaninka's pride, and he knew that Mario was a good person. We set a date for the following May.

Returning to San Ramón, the bishop spread the word via his news bulletin that the first Ashaninka was to be ordained a deacon. Unfortunately, before the great day arrived, Bishop Máestu died. Eventually Father Julio Ojeda, our religious superior for the province, was named the new bishop of San Ramón, and he rejected the idea.

It was an afternoon in 1984. I was awaiting the arrival of François with a planeload of supplies when Roy rushed into my office, gasping, "The Sinchis are invading the clinic!"

But a boy was at Roy's heels with the news, "The terrorists are invading the clinic."

I stepped outside and stared down the barrel of a machine gun. Several men in jungle fatigues glowered at me. I did not know whether they were an official Peruvian force or a Sendero unit, but I suspected that they were military by the combat boots that they wore. The man in charge asked, "Are you the padre?"

"Yes."

"We want to talk with you. How many settlers do you have here?"

"There are no settlers, only natives."

He gestured down below and asked, "What's the name of that river?"

"The Mamiri."

"Walk down to the river with me," the leader snapped.

I agreed, but asked if I could go to my room first. The leader nodded.

I went to my room, opened my safe and grabbed my keys, whatever money was in there, and all the important business papers relating to the mission. I planned to take these to Fortunato, who was with a work crew, laying a cement foundation for a new chapel building. As I approached the site, I saw Fortunato standing idle, with a trowel in his hand, watching the strangers with a wary eye. As he watched, the cement that he was supposed to be working was getting drier by the moment. I attempted to ease the tension by growling, "What am I paying you for—watching or working?"

Then I remembered my reason for seeking him out.

I thrust a stack of papers, keys, and money into his hands and said, "If anything happens to me, you take care of things." I told him how much to pay François when he arrived with supplies.

Fortunato said fearfully, *"No seas loco, padre."* ("Don't be crazy, Father.")

"Look, Fortunato," I explained, "if you've got a fucking gun up your ass, you don't refuse to go to the river."

"Take some natives with you," he suggested.

"No. I think these men are from the military; I don't think they are terrorists. But if something is going to happen, it will happen anyway. So why take the natives?"

Back outside, I fell in stride with the intruders. The group numbered more than thirty. As we made our way downhill, past the clinic and around the near end of the airstrip, I thought: I'm scared shitless, but I refuse to give them the satisfaction of seeing that I'm scared.

We neared a narrow log that served as a bridge across a small brook, and I thought that my quaking legs would surely fail me and I would tumble into the water. Suddenly I ran forward a few steps and bounded across the log.

"¿Qué pasa?" the leader yelled.

I turned to see him aiming his machine gun at me.

"Nada," I replied. "I wanted to cross the stream."

"Don't do that, Padre," he advised.

Who *are* these men? I wondered. Are they just going to put a bullet through me and leave me here?

When we reached the banks of the Mamiri, the leader asked, "You go swimming?"

"Yeah."

"Let's go for a swim."

He began to strip, and so did I. Several of the others joined us while a few stood guard. The cool water was refreshing, and the tension eased. As we talked, I realized that this was, indeed, an official army unit and that the leader was a lieutenant.

Above us, a sand ledge surrounded the jungle oasis. I glanced up and saw an Ashaninka boy watching, but I did not think that the lieutenant spotted him. A flash of movement caught my eye, and I turned to see a second boy. The lieutenant did notice him, and he said, "The little Campa kids are watching us."

"Well, we are quite a show," I remarked. "They probably never saw so many naked men in their lives."

This brought loud barks of laughter from the lieutenant and his men. In an instant, the entire ledge was blanketed with more than thirty Ashaninka men, matching the size of the military detachment. The natives' posture was not threatening, but each man had a bow at his side and an arrow in his hand. It was a mystery to me how they had managed to get across to the far bank of the river without us seeing or hearing them.

I flashed a reassuring wave, and as quickly as they had appeared, the Ashaninka melted back into the scenery.

The lieutenant was impressed with the show of loyalty toward me. He said, "We will go back to the mission now."

During the uphill march, the lieutenant informed me that he and his men would stay at our mission for some time. As an alternative, I suggested that they set up a barracks in the cement-block building at the far end of the airstrip, close to the river. This, I reasoned, would place them at a point where surveillance of the Ene would be easy—and it would keep them out of my way.

At the airstrip we encountered a larger contingent of soldiers, more than a hundred in all, who were inspecting the cargo of a single-engine plane and questioning its white-faced pilot.

A small, wiry, mustachioed captain approached the lieutenant and, gesturing toward me, demanded, "Who is this guy?"

"The padre," the lieutenant replied.

The captain eyed me quizzically. He could not believe that a crazy padre would be out here in the wilderness with the natives. He muttered, *"Gr-r-r-ringo?"* and his eyes regarded me as if I were a leper.

I matched his gaze.

"Norteamericano," he said, all but spitting the words.

"Yes," I answered. *"Norteamericano.* I don't think you are ashamed for being Peruvian, and I'm not ashamed of being a North American."

69

For a moment he said nothing. Then he turned to the lieutenant and asked if he had checked out the mission.

"Yes," the lieutenant assured, "it is okay."

"Is there a place to stay?" the captain asked.

The lieutenant said, "The padre doesn't want us to stay at the mission. He wants us to stay in the other building, away from the mission compound." He pointed toward the far end of the airstrip, but the cement-block building was not visible from here.

I did not want to risk offending them. "It's not that I want to throw you out," I explained. "But it is much more logical. It's right by the river."

The captain decreed, "Well, we'll go up to the mission and see what it is like."

Oh God, I thought, I don't want all of these soldiers at my mission, but there's not much I can do about it.

The captain grew more friendly as we walked up the hillside toward the compound. I decided that he was not such a difficult man after all, so when we arrived at my house, I offered him a cold beer and a few slices of cheese. He accepted these with a smile and said, "We're going to settle here."

Why did I bring out the beer and cheese? I chastised myself.

The large detachment of soldiers immediately began to sort itself out according to the hierarchy of the Peruvian military. There were three officers from PIP (Policía de Investigacíon del Peru), the dreaded and—in my view—corrupt secret police, and they did not wish to share quarters with the others, so they commandeered one side of the guest house. The captain and lieutenant took the other side. Members of the Guardia Republicana wanted their own quarters, so they commandeered the chapel. The rank-and-file soldiers were left to fend for themselves.

The soldiers declared a 6:00 P.M. curfew, and I was concerned that the Ashaninka would understand neither the concept nor the consequences. "Tell the people not to go out of their houses, not even to pee," I instructed Mario. "If they do, the soldiers will shoot them."

I retired to my room, hoping to calm my nerves. Suddenly, from a distance, I heard what sounded like a burst of machine-gun fire. I raced outside and found the captain, who was also wondering about the noise. "Did you hear anything?" he asked.

"Yes."

"What do you think it was?"

I tried to put the best interpretation on it, suggesting, rather absurdly, that maybe a tree had fallen in the jungle. But just then, we heard more gunfire. This came from the direction of the Ene.

"We have another group of soldiers down there," the captain said. "I'll send a man to see what is happening."

I, too, wanted to know, and I wanted desperately to get away from these men, at least for a time, so I suggested, "Let me go down there on my motorbike." It was more than a mile away.

The captain agreed and briefed me: When I heard a sentry scream *"Alta!"* I was to stop and give the password.

I was well on my way before I realized that I could not possibly hear the voice of a sentry over the sound of the bike's engine. This is so ridiculous, I thought. Do they shoot at anything that moves? If they are such damn fools, let them shoot me.

On the banks of the Ene I encountered a PIP agent who recognized me and did not shoot. He was enjoying his afternoon immensely, and he asked with a leer, "Did you hear the shots?"

Just as I acknowledged this, we heard a third burst of gunfire.

I did not wait around for details. Rather, I decided to make the round of the Ashaninka huts, to warn the natives to stay inside.

Despite the curfew, the Ashaninka did not curtail their evening activities. Throughout the night they met secretly and conducted their private business, but the soldiers never heard or saw any movement.

It was a difficult time. The Peruvian soldiers experienced severe problems in attempting to coordinate basic military activities. Once, they called in a flight of cargo planes—known as Buffaloes—but the pilots flew right past our airstrip without seeing it. The soldiers asked politely but firmly for our supplies, digging deeply into our food reserves. They brought prisoners into our compound and held them in our buildings. One day the PIP agents went downstream and raided a drug-smuggling base. They returned with booty, and offered me a large stereo set. "My God, no!" I responded. If the settlers saw me with something like that, obviously taken by the PIP, they would shoot me for sure.

Some of the natives reported to me and Sister Primitiva that the military had killed three men and that the force of the bayonet blows to their necks had decapitated them. The bodies had been left to rot in the jungle.

"Don't get involved," I warned the Ashaninka. "Just stay away from there. Stay away from all of them."

I managed to befriend a few of the rank-and-file troops, and they spun horror stories for me of how they subjected some of the settlers to torture. If a settler was suspected of supporting the rebel troops or of concealing critical information, the army interrogators cut them with knives and sometimes forced their own troops to drink the victims' blood. I heard that some prisoners were simply dropped to their deaths from helicopters.

I did not know what to believe. Around me, the soldiers were very cordial. The captain and I, sharing several bottles of beer in the evenings, became such good friends that when it was time for him to leave, he hugged me with tears in his eyes.

He extracted a promise from me that I would report any suspicious activity at the mission. And he also warned me that the nuns were not safe here. I asked him to convey that message to the nuns directly, and he did so, informing Sister Primitiva that he felt they should leave the area, at least for a few months, for their own safety.

Sister Primitiva asked me what I thought about the warning, and I suggested that she take her query to her superiors in Lima. She did not want to leave the mission, but she did write a letter to her mother superior informing her of the situation.

The day the soldiers left, Sister Primitiva and her colleagues headed into the jungle. They walked more than a mile until the stench of decomposing bodies led them to the site where the three men had died more than a week earlier. Repressing their senses, they buried them and erected crosses over their graves.

When they returned, I said a mass for the deceased and found myself regarding the nuns with new respect.

Shortly thereafter, the nuns received orders to leave Cuti. As Sister Primitiva climbed aboard the light airplane, I viewed her with grudging admiration, but I couldn't help muttering, "God love her, because I sure can't."

CHAPTER FIVE

Nicolás and I were at the Mamiri end of the airstrip when a strange plane appeared overhead and circled. It was a modern, twin-engine Seneca, far larger and more powerful than the small airplanes that serviced our needs. It came in past us for a landing and taxied to the far end of the runway nearest the Ene. The engines remained in operation. We watched from a distance as several amigos approached from the Ene, with black plastic bags slung over their shoulders. They hoisted the bags up to the two pilots, who appeared to be clean-cut, blond American boys in their twenties. I noticed that the airplane did not carry a Peruvian emblem, nor was the tail emblazoned with Peruvian colors, as the law required. We also realized that there was suddenly a great deal of boat traffic on the Ene.

Nicolás, who was always primed for a fight, suggested, "Let's put a hole in the tires."

"Nah, nah," I replied.

Nicolás and several other natives went off to the riverbank, encountered settlers arriving in a boat, and asked, "What is in the bags?"

"Samples of earth, samples of earth," the settlers said, laughing.

Back at the airstrip, one of the amigos spotted me and approached with a grin on his face wider than the Mamiri in the rainy season. His garish diamond pinkie ring sparkled in the sunlight. I did not recognize him, but he knew me.

"Ah, Padre," he said. He extended a hand, which I shook. Then he pulled away, waved his arm in a sweeping gesture, and explained, "We are collecting samples of peanuts." He laughed.

I did not comment upon his ludicrous lie. Rather, I told him a solemn truth: "There are some people visiting the mission right now, from the Ministry of Agriculture." Hearing this, the visitor scurried off toward the airstrip and speeded up the course of his business. Within ten minutes the plane was ready for takeoff. One unloaded bag remained on the airstrip as the amigo hopped aboard and the nervous pilot gunned his engine. The plane disappeared into the distance. Just as quickly, the settlers gathered the leftover bag and disappeared onto the path leading back down to the Ene.

I ran to my house and switched on my two-way radio. I raised the Wings of Hope office at the Satipo airport and asked them to relay my report to the Sinchi base at Mazamari: "A plane has landed at our airstrip. It did not have a Peruvian emblem. I don't know what the cargo is, but it seems a bit suspicious." Then I typed out a report, including all the details I could recall concerning the type of plane, the date and time it landed, the direction it headed, and my suspicions about the cargo. I sent the letter to Mazamari on our next supply flight.

Less than two weeks later, as I was helping Fortunato and a couple of the native workers build the roof of our new chapel, two young men appeared. "Don't you recognize me?" one of them asked. "I was your altar boy back in Flor de Punga." It was my first parish, and indeed, I did recognize the face from more than twenty years earlier. He was the Vásquez boy, now in his early thirties.

Upon closer examination, I recognized his older friend, too. He was a Pereira, one of the leading families of Requena, near my second parish in San Helena, and his presence here disturbed me. He was the black sheep of the family, and I knew that he had been in jail for various offenses. His appearance was sinister, but his words and manner were polite as he asked if they could stay at the

mission for the night. I offered them the use of one of the con-
crete-block warehouse buildings on the inland edge of the airstrip.

The two men disappeared the next day, but about two weeks
later they returned to Cuti on an incoming flight, bearing gifts:
cecina (a dried pork resembling beef jerky) and salted turtle eggs—
which they knew I loved. I thanked them, stashed the food, and
went to check on Fortunato's progress.

We were still at work on the chapel roof. The visitors followed me
to the construction site and watched idly for a time. Then Vásquez
asked, "How much is the roof costing?" He and his friend offered
to pay the entire bill for the materials.

"No," I snapped.

Pereira laughed at what he obviously believed was my lack of
sophistication. He confirmed my suspicions, freely admitting that
he and Vásquez were involved in the local drug trafficking operations.

"Padre," he said pointedly, "we know all about the letter you
sent to Mazamari." He repeated verbatim the contents of my note
warning about the clandestine activity at our airstrip. Laughing in
my face, he bragged, "We were informed by Peruvian intelligence."

Oh, God! I thought, I've got to watch my step. I resolved that in
the future I would be more careful about who I talked to in this
crazy, corrupt government. You are walking on eggshells, Mariano,
I thought. I glared at them for a few moments as I formulated my
response. "Look, I'm not going to kick you out of here," I said.
"I've never kicked anybody out of the mission. But I hope you will
have sense enough to keep the mission out of your business."

I was in Lima soon after that, discussing the mission's problems
with some close friends. "You should speak with Paul," one of
them suggested. "He is a very fine man. Why don't you talk with
him?" They were referring to DEA agent Paul Prudencio.

I followed their advice. Prudencio was attentive to the details of
my story—particularly when I told him that the drug dealers knew
all about my report to the Sinchis—but could offer little help. He
declared, "The American embassy knows what is going on, but
unfortunately, there is very little they can do about the situation."

He warned me about taking my concerns to Peruvian officials because, he said, "They are very corrupt." His best advice was, "Be careful."

From this time on, planes began to frequent our airstrip without so much as a by your leave. We tried to joke about this new phenomenon—someone dubbed the flights Aero Narcos—but we knew that they were serious business. I told the Ashaninka to stay away, just to leave the amigos, the settlers, and the pilots to themselves. "I want no one going to the airstrip unless it is a plane that we asked for," I commanded. "Don't get involved." To myself, I lectured: Play it cool. You are not a customs agent.

Now, whenever the authorities spotted me in Satipo, we carried on an uneasy conversation that went something like this:

"Are planes coming in?"

"Yes."

"Do you know where they come from?"

"No."

"Do you know what they are taking out?"

"No."

We maintained a nervous truce until, one day, a pilot emerged from his airplane and fell into a heated argument with some amigos who were waiting for him.

Roy's curiosity got the better of him, and despite my warnings, he scooted down to the edge of the airstrip to observe.

Within several minutes, the men had concluded their business. The plane was loaded and money changed hands.

After the amigos left, Roy hung around, eyeing the aircraft.

The pilot regarded Roy as a pesky insect. He reached into the cockpit and emerged with a gun. Grabbing Roy with one hand, he aimed the pistol at the young man's temple. Roy's good eye grew wide with alarm. The pilot screamed at Roy for a few moments, then let him go.

When Roy told me what happened, I fumed with anger. "Why did you go there?" I asked him. "I told you to leave them alone!" But I was more furious with the pilot. I kept my eyes open and waited for him to return. I knew him casually from the airport at Satipo. He had always seemed a bit gruff and shady.

Within a few days he returned. I waited for a moment when I could catch him alone, then marched up to his plane, collared him, and roared, *"No me joda!"* His face flushed, for I had literally demanded, "Don't fuck with me!" I asked, "What are you trying to prove? I'm not going to take that kind of crap."

He backed away, with his hands apart in submission, and promised that he would never again menace the natives.

A few days later, I was busy in my office when Roy came in to report that a group of amigos were here. He said there were about fifteen in all. "They want to see you," he said.

I sighed and responded, "Tell them to come in."

The amigos filed into my tiny office. I recognized a settler named Chavis, but in this company he was definitely low in the hierarchy. The designated spokesman was a Colombian, who was sinister but smooth and oh so polite. With a smile he announced that he had brought a gift for the natives, an entire crate of sharp, new machetes. Even now, he said, some of the Ashaninka were at the airstrip, happily accepting the coveted tools.

I responded with silence.

The Colombian shrugged and said, "Well, you must know what our business is."

I replied, "I'm not going to waste my time and try to give you a sermon."

"We'd like to make a deal." He said that he and his people would pay a thousand dollars for every flight that came in. There were no strings attached. The money was for the mission, or for me— however I wanted to use it. And he was talking about a lot of money, for by now, five flights came in during an average week.

"No way," I snapped. "Don't think you are going to buy me off with money. I want nothing to do with this."

I sensed immediately that I had made a mistake. The eyes of these men met, sharing an unspoken message. The Colombian's facial expression said: You son of a bitch. But, unlike me, he maintained his composure. With a grin, he stalked off to attend to business in the settlers' town on the other side of the Ene.

***

It was Good Friday when distressing news came in on the short-wave radio from the mission at Cheni, which was a relatively new settlement established by Father Carlos Cantella to serve a population of Ashaninka in the region of the Tambo River. A distraught nun reported that Father Cantella had gone out on a boat with several native boys. It was the rainy season and the river was swollen, and the boat had capsized; Father Cantella and one of the boys had drowned. The nun was frantic because she had been unable to contact anyone in Lima.

"I will come," I promised her on the radio.

I asked Mario to help me prepare for the trip. He said he would but warned me that the journey was perilous at this time of year.

Mario readied a boat. He made sure that the motor worked, and then found someone to act as *puntero*—to sit in the prow and plumb the depth of the water with a pole, so that we did not run aground.

As Mario packed food and fuel, I threw a few things into a bag. Suddenly Fortunato told me that some amigos at the airstrip wanted to speak with me. I rode my motorbike over to them, wondering what was on their minds now. The amigos greeted me pleasantly, and one of them asked why Mario was preparing a boat. When I explained, he responded, "Father, our plane is at your disposal, for whatever you need. We will fly you to Cheni."

I did not want to ally myself with these men in any way, but I did want to get to Cheni the fastest and safest way possible. I nodded.

"What time?" the amigo asked.

"How about two o'clock?"

"*Bueno.*"

Fortunato was concerned. "Padre, don't you think it's a big chance you're taking?" he asked.

I shrugged.

The plane landed at Cuti precisely at 2:00 P.M. I tossed my bag aboard and climbed on to find myself in the company of the pilot and two men dressed in ragged, dirty, jungle clothes. Terrorists! I thought.

The two men regarded me with ill-disguised hate. Throughout

the twenty-five-minute flight, they said nothing.

The aircraft deposited me at Cheni and took off immediately.

I thought: They have their business, and I have mine.

All too often the silence of the morning was broken by the excited squeals of the Ashaninka children as they pointed to the sky and shouted, "Aero Narcos! Aero Narcos!"

I could not ignore the increasing reports from some of the natives about other airplanes that came into Cutivireni and unloaded machine guns, artillery, and ammunition. The inquisitive Ashaninka watched these transactions while hiding in the nearby jungle. Nicolás, Mario, and several others told the same story.

Were these arms intended for the drug smugglers or Sendero? I wondered. Then I realized that it did not matter. The two groups seemed to be very cooperative with one another.

On a Wednesday, I journeyed to Lima to speak with my good friend, Miguel Vega Alvear, whom I had known for many years. He was one of Peru's most capable politicians and was working his way up into a position of greater power. I knew him to be one of the honest officials in a governmental bureaucracy that was highly corrupt. Mickey was alarmed by my report and mentioned the names of several politicians and government officials whom he considered honest and trustworthy; he said I could speak freely with them.

I decided that the most prudent course of action was to present my story only to General Rojas, whom I had befriended when he commanded the Sinchi base at Mazamari. The general expressed some concern over my reports of drug trafficking in the Ene River valley, but his ears really pricked up when I mentioned arms shipments that appeared to be making their way to Sendero.

"Please," I implored, "I don't want this coming back on me."

"I have to inform the Ministry of the Interior, but I won't get you involved," he promised.

I had a bus ticket for Thursday, the next day, back to Satipo, but my friend Chino Luy, a former bush pilot, said that if I could wait an extra day, he would drive me. Then he would fly to the mission with me to inspect our growing array of mechanical equipment.

This was great, for I enjoyed Chino's company and the roadway would take us through Tarma, the beautiful mountain town known as the Pearl of the Andes. We could spend a pleasant night in the hotel there and enjoy a relaxing meal.

On May 3, 1984, two days after my meeting with General Rojas, a group of men armed with machine guns suddenly appeared at Cutivireni. Roy and his girlfriend fled in haste—so fast that Roy forgot to retrieve his glass eye—and took refuge in an outhouse located in, and obscured from view by, a deep gully. Fortunato joined them there. They heard someone order sharply, *"Díganos, carajo."* ("Tell us, you bastard.") Then they heard sounds of pain, as if someone's arm was being twisted.

In the chapel, another assailant threw frail old Brother Pío to the ground, placed the barrel of his machine gun at Pío's temple, and growled, "Where is the gringo priest?"

"He's in Lima."

"Where do you keep your gasoline?"

When Pío told them, the men ran off, leaving the old brother in the dirt.

Pío scrambled to his feet. His mind whirred. He guessed that these attackers were from the settlers' community on the other side of the Ene, although he did not recognize any of them. He also guessed that they did not want the gasoline for their motorboats but to set fire to the mission buildings. He ran inside the chapel, opened the tabernacle, and ate the supply of communion wafers kept in the gold-plated ciborium. Then he raced back outside, stood hopelessly, and watched from only a short distance as the bullies returned, carrying cans of gasoline.

The assailants entered the chapel and began to smash the altar and tabernacle. They threw the ciborium to the ground. Another group raided the sacristy and trashed the vessels and vestments. When they were finished with their vandalism, they set fire to the building.

Then they moved through the compound, systematically torching the clinic, the store, and my house. For some reason they spared the school, and they apparently did not notice the guesthouse, hidden from view by a large stand of bamboo trees.

Next, they set their sights on our prized Ford tractor and demolished it.

Before they left, one of them spotted Pío and suggested, "Why don't you come with us, old man? You are going to starve to death here."

But Pío refused to leave.

The men ran off, leaving the mission in flames.

Later that day three boats, overloaded with stolen supplies, stopped at a hut far down the Ene, which happened to be the home of Roy's mother. She did not comprehend what the visitors meant when they said menacingly, "This is what happens to the padre for being a bastard informant."

Meanwhile, Roy and a few other natives gathered with Fortunato and Brother Pío to view the embers of our long labors. They were filled by sadness tinged with fear. They all wanted to leave quickly, lest the attackers return to exact more vengeance. Roy volunteered to go for help. He ran off along a jungle trail to the village of Quimpiri, where a shortwave radio was available. From there, he called the Wings of Hope office at the Satipo airport, knowing that they monitored our frequency. He relayed his story, and a Wings of Hope pilot made an emergency flight to Cuti. The pilot circled overhead for a time, wary of landing amid the smoke that still poured from the ruins. When he finally gathered his courage and put down, Pío and Fortunato scrambled aboard.

The pilot dropped off Fortunato at Satipo, where his family lived. Then he flew Pío on to San Ramón so that he could report to the superior.

On Saturday morning in Lima, unaware of the carnage that had taken place, I climbed into Chino's car, along with his wife, their daughter, Rosa, and their sons, Alfredo and Eduardo. We set off to navigate the treacherous roads that snake up the western slope of the Andes; within three hours, the road climbs from sea level to fifteen thousand feet. Past Ticlio, on the eastern, downslope side, the roadway spins through a seemingly endless series of hairpin curves, working its way up and around rugged ridgelines. No guardrails edge the route. Until only a few years ago, the roads were so narrow that traffic was limited to one direction—alternating daily between eastbound and westbound.

About a six hours' drive north-northeast of Lima, the road reaches Tarma, which lies at a pass in the mountains. The surrounding peaks reach to an altitude of more than three miles. At Tarma, we enjoyed dinner, and I settled into a comfortable hotel room.

Late that night I was awakened by a phone call from Felix, my provincial. "How did you know I was here?" I asked.

"I know you, gringo," he said. He knew that I loved this particular hotel. "Listen, make very sure you stop and see me when you go through San Ramón tomorrow." He explained that one of our colleagues, Father Ortiz, was to receive a well-deserved reward for his literary works concerning the history of the Franciscans in the Peruvian outlands. Felix hoped that I could arrive for the ten o'clock mass and the awards ceremony that would follow. "You must not pass San Ramón without seeing me," he instructed. Because it was so late at night, I missed the significance of his insistent tone.

At breakfast the next morning, Chino's son Eduardo dawdled, and we were late getting started. Our destination was about an hour and a half to the northeast. San Ramón, known as the Golden Gate to the Jungle, lies just below the tree line, so that upon entering from the Andes side, one moves from barren landscape to a tropical paradise.

Mass was already under way by the time we arrived. I stepped inside the church and caught Felix's eye. Waving slightly, he indicated that he wanted to speak with me. He moved quietly out of the chapel, drew me aside, and asked, "How is your blood pressure?"

Uh oh, I thought. My mother must have died. Well into her eighties, she was already in poor health the last time I had been able to visit her back in New Hampshire. "My blood pressure is fine," I said.

"Sit down. I've got bad news to give you."

"Go ahead and tell me."

"They have burned the mission down."

"My God!" I exclaimed. "How's the brother?"

"He's here," Felix said. "I'll call him in. He's been waiting for you."

Brother Pío was in tears, and his sobs increased when he saw me. "What happened?" I asked.

It took him some time to compose himself. He assured me that no one had been hurt, but the mission was destroyed. He told me how he had consumed the sacred host and asked, "Do you realize how lucky we were? I was able to save our most precious possession so that it would not be desecrated."

After I collected my thoughts, Chino piled his family back into the car and we raced for Satipo. On a map, this was not very far, but it was a lumbering, five-hour-long ride, more or less following the course of the Perené River. At several points the roadway was crossed by rapid-flowing brooks. Each time we forded these, Chino had to slam on the brakes several times in succession in order to dry them.

Chino wanted to come into the mission with me, but I said, "No, you've got your family with you. You must stay with them." So, at Satipo, Chino reluctantly left me at the airport, where I searched for a pilot willing to take me to Cuti immediately. By the time I was able to arrange a flight, Felix had joined me. He, too, wanted to assess the situation. I could sense that he was genuinely concerned about my state of mind.

When we flew over Cuti, wisps of smoke were still rising from the burned-out buildings. Almost nothing was left. I peered out the side window at the wreckage of my dreams, and I tried to hide my face, both from Felix and the pilot. But Felix saw the tears that flowed down my cheeks. His hand reached out and rested upon my wrist, but he was smart enough to say nothing. I was grateful for his compassion.

The moment we landed at the airstrip, the plane was surrounded by Ashaninka, all chattering, "Padre! Padre!" Their words were jumbled into an incomprehensible babble. I raised my hands, asking for calm, and said simply, "Let me see."

The pilot waited at the airstrip while Matías led Felix and me to the site of the devastation. As we cleared the top of the rise and I saw, close at hand, the ashes of Cuti, my tears once more ran freely.

We walked on to the guesthouse. I fell into a chair and felt an unaccountable weakness beset my body. Felix allowed me several minutes of silence. Then he said, "I want you to return to Lima with me tonight."

The request jarred me. I tried not to show my reaction, but now I knew the truth: Yes, Felix was genuinely and deeply concerned about me—but that compassion did not extend to the Ashaninka. They needed me here.

"No way am I going back to Lima now," I replied.

Felix was intelligent enough not to press the point. He stayed with me a bit longer, and once again we walked past the devastation. I ushered him back to the airplane. He offered a few final, obligatory words of consolation, and then he was gone.

Matías asked, "Where are you going to stay tonight?"

"In the guesthouse," I said.

"Don't stay alone." Matías and all the others were concerned that the attackers might return, looking especially for me.

"I will stay alone in the guesthouse," I insisted. Somehow, I had to show the Ashaninka that there was no cause for fear. We had to deal with this, and pick up the pieces.

That night, each time a dog barked or a twig snapped, I reacted with a twinge of fear.

Matías checked on me first thing in the morning. Olga came with him to cook me some breakfast.

"Here," Matías said, thrusting my 12-gauge shotgun at me. "I managed to save this for you."

"It's yours now," I replied. I could always get a new one in Satipo, and I knew that Matías would appreciate the extra protection. He beamed.

After breakfast, both Matías and Olga said, "Why don't you stay with us?"

I agreed. We gathered my few possessions and moved up and down the hills, past the Ashaninka town to Matías's house, which was set apart from the main village on the way to the airstrip. Matías spent the day creating a private space for me within their hut. He used what he called *pona,* slatlike boards of chonta bark lashed together with vines, to screen off my quarters.

"We should hide the radio," I suggested. Matías and I found an appropriate place, in a deep gully just down the hillside from the village.

On Tuesday, just before nightfall, word suddenly spread through the village that there was activity on the Ene. Someone had heard the sound of motorboat engines. Several people screamed out their fears that the settlers might attack. Women and children wailed; many of the men ran about in circles, not knowing what to do.

Matías grabbed my arm and pushed and pulled at me until I agreed to hide in the gully, alongside the radio. As I moved away from the village, I saw that Mario and Nicolás were organizing a small party of men to scout the area near the Ene.

Within a half hour Mario, Nicolás, and the others returned with the news that we had lived through a false alarm. No one seemed to know how the panic had begun, but there was no evidence of a new attack.

The men of the village gathered, and Matías suggested a contingency plan in case there really was another attack. His chief concern seemed to be my protection. He said, "If this should happen again, the padre will go with my son Carlos to Tinkarini." This was another, very small Ashaninka settlement about an hour and a half's hike through the forest.

Everyone agreed with this plan, but the Ashaninka were still obviously nervous as they went to their huts to face an uncertain night.

In the seclusion of his own house, Matías said to me, "If we are attacked, do not go to Tinkarini."

My face must have showed my confusion.

"In case the settlers or the terrorists grab us and torture us," he explained, "you must go in a completely different direction. You must go to Anaro. Then no one can tell them where you are. They will think you are in Tinkarini."

I was impressed with Matías's caution. Yes, it was quite possible that these savage attackers would attempt to torture the truth out of the people. Left unspoken was the suspicion that some of the Ashaninka might already be aligned with our enemies.

During the next two days, natives gathered at Cutivireni, emerging from isolated spots of the forest. Some came from faraway mountain retreats. I did not know them all, but they seemed to know me and the work of the mission. Their faces were painted only with black pigment, indicating the prevailing mood.

"We are going to have a *reunión,*" Mario explained. "They want to have revenge against the settlers."

The meeting took place on Thursday, six days after the attack. I had never seen so many Ashaninka together in one area. Hundreds assembled, the men gathering into a circle, the women hovering at the edges. The talk was rapid and loud, and it was very easy for me to grasp its import. Men held arrows in the middle of the shaft and thrust the sharp points repeatedly into the air. The chanting took on a vicious, angry cadence.

I sat to one side, stone-faced, observing.

"They demand revenge," Mario said, translating loosely. "They want you to stay here. We don't want anything to happen to you." He explained that the simple plan was to cross the Ene, ambush the settlers, kill as many as they could, and burn all of the houses. "What they did to us, we must do to them."

"And what do you think about this, Mario?" I asked.

"We must have our revenge."

My heart sank. "Mario," I said quietly, "did I baptize you?"

He nodded.

"And did I tell you that you *had* to be baptized?"

"No."

I raised my voice and addressed the group. Mario translated: "Didn't I tell you that you were born children of God? And when you asked to receive the sacrament of baptism, did I not explain that you were making a commitment to try to live a Christ-like life, to renounce Satan and not to brood over envy, not to have revenge, to love your neighbors, and even to love your enemies? Didn't we go through all that?"

"Yes," Mario admitted. As he translated, several heads nodded.

"Then you lied to me!" I accused. The words cut deeply. "Now you are traitors to your vows of baptism."

The Ashaninka are a stoic people. They seldom show emotion. I saw that Matías, sitting at a table in front of me, had lowered his head so as not to meet my gaze, and I singled him out. "Matías!" I snapped. "Did I ever tell you to baptize your children?"

"No, Padre, no."

"Matías, then what are you saying to me? Are you telling me that you lied and that you are a traitor to the promises you made?"

Matías's shoulders slumped, and he placed his head down upon the table and began to cry. His chest heaved as he sobbed unmanly tears, and I twisted the knife. "Now the only thing you can do about it is cry, isn't that right?"

Still, no answer.

I turned to others. "Nicolás! Gregorio!" I said. "Obviously, I have wasted my time here. I don't even know why I came. I never asked you to be baptized, but once you were, I told you the obligations you have. We don't even know the individuals responsible for this. To burn and kill indiscriminately would make us no better than our tormentors."

Nicolás and Gregorio stared at the ground. Roy shivered and turned away from me.

The violence was defused. There was no massacre. And as I saw these noble people turn the other cheek, I wondered: How many of us, who smugly call ourselves Christians, feel our baptismal vows this deeply?

Mario asked softly, "What are we going to do?"

With a sigh I responded, "We will rebuild. We will start all over again."

CHAPTER SIX

*P*resident Belaúnde Terry issued an order for the Sinchis to come to Cuti to track the the culprits, but the paperwork was mysteriously mislaid, and it was a full week before the Sinchis received the order. By then, the trail was cold, and when they did arrive, they were completely useless. They stayed for months, but never bothered to go across the river to investigate the violence. They were billeted in one of the warehouse buildings at the Ene end of the airstrip. Too lazy to walk the few yards to the outhouse facilities, they relieved themselves on the floor, and used some of our valuable lumber for firewood. It almost seemed as if they had been instructed to do nothing but get in our way, eat our food, and recklessly destroy our property.

My mood was surly and despondent as we sifted through the rubble, trying to salvage what we could, when one of the Ashaninka muttered, "We might as well forget it." The comment slapped me in the face and underscored my sense of urgency. I knew that I had to do something quickly to raise the morale of the Ashaninka, but what? I realized that our tractor was long viewed as our most valuable possession, and that a new one would be the most visible sign of a fresh beginning. So I made the arduous journey to Lima to see if I could persuade my friends to help me raise enough money.

In Lima, I learned that newspapers had reported the attack on

89

Cuti and speculated that Colombian drug dealers were behind the assault, but I doubted that. Was it the settlers, the amigos, or Sendero? I did not know, and there seemed no way to find out. So many groups had motives. Perhaps it was a combined attack. The worst part of the press coverage was the headline: PRIEST DENOUNCES DRUG TRAFFIC AND TERRORISM IN JUNGLE.

I knew that this marked me as an informant—and a target.

I ran into further trouble when Father Julio Ojeda, superior of the Franciscan province, asked to see me. We had been classmates at the Monastery of Santa Rosa de Ocopa, but we had traveled divergent pathways in thirty-two years. He was a mild-mannered, introverted scholar, a Church bureaucrat, and a *burgalés*—a member of a clique of churchmen who hailed from the Burgos province of Spain. I considered him to be an excessively meek pessimist; he probably viewed me as a royal pain in his frock. There was much that we respected in one another, and some bitter points of contention that had surfaced shortly after he succeeded Bishop Máestu as bishop of San Ramón.

He stared at me through thick-lensed glasses. His voice trembled slightly as he speculated that my actions may have precipitated the burning of the mission and even implied that I may have done it myself, to focus attention on the plight of the Ashaninka.

I was stunned into silence; for once in my life, I could think of nothing to say. I thought: Now, in addition to the physical destruction, I have to cope with innuendo and absurd accusations from within the religious community. I wanted to lash out, but forced myself to hold my temper in check.

"Why don't we go upstairs to get a coffee or something?" he suggested.

We adjourned to the mission quarters on the second floor, got two cups of coffee, and sat at a small table.

"We received a letter from Father John Vaughn, minister general in Rome," he announced. I was very interested to hear this, for the minister general was the worldwide director of Franciscan missions. "Rome offered to help finance the rebuilding of the mission at Cuti."

I was so excited that I nearly spilled hot coffee all over myself.

"We refused the offer," Father Ojeda said. As he spoke, the flesh at the left corner of his mouth twitched.

I was simultaneously saddened by the news and supremely angered. If Father Ojeda and I had a personality conflict—well, that was one thing. But to allow that conflict to prolong the suffering of the natives was, to me, intolerable. I raged, "Well, maybe if I was a *burgalés* you would have accepted."

Father Ojeda rose and stalked off.

He always runs away from problems, I thought.

I had no recourse now but to concentrate my attention on private donors and government offices. Before long, I had received commitments from my friends to finance the purchase of a new Fiat tractor and a new diesel generator, which General Pérez of the Peruvian Air Force agreed to fly to Cuti on a Buffalo cargo plane.

Mickey Vega's wife, Bertha, and our mutual friend Astríd de Almenara took the lead in planning a special fund-raising event. Together we compiled a list of all the people who had assisted the mission over the years. Father Ojeda authorized us to use the huge mission cloisters at the Monastery Descalzos for the event, but remained less than enthusiastic; he was concerned about what others might think. "Can we have the student choir sing?" I asked. He was hesitant about this, but he agreed.

Bertha and Astríd hosted a wonderful party. Our new tractor and generator stood at the main entrance, near a table where donations could be placed. The cloister patios were bedecked with a massive array of flowers. My friend Moya, who owned a large farm, donated scores of chickens as well as numerous pigs, which we roasted on spits. A beautiful tableau of wine and cheese stood in the center of the hall.

When the guests were assembled, I celebrated mass, with liturgical accompaniment from the student choir. We said little about the need for special donations to the mission at Cutivireni; our guests already knew this.

At one point, as we ate and drank, two of my good Jewish friends approached me. They were Sam Burtman, owner of a major textile manufacturing firm, and George Grueberg, whose Fábrica de la Unión produced metal building supplies. George, an inveterate joker, asked me, "What is the ultimate Jewish dilemma?"

"I don't know?"

He grinned and explained, "Attending mass in a Catholic monastery and being offered free pork."

I added, "And getting money out of you?"

Sam and George both laughed, and I knew that they were ready with their checkbooks.

By the end of the evening, we had raised more than sixty thousand dollars in cash.

While I was in Lima, I confronted General Rojas. I told him that I had heard that the attackers had called me an informer. Somehow, they had learned of my reports to Peruvian authorities, and I wanted to trace the source of the leak.

"I never mentioned your name," General Rojas replied. He searched his files and produced a copy of a memo he had sent to the Ministry of the Interior. Indeed, the letter did not mention me, but it reported that an unnamed source had leveled accusations of drug running and weapons smuggling via the Cutivireni airstrip.

"Rojas!" I said resignedly, "you don't have to be very intelligent to figure out who came to Lima to make the accusations."

The general argued, "No, no," adding, "It just couldn't be."

I returned to Cuti triumphantly, climbing down from a Peruvian Air Force Buffalo to announce to the Ashaninka that I had arrived with a tractor, building supplies, and much food. A TV camera crew captured the native faces on film, beaming brilliant smiles. The children jumped up and down in excitement.

As construction work began, I said, "See, the terrorists did us a favor. We will learn from the mistakes we made the first time."

My aching bones would long remember the labor of rebuilding. We were able to salvage the foundations of several of the structures, and before long, new walls rose. Fortunato developed into the finest concrete contractor the mission ever produced. The huge tree trunk that had served as the base of our old altar was too grizzled and iron-hard to burn, so we were able to reinstall it in the new chapel. Fortunato fashioned an exquisite entranceway out of multicolored stonework. The chapel came out better than ever.

Brother Pío returned to Cuti on a temporary basis, but soon moved to Puerto Ocopa to work with Father Castillo. We developed strong new allies in Diego de Almenara, the eldest son of our Lima benefactor Patricio de Almenara, and French explorer Michel Saenz, whom we called Mickey. The two had met in Satipo and become champions of the almost-forgotten plan to persuade the government to designate the Cutivireni area as a national park.

Diego and Mickey arrived in Cuti via our airstrip, but since they did not wish to impose upon our hospitality, they settled in another area of the valley. Striking out from the mission, they headed east along the Cutivireni toward a huge waterfall at Parijaro that tumbled more than a thousand feet down a sheer cliffside.

The leader of the Ashaninka settlement at Parijaro was Lorenzo, a brawny, muscular, formidable fellow whom Brother Pío had dubbed Shirampari Potente ("Strong Man") and was now known throughout the valley simply as Shirampari.

Diego was a sharp businessman who knew how to attract attention to the venture. He and Mickey established the Association for the Conservation and Patrimony of Cutivireni. Diego then wrote an articulate appeal and approached several groups, seeking to build interest. Both the Smithsonian Institution and the National Geographic Society responded favorably. Several influential people in Lima volunteered their services, including Alfredo Paino, an attorney who provided legal services free of charge. The group produced a program for Peruvian TV, which elicited additional support.

Just as the project was poised for success, Diego was killed in the tragic crash of a Peruvian Air Force plane that went down in the Andes. Mickey was devastated, but he was more determined than ever to carry on the work of preserving the Cutivireni area as a national park and as a memorial to Diego. It was the natives' last, best hope.

Over time, Mickey developed into a true devotee of the Ashaninka culture and adopted some of its customs with an ease that, I had to admit, I envied. He loved to have his face painted like the natives; his own natural laugh gradually escalated in pitch to mimic the Ashaninka. Such adaptations were natural for Mickey.

He was a tall, slim Frenchman with a mop of graying hair, but he appeared comfortable in a *cushma*. He and Shirampari grew to be genuine friends.

On May 14, 1986, two years after the mission was burned, we held a rededication ceremony. A Peruvian Air Force Buffalo flew in our major benefactors, as well as the by-now ex-president, Belaúnde Terry. Brother Pío, appearing ancient and tired, was there, too. He managed a smile when, during my sermon, I thanked him for his long labors at Cuti and characterized him as the only man I knew who could manage to squeeze thirty-five hours of prayer into a twenty-four-hour day.

After the service, the Ashaninka hosted a banquet that featured barbecued deer.

There was real hope for economic and democratic change in Peru. President Alan García, of the American Popular Revolutionary Alliance, instituted unorthodox policies designed to redistribute income to the poor. He enlisted the aid of a dozen key business figures, dubbed the Apostles, who signed letters of intent to invest in Peru.

For a few blessed years, things were peaceful at Cutivireni. The word was out: If a settler dared set foot on Ashaninka ground, he would get an arrow in his belly. No drug dealers landed at our airstrip.

But President García's reforms did not have the desired effect. Some of the Apostles reneged on their agreements, production fell, and inflation spiraled out of control. García refused to make loan payments to U.S. banks, and the International Monetary Fund blacklisted Peru, making it ineligible for new loans. The minimum wage fell; the poor grew poorer. Only the illegal export of coca, which brought in more than a billion dollars a year, kept the country going. There were rumors of a military coup.

Tranquillity did not last at Cuti, either. The trouble started once again with the damned *fútbol*. The Ashaninka simply could not resist the temptation to challenge the settlers to soccer games.

With the ice freshly broken, the settlers began visiting the clinic with regularity.

Moisés Medina had taken over the management of our new clinic. Sister Primitiva had trained him in first-aid techniques, and he applied his skills effectively. More sophisticated than most of the Ashaninka, he managed to arrange for a government salary. I soon came to realize that he augmented this by selling off some of our medicines and other supplies to his contacts in the settlers' community. I tried to stop, or at least slow, this activity, but Moisés was a shrewd operator. Once, I warned him, "It's going to backfire on you."

Undaunted, Moisés continued to fashion his own small empire within our mission, and he also was the center of a scandal. He and his wife, Tsinani, lived in the house between those of the sisters Cecilia and Claudia. Cecilia's happy marriage to Mario filled her widowed sister with envy; she *had* to have a man of her own, and she took up with Moisés. Tsinani bore this shame in silence, as is the way with the Ashaninka wife.

Claudia caused us increasing amounts of trouble. When her young daughter died, Claudia claimed—to anyone who would listen—that the girl had been bewitched by her brother-in-law Mario.

Before too long, another caravan of mysterious airplanes with shady-looking pilots began to frequent our airstrip. Once again I warned the people to stay away from them.

A triangle of terror took shape, closing in on the Ashaninka and the mission. The settlers, with their slash-and-burn techniques, grabbed ever more forest land. The drug traffickers, even as they usurped our airstrip, offered the temptations of indulgence. Recruiters from the Shining Path continued to whisper into Ashaninka ears: You have nothing; all those people in the towns have everything; it is not right; join us; take this shotgun. The despicable rumors resurfaced: The padre was enslaving the Indians; all he wanted was to take the Ashaninka land.

As time passed, the basic infrastructure of the Ashaninka culture grew ever weaker. Little by little, settlers continued to encroach upon the land, and even upon the women. More and more of them took wives from among the natives. By the late 1980s there were only two remaining strongholds of Ashaninka life: Camantavesti and Cutivireni.

Somehow, we maintained a delicate truce.

I heard incredible stories of evil invading the valley. One report, spread quickly by rumor, was that a Colombian pilot had attempted to pay for a load of cocaine with eighty thousand dollars in counterfeit currency. His body was found floating in the river, with its fingers, toes, and penis cut off.

The Ashaninka learned to avoid the banks of the Ene whenever they heard speedboat activity, for they knew that the narcos would not hesitate to turn their machine guns on prying eyes. In fact, the natives began to avoid fishing in the Ene altogether, fearful that it was contaminated by too many dead bodies.

Cuti was a magnet that attracted many visitors. One of them was a British woman named Bridget Tempest, a renowned painter who came from one of the reigning families of British Catholic aristocracy. She was a lovely, cultured young woman who was referred to us by Javier Pardo. With her brush and paints, Bridget sought to capture the beauty of the Ashaninka culture. One of her greatest works was an immense mural painted on the plywood sheeting above the inside back wall of our sanctuary. It depicted Christ, dressed as an Ashaninka. The Lord wore a *cushma* and had a painted face. In the open palm of His left hand He held Tasorensi, the white-tailed hummingbird, the symbol of the Holy Spirit. *Piarinsti* flowed from a gourd. The background was a vista of whitewater cascades, deer, birds, and other gifts given freely by God to the Ashaninka.

Bridget was at the mission when three members of the Guardia Republicana, who had been camping on the far bank of the Cuti, came to us for temporary refuge, fearful of rumors of terrorist activity. We had imported a group of construction craftsmen from Satipo, and they and Mickey were there, too. Our various facilities were overflowing with guests.

96

In the midst of this activity, one of the drug kingpins, a Colombian, showed up, seemingly unconcerned over the presence of my other visitors. He explained politely that he was awaiting a flight out; the plane was delayed, and he wondered if he and his bodyguards could stay with us for a few days. I agreed to let them use half of the guest house, which had a separate entrance from the side occupied by Bridget.

That night, we shared dinner, and he was very cordial. He was a heavyset man with a healthy appetite. He asked me if he could buy some of our chickens. "I will pay for them," he offered. "You name the price."

I told him that since our chicken supply had dwindled, I had refused to sell them to the natives and therefore could not sell them to anyone else.

"How about one hundred dollars?" His face beamed, appreciating his own generosity.

"It's not a matter of money," I said.

He understood my position, but flashed a smile once more and suggested, "Why don't you take the money anyway?"

"No." I tried to keep my voice extremely polite as I explained that we had private donors in Lima who supported us.

We stayed up late, talking. He told me how he got involved in the drug business. His father was arrested and thrown into jail, held on what he assured me were false charges. He could not raise bail money. Then an acquaintance offered to supply the bail money in return for a favor. From that start, he worked his way slowly into the business until now, he boasted, he was one of the most powerful men in the Colombian cartel. "I have a yacht in Miami," he said. He claimed to be a charitable man who wanted to create some sort of foundation to aid abandoned children and the elderly.

He was proud of his creative approach to the drug-smuggling business. He explained that one of his favorite tactics was to ship cocaine in the false bottoms of bottles of *pisco,* a grape-based liquor.

Late that night, shortly after the drug dealer crawled into bed, Bridget ran to me, wrapped in blankets, and declared, "I don't want to sleep in the room next to him." She went to the workers' hut, where Fortunato and his crew bunked.

In the morning, Mickey told me that the narcos had been speaking on the radio in the woods. The Frenchman said he had overheard the drug smuggler arranging a flight.

I was very edgy. Walk this tightrope, I commanded myself. Stay out of the troubles around you so that you can help the people. I snapped, "Look, Mickey, I didn't ask you to stay here. Look for another place. This is not a hotel. If you stay here, you mind your own goddamn business, and don't ask any questions." Mickey, hurt and confused, was unaware of the pressures that caused me to berate him.

Later that day a flight came in, and after it left, the drug lord showed me a plastic bag stuffed with money. "Can you keep it in your bedroom for me?" he asked.

"No way," I replied.

My curt refusal did not faze him, but he was really upset about Bridget. He complained, "Last night, she called me a fat pig."

From time to time, even the terrorists sought our help. In the midst of a torrential rainstorm, a young Quechua woman ran to the mission and reported that a group of her friends were at one of the warehouses adjacent to the airstrip. One of them was experiencing severe stomach pains, and she asked if she could bring him to our clinic.

The woman was an agitator and an informant, and since I did not want her friends at our mission, I said quickly, "Why don't I just go down there and see what I can do?"

Along with Mario, I followed her to the warehouse. There, we found a group of young men whose faces showed their resentment. They did not want me around, but they knew that they needed me at the moment, for the man who was obviously their leader was laid out on the ground, weakened, and in pain.

"He is fooling us," Mario whispered. "It is not a bad stomach. It is a bullet."

I leaned over to examine the man. He appeared to be in his early twenties and, despite his travail, presented a more sophisticated appearance than his comrades. I guessed that he had been a

An aerial view of the mission of San José de Cutivireni

Caretas/OSCAR MEDRANO P.

More play before school. At the rear of the picture, in the center, stands the teacher, Mario.

In happier days, before he became a renegade member of the Shining Path, Moisés (*at left*) inspects our new Fiat tractor, along with Matías and me.

Mario was our finest teacher, with a burning desire to train the Ashaninka children.

Caretas/OSCAR MEDRANO P.

The angels of Cuti at the beginning of the school day. We viewed education as their best hope of adapting to the encroachment of "civilization."

Caretas/OSCAR MEDRANO P.

The chapel, the crowning glory of our mission at San José de Cutivireni

Celebrating mass in the chapel at Cuti

In the chapel at Cuti, with a statue of Joseph and Christ child

Caretas/OSCAR MEDRANO P.

Another day of school. In these faces, I saw the glorious reflection of the Christ child.

Caretas/OSCAR MEDRANO P.

Taking our new Fiat tractor for a test drive

Caretas/OSCAR MEDRANO P.

university student; Sendero was very successful at recruiting from the youthful intelligentsia.

"I'd like to talk to you alone," I said.

He gestured for the others to move away.

When we were alone, I asked, "Where's the bullet?"

"No, I have stomach problems," he answered.

I agreed, "You really have stomach problems. Did they shoot you in the stomach?" He refused to answer. "There is no nurse here," I informed him. "I know you don't want to go to Satipo." There, he would surely be pegged as a terrorist and arrested by the army. "I can give you some gasoline," I suggested. "Then your friends can take you somewhere by boat."

He nodded his agreement.

Mario and I retraced our steps to the mission and returned with gasoline and a supply of milk, bread, and canned foods. They accepted the supplies, and it was the last I saw of them.

June 1989. Mario greeted me the moment I stepped out of the Cessna. "They are here," he said. "They want to talk with you."

"Okay," I replied. I had just returned from a brief flight to Satipo, a routine hop to purchase supplies.

I was surprised to see the sloping trail leading up from the airstrip to the mission lined with Ashaninka, armed with bows and arrows and a few shotguns. The natives watched carefully as a young, dark-skinned man in jungle fatigues strode purposely toward me and called out, "Padre, we want to talk to you."

He directed me toward a small hut at the Mamiri end of our airstrip. Three others accompanied us and, armed with machine guns, took up sentry posts.

Sendero's terrorists routinely covered their faces with hoods similar to ski masks to avoid recognition. These men were uncovered, indicating a degree of trust. Although they were armed, their posture was not threatening, and I was not frightened.

The youthful leader presented me with what he described as Sendero's code of honor. Printed neatly in blue ink on a piece of tracing paper, it read:

The Poison

Three Cardinal Rules

1. *Obey orders in all actions.*
2. *Do not touch or take anything not even a needle or a stray hair from your own people.*
3. *Turn over everything that is captured or taken as trophies.*

Eight Admonitions

1. *Speak cautiously.*
2. *Pay with honor what you take.*
3. *Give back what you borrow.*
4. *Make indemnification for what you break or ruin.*
5. *Do not hit or infuriate people.*
6. *Do not ruin or destroy crops or fields.*
7. *Do not take liberties with women or men.*
8. *Do not maltreat prisoners of war.*

This travesty would put the Golden Rule to shame, I thought. I wondered what the terrorists were up to now. Why were they attempting to make me think that they had changed into innocent schoolchildren?

The Sendero spokesman's next statement belied the carefully penned words. He intoned catchphrases of the party line with the same robotlike quality one might expect from a youngster reciting the catechism. Although the speaker delivered the words by rote, I sensed that he was a bit more educated and cultured than the others. With ramrod posture, he intoned, "We start from a principle established by Chairman Mao—violence is a universal law with no exception. Without revolutionary violence we cannot replace one class with another. The revolution will triumph after the Peruvian people cross over the river of blood to the other side."

I pretended to listen, but there was no point. I had heard it all before, and I knew that Sendero was an indiscriminate killer bent on destruction, with no respect for human life.

Finished with his speech, the rebel demanded, "Give us ten of your boys to train."

"I can't do that," I protested. "They are not mine to give. I can't just hand people over. Talk to their fathers."

Undaunted, the terrorist proclaimed, "For the coming year, you will either join us or suffer the consequences."

I said nothing. By now, some experts estimated that the terrorist ranks numbered about five thousand, and their strength was magnified by the quiet support of an increasing number of sympathizers and fellow travelers. Sendero's presence had forced the government to place more than half of the country under an official state of emergency. But I was naive enough to wonder what they wanted from me—and from Cuti. The danger, as far as Sendero was concerned, was all to the north, the west, and the south—where the military bases were located. The Ashaninka were no threat to them.

Impatient with my silence, the terrorist asked, "Can you help?"

"What do you need?"

"Guns."

"I can't get you guns. I can't even get shotguns for my people for hunting."

"Shells for sixteen-gauge shotguns."

"I can't get those things either," I repeated. "You need a license for that."

He softened his demands. "How about clothes? Sneakers?"

"I don't have any."

He consulted with his compatriots as he assembled a list and added other needs: medicine, copybooks, five thousand sheets of bond paper, and stencils for a mimeograph machine.

"Look," I said, "I am not going to promise anything. I don't have these things here. I just returned from Satipo, and I don't know when I'll get out again. When I go to Satipo or to Lima, I will do my best to get them for you."

"We want some chickens."

A moment of inspiration hit me. I replied, "We are very low on chickens, but I will give you some ducks." The damn ducks, I thought, are always crapping on everything anyway. I yelled out a window, "Mario, go grab three or four ducks."

As Mario trudged off for the ducks, the rebel spokesman asked for gasoline and oil for their boat. I asked Matías to drive the tractor to the mission and return with fuel supplies.

The four guerrillas presented a comical sight when they were loaded and ready to leave. Each wielded a heavy machine gun and held a squawking, wriggling duck by the feet.

"I'll drive you to the river," I offered.

As the men piled onto the trailer hitched to the back of our tractor, one of them inadvertently jabbed me in the stomach with the barrel of his machine gun.

"Cuidado" ("Be careful"), one of his partners yelled.

The offender replied, *"Desculpa, padre."* ("Excuse me, Father.")

We bantered easily as I drove to the far end of the airstrip and down the path to the point where the Cutivireni empties into the Ene. I pulled to a stop and was surprised to see more than twenty settlers from the nearby town, waiting expectantly. Ah, yes, I thought. It is as I suspected. It is as Mario has warned me. Here is more evidence that the settlers and the terrorists are all in this together.

The four rebels clambered down from the trailer with their load of squawking ducks. The leader turned to me and said, not unkindly, "We'll be back for the supplies we hope you will get for us."

They slid down the riverbank and exchanged greetings with the settlers.

The entire community was saddened by Fortunato's decision to leave us. The genial, giant Quechua had worked with us for years, building and rebuilding. His handiwork was evident throughout Cuti.

But our personal sense of loss was tempered by his own happiness. He was returning to Satipo to marry his girlfriend, and they planned to work together in her café on the south side of the town's central plaza.

I wished him Godspeed.

On a routine trip to Satipo, I was on my way to the Wings of Hope hangar when I suddenly became aware of someone running up behind me.

"Are you Father Mariano?" a voice asked.

I turned to see a man, perhaps in his early forties, slim, dark, and wiry. He was all muscle and sinew. His gaze was cool and business-like. "Yes," I replied.

He introduced himself as Lucas Adins and said that he was from Belgium. "I'd like to talk to you for a moment."

"About what?" I asked.

"About the mission," he declared. "I'd like to do something for the mission."

We could always use help. I told him that I had to go to the bank in town. It always took them an hour or so to process my paper-work, so we could go to Fortunato's Bar Azul, across the street, share some refreshment, and speak further. I received a huge bear hug from Fortunato, the mason turned capitalist.

Over coffee, Lucas explained that he wanted to visit Cuti to assess the possibilities of creating a development project. He elaborated a plan that included sophisticated machinery and personnel. "Your plan is too ambitious for us," I said, "but there are some areas where we could use assistance." When I told him of our efforts to improve our cacao crops, he contended that he was an expert in this area. He also indicated that he could improve our clinic facilities and supply us with a doctor and nurse. Intrigued, I extended an open invitation for him to visit.

Lucas arrived at Cuti shortly after my return, on a Wings of Hope flight, and announced that his organization had half a million dollars to invest—in the first year alone. I again cautioned him that his plans might be overly ambitious, but I was excited. We walked off on an inspection tour of the Ashaninka cacao fields, whereupon Lucas announced that he could more than double the yield by implementing modern agricultural techniques.

Lucas and I held lengthy discussions. He studied the terrain and suggested that we might transport water from Tinkarini by pipe-line. Perhaps we could employ solar energy. I felt it only fair to be candid about our situation. "The narcos are here, and the terror-ists are here," I said, "and the mission has already been destroyed once." The information did nothing to dissuade him. Since I was scheduled to travel to the U.S. in October for a rare and long-

awaited visit with my friends and family, I decided to add the
Belgian embassy in Lima to my itinerary to see what more I could
learn about this enigmatic man before I agreed to his plans.

Mickey took an uncharacteristic, instant dislike to Lucas and
warned me that although Lucas said all the right things, his eyes
remained fixed and cool. "I don't feel *vibrations* from him," he
said.

I eyed Mickey, grinned, and shook my head in frustration. The
Frenchman's tall, lanky body was draped in a striped *cushma*. His
face was painted with achiote berry. I suspected that already this
day he had a bellyful of *piarinsti*. More than ever, he seemed to feel
the need to be accepted by the Ashaninka as one of them, and I
sensed that he was jealous of anyone new who might come in to
steal their affection and attention. I agreed that this man, Lucas,
was aloof and a bit of a loner, but he seemed to adapt well to jungle
life, and I reminded him that the Ashaninka could use all the help
they could get.

On the first leg of my long journey back to the U.S., I flew on the
short hop from the Cuti airstrip to Satipo. The border town had
become a center of intrigue, rife with operations of various international drug-smuggling rings, terrorist members and sympathizers, and a variety of civilian and military agents; informants walked
on both sides of the street. One could find out almost anything in
Satipo; the difficult part was separating the truth from the lies.

I made my rounds, checking with friends and acquaintances. I
wanted to be sure that it was a safe time to leave my people in the
care of Mario, Roy, and Matías. It was also necessary for me to
discern how Sendero might react to Lucas's plans. Through an
informant, I was told that the terrorists would have no objections
to our efforts to improve the clinic—as long as they were permitted
to use it when necessary. But the water-pipeline project from Tinkarini and the improved cacao fields would not be permitted.
Sendero would not tolerate progress until such time as it was in
power and could take the credit.

With this information in hand, I caught a bus for the three-hour
ride to San Ramón and was surprised to realize that one of my

fellow travelers was an old acquaintance named Antonio. For years I had known that Antonio was allied with Sendero, but I considered him harmless. I enjoyed bantering with him, trading political rhetoric.

As the ancient vehicle worked its way slowly up the foothills of the Andes—with each revolution of the wheels it emitted a variety of sounds, threatening to leave us stranded at any moment—Antonio told me that he was on his way to Lima for a meeting with some of the Sendero leaders. I was surprised that he was so open with this information, and I took his candor as a sign of trust.

When we spoke of the future of Peru and its people, he admitted directly, "I don't trust the Church. The Church has always been with the wealthy." But his stated dislike for the Church did not keep him from trying to persuade me to join Sendero's cause.

My response was diplomatic. I told Antonio that I approved of Sendero's broad goal of justice for the people, but I could not condone the methods.

Antonio smiled and predicted that someday I would understand the necessity to resort to violence.

He is a slimy one, I decided. Watch yourself.

At San Ramón, Antonio and I parted company. As I waited for the next bus to Tarma, I encountered a group of men whom I recognized as members of one of the cocaine smuggling rings that constantly used our airstrip. Upon learning my destination, they told me that they, too, were on their way to Lima, and cordially invited me to join them in their car. I accepted.

My hosts were talkative. As we rode, they spoke openly about the particulars of the drug trade, describing their hidden jungle laboratories where they turned stores of coca leaves into the easily exportable paste. They boasted that it cost them about twenty-five thousand dollars in bribes to get each shipment safely out of the country.

I was not displeased when we experienced car trouble near Tarma, because it afforded me the opportunity to enjoy another night at my favorite hotel. In the morning the car was repaired, and we headed off along the treacherous downhill roadways of the western slope. The smugglers spoke about the terrorists, and admitted that they paid Sendero a protection fee of a thousand dollars each time one of their planes used our airstrip. By now, there were weeks when as many as a dozen flights were registered. The smugglers wanted to know if our mission ever received any of the money, since we were the ones who maintained the airstrip.

"No!" I said, and attempting to be diplomatic, I explained once more that we were willing to coexist, but we wanted nothing to do with drugs, nothing to do with terrorists.

In Lima, I paid a visit to the Belgian embassy and asked some questions about Lucas Adins. The response was vague. An official told me that, yes, Lucas was from Belgium and his credentials appeared legitimate, but offered very little additional information.

I did not comprehend everything that was happening around me. I was uneasy, but I did not know why.

CHAPTER SEVEN

November 11, 1989. Nationwide mayoral elections were scheduled for the following day, and Sendero wished to make a show of defiance against the democratic process. Throughout Peru, they intimidated citizens with threats of violence, should they attempt to vote. And they chose this day to confront the Ashaninka.

A group of terrorists encountered Mario and Roy at the mission, delivered yet another Maoist harangue, and issued their demands. They proclaimed that from now on the mission was forbidden to fly the Peruvian flag. Instead, Cuti was to display the bright red banner, with a white hammer-and-sickle insignia, of the Shining Path. The terrorists also instructed Mario and Roy to spread the word to the rest of the Ashaninka that the elections were to be boycotted.

The two Ashaninka men held their tongues. The Ashaninka are not easily excited, nor are they demonstrative. Neither Mario nor Roy confronted the terrorists with a direct refusal.

But shortly after the invaders left, Mario calmly lowered the rebel flag, removed it from its rope, shredded it, and stomped it into the ground. Then he proudly raised the Peruvian flag, with its three, broad, vertical fields of red, white, and red.

Roy, fearing repercussions from their defiance, drove our most precious possession—the Fiat tractor—into an out-of-the-way clearing and camouflaged it with tree limbs and palm fronds.

Tension filled the homes at Cuti. Matías spoke about the situation with his brother-in-law Capitán. The passing years had blessed Capitán with four vivacious, wide-eyed daughters, and he was concerned about their safety. The two men were both quiet, mild-mannered Ashaninka who now faced a serious question. If there was trouble, where could they flee? Where was the best haven for their families?

Eleven days passed.

November 22. A force of about sixty Senderos, young men and women, armed with submachine guns and assault rifles, crossed the Ene by boat and landed on the bank that gave access to our mission. They trekked one mile up the path to the far end of the airstrip, traversed its length, moved on uphill to the mission compound, and confronted Roy, demanding, "Where's Mario?"

"I do not know," Roy answered. In fact, he knew that Mario had gone to Sankatiaro to play *fútbol* and was due back the next day.

Deprived of their primary target, the terrorists moved toward their secondary goal, which was to loot the mission. At gunpoint, they marched Roy to the schoolhouse, where they captured Alberto, one of our teachers. Then they went to the guesthouse, where they surprised Lucas, who had returned from Belgium weeks before and was awaiting my arrival.

They surrounded the guesthouse with armed sentries. Roy, Alberto, Lucas, and Roy's pregnant wife, Antonia, were imprisoned inside.

The terrorists moved systematically through the compound, stripping everything of value from the mission house, the school, the clinic, and the cooperative store. Throughout the afternoon they forced Lucas into the unfamiliar task of driving the tractor, pulling a trailer filled with booty to the end of the airstrip and then down to the riverbank, where boats awaited them.

Groups of Ashaninka watched silently and unnoticed from the edges of the jungle.

That night, the terrorists feasted on more than twenty of our chickens.

Inside the guesthouse, some of the terrorists played cards with

113

Roy and Alberto as Lucas asked repeatedly, "Why are you doing this?" He was answered with revolutionary platitudes.

When Mario returned to Cuti the next morning, he was quickly met by his neighbors, who warned, "The terrorists have arrived. You must run!" Mario reacted to this news with a touch of machismo. Shrugging aside any thought of danger, he ignored the advice.

It was Mario's own sister-in-law, the devious Claudia, who sold him out. By now, Claudia and her lover Moisés had become a source of even greater tension in the community. Claudia must have reasoned that in the absence of the padre the Ashaninka were at the mercy of Sendero, and she sought to ingratiate herself. It was time for her—and Moisés—to break their bonds with Cuti. In a supreme act of treachery, she informed the terrorists that Mario was back and led them to his house.

At gunpoint, the terrorists took Mario to the guesthouse. With their prize now in hand, they made plans to leave. They torched our mission, burning to the ground every building except the guesthouse. Once again, Cuti was a blazing inferno.

The terrorists placed Mario, Roy, and Alberto into the trailer at the back of the tractor and commanded Lucas to drive them toward the river. When they reached the end of the airstrip, the guerrillas instructed Lucas to remain seated, spread his hands, and keep them rested on the fenders. "Look straight ahead," they warned. Then they marched their three Ashaninka prisoners away.

Within minutes, Lucas heard three gunshots. He assumed that all had been executed.

In fact, the guerrillas shot Roy and Alberto in quick succession, but the attackers had other plans for Mario. To Sendero, our mission at Cuti had become a symbol of imperial oppression, and Mario was a puppet of the padre. Eleven days earlier he had openly defied them by lowering their flag, and they now demanded retribution. They took him across the river, marched him to the settlers' town nearby, and staged a public spectacle.

A terrorist proclaimed, "Your padre is an imperialist *yanqui!*"

"He is a good man," Mario replied.

"You must join our cause," the Sendero speaker retorted.

"No," Mario replied. "Go ahead and kill me if you want to."

First they cut out Mario's tongue. Then they castrated him. They crucified him, fastening him to a makeshift cross. As he hung there, they jabbed sharp sticks into his belly, taunting, "Where is your God now?"

When Mario was dead, they sliced open his belly and filled the body with stones to weight it down. Then they threw his remains into the rapid, muddy waters of the Ene.

Seven hundred Ashaninka vanished into the jungle, leaving Lucas alone at Cuti.

An endless week passed. By day, Lucas wandered through the smoldering rubble and hoped that word of his survival filtered to the authorities, and that they would send someone to rescue him. By night, only the ever-present buzz of the bugs kept him company. Periodically, Ashaninka women appeared, offered him food, and suggested that he flee with them and their families. Lucas accepted the food, but refused to run.

A week after the initial raid, the rebels returned to Cuti, sent to retrieve the one major remaining asset—the tractor. Lucas managed to evade them, but they encountered Martín, the medicine man, who was there along with two young men. The terrorists demanded that Martín talk with them, and when he refused, the attackers killed all three of the natives.

It was on this day that Sendero was to realize that it had miscalculated the Ashaninka personality. For years, the terrorists had watched the Indians retreat from the encroachment of the settlers and had seen them flee from the initial attack. But the terrorists simply did not comprehend that the Ashaninka lack the concept of defense. Running from an attack is not a manifestation of cowardice; rather, the Ashaninka flee in order to regroup and counterattack.

After murdering Martín and the two young men, the rebels drove the tractor to the edge of the airstrip and began to maneuver it slowly downslope toward the Ene. Suddenly, a large force of Ashaninka appeared at the edges of the trail and attacked with bows, arrows, and shotguns. In a brief flurry, the natives killed sixteen guerrillas—one terrorist died with an arrow piercing his throat.

Now it was war, and the Ashaninka knew what that meant. Sendero's message was clear: If you dared defy President Gonzalo, you must die.

After the retaliatory attack, most of the families of Cuti fled southeast along the Mamiri River, which parallels the Cuti River, through a narrow canyon to Tinkarini. This was the haven where, six years earlier, Matías had publicly suggested that I take refuge. A few other families went to the other side of the Mamiri.

Their plan was simply to wait for the padre to return.

PART THREE

The Passage

December 2, 1989. Somehow, word got out to the authorities. Two American helicopters, each of them manned by three U.S. soldiers and six Peruvian Sinchis, swooped into Cuti and evacuated Lucas. Dazed, starving, and grieving, he was taken to the military base at Mazamari, where he was debriefed by Peruvian authorities. Following this, he was flown to Lima on a special U.S. aircraft for further debriefing by Colonel Robert Froude, military attaché to the U.S. embassy, and by another embassy official, Fred Hamiliton.

Following my trip to the States, I had accepted the invitation of a friend to return to Peru aboard an itinerant freighter. It was glorious to spend three weeks on the open sea, away from the concerns of the world. The captain and first mate—both Hindus from India—befriended me, and we held many a late-night philosophical discussion. My only agenda was to return to Cuti in time to celebrate Christmas with my people.

The ship docked in Lima early in December. It was near dawn, so I was somewhat surprised to see Father Felix waiting to greet me.

My provincial chatted with me and the captain as if everything were normal. Only after I had said good-bye to my shipmates and joined him in a car for the drive to his quarters at the Convento de

119

los Padres Descalzos ("Monastery of the Barefoot Friars") did he say, "I have something to tell you." Then he blurted out, "They burned down the mission."

A crushing wave of déjà vu washed over me. It was Felix who had told me about the burning of the mission five years earlier. "How are the people?" I asked immediately.

As gently as he could, Felix told me that the terrorists had killed Roy, Mario, and several other Ashaninka. My mind went numb. Felix's words seemed to emanate from a cloud. Roy was dead? Mario was dead? How could this be? I was assaulted by pangs of guilt. Had I done something to trigger this tragedy? I berated myself for leaving the people alone, but my mind countered with the argument that everything was peaceful when I left. I could not have foreseen this, could I?

I pressed for details. Felix explained that all he knew was what he had learned from the American authorities who had debriefed Lucas. He knew that Cuti was destroyed and abandoned, but nothing of the whereabouts of the people. The seven hundred men, women, and children who had lived, worked, played, and studied in and around Cuti had vanished.

This all sounded very strange. Lucas was there at the time? The terrorists killed Roy and Mario, but spared Lucas? He was a Belgian, but in their minds he must have simply been another gringo, an enemy. The information was confusing, and I knew that I needed more facts. I said, "I must get back to Cuti as soon as possible."

Felix warned me that both Colonel Froude and Fred Hamilton of the American embassy had given him the same insistent advice. Felix repeated it now with compassion in his voice: "For your own safety, you should not go back in there."

I asked, "What did you tell them?"

Felix looked resigned as he smiled and answered, "I told them they don't know you."

Where are the people? I screamed to myself. How are they doing? What has happened to Matías and Olga and Nicolás? How is Mario's widow, Claudia? What has happened to the bright-eyed children? How is Antonia, Roy's pregnant wife? No one could, or would, tell me.

I cried silently: How did it all come to this?

The only issue on my mind was somehow to get back into the Ene River valley and find the people. Only then could we figure out what to do next. I searched my mind for possible locations, and I remembered the long-ago conversation when Matías had publicly suggested Tinkarini; I also thought of the remote location at Cubeja. I was sure that the people had gone to one—or both—of these refuges. But how could I find out? How could I get in to see them? I supposed that for the right price I could persuade one of the Satipo bush pilots to fly me to the airstrip at Cuti, but what would I do then? I could not traipse through the jungle alone, searching for a frightened, nebulous group sequestered in any one of several locations.

It was time to tap my resources. I had been in Peru for forty years, and had come to know many persons who had risen to positions of power and influence. Again my thoughts centered on General Pérez of the Peruvian Air Force. I had known him since my days as a parish priest in Santa Helena, when he was a mere lieutenant, fresh out of officers' school. Over numerous late-night drinking sessions, we established a deep friendship. He was an enthusiastic supporter of all mission work in Peru, and I was certain that he would do what he could to help. What's more, he was stationed here in Lima.

General Pérez listened to my report with genuine concern. He spoke with several officers and then assured me that the Peruvian Air Force would, indeed, support my efforts to reach the Ashaninka. Air force helicopters stationed at San Ramón would be made available to take me—and shipments of emergency supplies—directly to the people.

But first, I had to determine where the people were.

My next step was to attempt to speak with Lucas, the only available eyewitness to the tragedy. Felix said that Lucas had been staying with Fred Hamilton of the American embassy. "I was told that he was going to go back to Belgium," Felix said, "but he might still be at Hamilton's."

121

I called Hamilton's apartment and was relieved to find Lucas there. He was eager to see me and agreed to meet me for a drink in the bar of the Bolívar Hotel in the Plaza San Martín.

Lucas appeared to be recovering from his ordeal. He spoke highly of the support provided by the American embassy. They had outfitted him with new clothes and had now bought him a plane ticket home to his native Belgium. "What my own embassy won't do for me, the Americans are doing," he said.

As we shared a drink in the quiet comfort of one of Lima's best hotels, Lucas related the grim, nightmarish story of Sendero's raid upon the mission. He told me how he was forced to drive the tractor that carried Mario, Roy, and Alberto to the end of the airstrip, to the path leading to the river. He reported that he heard three gunshots. He assumed that the men were dead, but he had not seen their bodies.

According to Lucas, Sendero's whispered propaganda campaign had begun to bear fruit. Several of the Ashaninka decided to cast their lot with the terrorists, and chief among them were Moisés Medina and his lover, Claudia. Lucas told me that it was Claudia who had betrayed Mario to the terrorists, and he had now heard that she had persuaded Moisés to join the rebels.

This was very painful to hear. Moisés, for all his faults, had accomplished much good through his work at the mission clinic. Sendero had turned him into a Judas.

When I told Lucas of my determination to return to the Ene River valley, he warned me, without emotion, "It is very dangerous."

Christmas approached. The holiday had always been a great occasion of celebration for us at Cuti. In twenty years, I had never before been absent for the festivities. My generous network of private benefactors in Lima supplied funds for salt, sugar, and other essentials. I bought candy and a few Christmas trinkets for the children. A reporter and photographer from the Peruvian weekly *Caretas* wanted to journey in with me to document the plight of the Ashaninka, so we all went to Satipo and attempted to arrange a flight into the airstrip at Cuti. To my dismay, no one would go. One pilot after another explained his fear that Sendero was guarding the airstrip and would butcher anyone who landed there.

The magazine crew gave up the quest and returned to Lima for Christmas, but I stayed on in Satipo. I realized that there was one way to find out what was going on. We could fly *over* Cuti and not attempt to land.

Finally my good friend Armando Velarde Torres agreed to make the flight. The twenty-eight-year-old bush pilot had about six thousand hours of flight time in his logbook, almost all of it over the jungle. He was a young, but exceptionally good, aviator. With his close-cropped black hair, a perennial smile beneath his mustache, and dark-surfaced glasses, he exuded confidence. He agreed to make two flights—one for reconnaissance and, if we were successful in making contact, another to deliver supplies.

In anticipation, I scrawled a note. I knew that at least a minimal form of leadership would evolve from the crisis. Mario would have been the natural choice, but he was gone, and I suspected that the even-tempered, soft-spoken Matías was the most likely one to assume the role, so I addressed my message to him:

This afternoon the plane will return (unless there is bad weather). In the case of bad weather, the plane will come the following day or the first day of good weather.

Wait for me at the same place you always do and where the plane unloads. In case it is dangerous for you to go and that it is dangerous for the plane to land give us a signal by waving a *cushma* or any other cloth in the air. Make this signal from Tinkarini.

I made three copies of this message and encased them in small plastic bags weighted with stones. I attached red plastic streamers to the bags so that they would be visible when dropped from the sky.

My heart pounded in anticipation as Armando taxied his Cessna to one end of the airstrip and turned for takeoff. Ahead was a flat straightaway of hard dirt and gravel, with patches of grass growing between the well-worn wheel ruts. Armando took off and banked left, climbing quickly to scale the surrounding mountaintops. For a half hour the plane's engine droned as we skimmed over the green-shrouded jungle. From here, the treetop canopy appeared soft and inviting. The ground below us undulated with wavelike formations of peaks and valleys. The terrain was cut by a maze of rivers and waterfalls. Here and there, gray-white fields of limestone were visible on the faces of cliffs.

The aerial view of Cuti produced a mixture of emotions within me. The deserted appearance of the mission made me feel cold and lonely. I told Armando over the sound of the Cessna engine, "It's not quite as bad as I thought." Although there were many burned-out buildings, the school and the chapel were still standing. The airstrip appeared to be in good shape. All in all, the destruction seemed less severe than when the compound was torched in 1984. Buildings could be replaced. It was for Mario and the other victims that I mourned.

But where were the survivors?

I asked Armando to fly over Tinkarini, only a few minutes away.

As we circled low over the mountain crest, I strained for a glimpse. Attracted by the drone of the engine, an Ashaninka man stepped into a clearing and gazed up. Soon, others joined him. I counted dozens here at Tinkarini.

At my request, Armando descended lower. One at a time, I dropped my three packages containing the note to Matías and watched the red streamers flutter to earth. The Ashaninka ran out to retrieve them, and then they disappeared, back to the security of the jungle.

It was the next day before Armando and I could return. As we approached the airstrip at Cuti, my eyes searched for a view of a welcoming party. If the Ashaninka were waiting for us, we were certain it would be safe to land.

But no one was there. To be sure, we circled for many minutes.

Deeply disappointed, we again headed for Tinkarini. Here, the natives were anticipating our arrival. As we flew over, we saw dozens of Ashaninka on the ground below. Each held a *cushma* high over his head, waving it in an exaggerated gesture, warning me that the area was not safe.

We returned to Satipo dispirited, and I spent Christmas in solitude.

I was determined to get the supplies to the Ashaninka, even if I could not deliver them personally. Shortly after Christmas, Armando flew me to Mazamari, where the Sinchi commander agreed to loan me parachutes and two men so that we could conduct an airdrop.

On December 29, I composed another letter to Matías, and placed it in with the supplies:

Seeing that there are no natives at the airstrip and that you gave me the signal not to land, I am returning to Satipo and then to Lima. I will try again at the end of January. Meanwhile, if possible, try to get information to me either at Satipo or Puerto Ocopa.

Before we left, Armando removed the passenger seats and the right door of his Cessna. The two Sinchis and I strapped ourselves in, and Armando guided his plane into the skies over Satipo, banking and climbing quickly to rise above the surrounding mountains.

When we reached Tinkarini a half hour later, the Ashaninka gathered on the ground below. The Sinchis pushed open the airplane door and kicked out the parachutes. I watched them float downward and veer toward the waters of the Mamiri. *"Se va al río"* ("They're going to fall into the river"), I moaned. But at the last moment, a stray wind current carried them onto the riverbank. The Ashaninka ran for them quickly.

"Feliz Navidad," I whispered.

January was the time for the provincial chapter, the meeting held every three years to conduct the business of the Franciscans throughout the province. My colleagues had elected me as a delegate, and I had to attend, so I decided to use this as an opportunity to see if I could get help from various sectors in Lima.

During the weeks of the sessions, I arranged to meet with Fred Hamilton of the American embassy. On the appointed evening, when I went to meet him at his apartment, I was surprised to see the front of the building guarded by two sentries armed with machine guns. An attendant in the lobby announced my arrival by telephone, and Hamilton came downstairs to fetch me, accompanied by a personal bodyguard.

His second-floor apartment was comfortable, but not ostentatious. To enter, we had to pass through a double set of doors. The inner one appeared to be made of cast iron, like something one might see at Fort Knox.

"All this security has been imposed upon me by the embassy," Hamilton explained. "All of us are obliged to abide by the rules."

He showed me to a couch and presented me with a drink, and our conversation turned quickly toward the plight of the Ashaninka. Hamilton expressed sympathy for my desire to return to the Ene River valley, but he warned, "It is crazy for you to go in there." His tone seemed genuine and sincere.

"I'm going to go in, and the Peruvian Air Force is going to support me," I replied.

Hamilton raised an eyebrow and commented, "You know how the Peruvian Air Force is. They will promise you, and—"

"I think I will be able to get in," I cut him off.

As the conversation continued, I found the man a bit haughty, trying to present an impression of urbane sophistication. His posture was as ramrod straight as the sharp crease in his trousers, and there was an almost robotlike air about him. He shocked me when he stated that he had been completely unaware of the drug trafficking in the valley, especially around Cutivireni.

I stared straight into his eyes and declared, "That is a complete lie!" His face reddened with embarrassment and anger, and I hastened to explain, "I do not mean to say that *you* are a liar. But it is obviously a lie to say that the *embassy* did not know what was going on in the Ene. The embassy had all the information. On several occasions, I have given them the details, and I am sure that those reports are on file."

Hamilton explained that his work was so unimportant—according to him, he was little more than a paperboy at the embassy, a small spoke in the wheel—that he would not have been informed. He said that the military attaché, Colonel Froude, occupied a much more important position in the embassy's hierarchy. I glanced about Hamilton's apartment and wondered why such an ineffectual peon needed such elaborate security.

I told him that I was acquainted with one of the DEA officers, Paul Prudencio. Several times in Lima I had discussed with him the drug problems in Cuti, and he had even visited the mission to see for himself how the smugglers had commandeered our airstrip for their own purposes.

"I do not even know of this man," Hamilton demurred.

When I told Hamilton of my meeting and conversation with Lucas before he returned to Belgium, he asked me to do him a favor: If and when I spoke to anyone about the terrorist attack, I was not to mention Lucas—"for his own security," Hamilton explained enigmatically.

I had no time to dwell on this statement, for Hamilton now suggested that we continue our conversation over dinner. Given the level of security I had already witnessed, I was surprised when we walked out onto the streets of Lima unaccompanied by any guards.

At the restaurant, Hamilton ordered a full meal, but I was not hungry and settled for a cup of coffee. Once more I began to detail for him what had happened to our mission at Cuti.

"I want very much to help," he said. "But I am very limited because I am such an unimportant man at the embassy." He repeated the comment that he was the "last spoke in the wheel," and said that he did not agree with the political decisions that had been coming in from the States and promulgated by the embassy. His mood seemed to turn suddenly. He growled that he was "fed up" with his work and claimed that he was ready to quit the Foreign Service. "I'm seriously thinking of joining the priesthood," he announced. He said that he wanted to return to the States and enter a seminary. However, he did not feel called to missionary work; rather, he wanted to be a parish priest back home in America, where it was more comfortable.

The words buzzed into my ears and bounced around in my head. This was a strange man, impressive and forceful, yet somehow weak and evasive. I decided to reserve my judgment and listen to him carefully. My bottom line was, What help could he provide for the people?

Hamilton's final words to me that evening were, "Okay, Father, we don't think you should go in. But if you do, why don't you go in with *our* men. We'll have two helicopters in Mazamari, and we'll help you out."

I thought: I'll take this man at face value. The Peruvian helicopters were stationed in San Ramón. American helicopters from Mazamari would be much more convenient and, given what I knew about the Peruvian military, were certain to be more reliable. What's more, Hamilton's words gave me hope that the Americans might help us rebuild Cuti, once order was reestablished. Deciding to rely upon the Americans rather than the Peruvians, I happily agreed.

By the time I returned to the Monastery Descalzos that evening, I hoped that in Hamilton I had found an important contact, and perhaps even a new friend. I could overlook his haughty exterior and his oh-so-careful diplomatic statements. I was a bit skeptical about his plans to enter the priesthood—his presentation had been a bit overblown—but I was convinced of his sincerity in wanting to help the natives. What else mattered?

While in Lima, I also came to know Colonel Robert Froude, the military attaché. Our first meeting occurred when Hamilton took me to Froude's home for a dinner party. The colonel lived in a splendid home in an upscale section of Lima known as San Isidro. The yard held a lovely terrace surrounding a swimming pool. Inside, the house was lavishly furnished, a bit pretentious for my taste. The bathroom featured a garish, mirrored ceiling, for which Froude apologized, noting that this was a rented house. I was surprised at the lack of security precautions, for according to Hamilton, Colonel Froude was on a higher level than he was. Yet here, I did not see a single armed sentry, nor anything resembling the heavy cast-iron door that guarded Hamilton's apartment.

The lavish feast began with a sideboard of hors d'oeuvres and a plentiful supply of liquor. The main course was a delicious barbecued filet mignon. After dinner, we sipped fine Napoleon cognac.

Colonel Froude attempted to evoke a machismo image, but he seemed to take his conversational cues from Hamilton. Like Hamilton, Froude offered me his friendship and told me that he would do everything within his power to help the Ashaninka, even if it meant sticking out his own neck. In a conspiratorial tone, he hinted that he might be willing to take certain actions that would have to be kept secret from other embassy personnel.

Both Hamilton and Froude pricked up their ears when I mentioned some of my Peruvian sources of support, such as the Pardo family and Senator Miguel Vega.

Late in the evening, Colonel Froude suggested, "You must take pictures of what is going on out there."

I nearly laughed in his face. I asked, "People are getting killed and you expect me to take photographs?"

"Well," he explained, "the embassy does not believe what is going on."

I thought: A revolution is underway in the jungle. Is it possible that the gringos are such idiots that they don't know that? Are they interested only in images?

Several dinner invitations followed, and each event at Colonel Froude's home was more elegant than the previous. One of these was attended by the second-in-command of the embassy, a Mr. Dion, who claimed that he came specifically to meet me. Colonel Froude added the comment that U.S. ambassador Anthony Quainton was also eager to talk to me.

On several occasions, the embassy men made unsubtle attempts to discern my political bent. Hamilton mentioned that the embassy used to have good relations with the Maryknolls, a Catholic foreign mission society that was active throughout Central and South America. The Maryknolls were among a group of activists who could be lumped together in a loosely defined movement of so-called liberation theologians. Their agenda was social justice, and their politics could be considered a bit to the left. They were not communists, but I knew that the U.S. government perceived them as such. Hamilton bemoaned the fact that the Maryknolls now snubbed the embassy, and said, "I don't think the politicians in the U.S. understand the situation in Peru." In a subdued tone, he ventured the thought that perhaps some form of socialist government was appropriate for this country. "What do *you* think?" he asked.

I thought: He's trying to loosen my tongue. I backed away from the topic, aware that to these bureaucrats, terms such as *liberation theology, leftist,* and *socialist* were synonymous with *communism.*

What is going on? I wondered. Why is the embassy so interested in what I think? Was the series of social events at Colonel Froude's home used, to a certain extent, for the specific purpose of evaluating me?

These questions deepened when I heard reports from some of the friars at the Convento de los Padres Descalzos, where I was staying. They said that a car from the American embassy (with bulletproof glass in the windows) had picked up Father Bill Brown. He was a good friend who had worked with me at Cuti in the distant past, and I was curious to know what dealings he had with the embassy. But when I confronted him with the report, he denied it. I found this very strange, for he had always been very open with me, and I doubted that he would lie. I suspected that he was told to keep quiet about this strange encounter.

In January, a band of terrorists invaded the village of San Martín, where they butchered numerous Quechua settlers, dousing some of their victims with gasoline and then setting them ablaze.

Another rebel contingent attacked an Ashaninka settlement at San Ramón de Pangoa on the western outskirts of the Ene River valley; we heard grisly rumors of children being forced to eat the tongues of their parents.

Following this assault, a Peruvian television crew managed to reach San Ramón de Pangoa, to tape an interview with an Ashaninka man known as Shinanki, the leader of the survivors. As he spoke to the reporter, Shinanki held a large bow in his hands, and rocked it back and forth nervously. Behind him, a young man whittled an arrow out of chontawood. A fearful child cried. Shinanki reminisced about the old days, when the Ashaninka lived in harmony with the land, when there was no need for money and the civilized conveniences it could buy. "We want to go back in time," he proclaimed. "We were ignorant, but we were clean."

February 2. Sendero did not know about the enclave at Tinkarini, but other Ashaninka did. It was Moisés who led a band of renegade Ashaninka to Tinkarini and surprised the Cuti refugees. Natives screamed and ran for the jungle, and the terrorists set upon the stragglers, hacking to death eighteen women and children. Matías's wife Olga took a volley of shotgun pellets in the shoulder and hand as she shielded her child.

Among the victims were Capitán's wife, and three of his four daughters.

Once again the survivors disappeared into the rain forest, and this time they ran for even deeper cover.

While I was still in Lima, Michel Saenz sought me out, suggesting that we find some way of going back into the Ene River valley together. This troubled me, for I worried that if additional people got involved, the Americans, who were obviously cautious, might back off from their promises of support. In addition, pride got the better of me; I reasoned that I alone was the one who should go in to save the people.

I snubbed Mickey at first, returning to Satipo alone. To my surprise, the Frenchman followed me there.

I said to myself: Mariano, you do not have a monopoly on the natives. Mickey is a good man, and he loves them, too. Besides, he is younger and stronger than you. How can you refuse his offer to help?

Armando flew Mickey and me on a reconnaissance mission over Tinkarini, but there was no sign of the natives. Following the most recent attack, the Ashaninka had vanished.

Mickey and I took up temporary residence at the mission house in Mazamari, where the Sinchi chaplain, Father Joaquín Ferrer, received us graciously. The Americans at the military base told us that within two weeks their helicopters would arrive from Santa Lucía to assist us.

As we waited for some news of the natives, Mickey and I held many spirited conversations. I wondered why the terrorists seemed so intent upon destroying the Ashaninka, and Mickey responded by pulling out a map. It was he who explained to me the strategic nature of the territory. The Sinchis could attack Sendero from their base here at Mazamari, located to the north of the terrorist stronghold. Similarly, the air force could strike from Huancayo to the west and the navy could move up from the base at Luisiana to the south. If pressed from these three logical points, Sendero's only line of retreat was to the east, along the Cutivireni River, through Ashaninka land. It was the unfortunate lot of the Ashaninka that they lived in the midst of Sendero's escape route.

As I pondered this knowledge, a vague plan took shape in my mind. I knew that the Ashaninka loved their land, and they loved the mission at Cutivireni. But it now appeared that Sendero was intent upon clearing the area of all opposition. Would the Ashaninka have to flee the valley altogether? Where could they go? The Ene was the only home they knew.

I thought of Father Adolfo and his mission at Kiriketi in the Urubamba region, far to the east, across the Vilcabamba Range. I knew that it was a favorable territory for hunting and fishing, for I had seen flights come into Satipo from Kiriketi with dried meats for sale. The Urubamba was far from Sendero, but would the Ashaninka consent to go there? Would their cousins, the Machiguenga, accept such a migration? I realized with a start that it was possible that some of the Ashaninka had already attempted the treacherous overland trek to the Urubamba. I had to find out.

On February 21, 1990, a Wings of Hope pilot named Hervé flew Mickey and me from Mazamari to Kiriketi, via a necessarily circuitous route. The fourteen-thousand-foot peaks of the Vilcabamba Range are nearly always shrouded by thick clouds, making flight treacherous. To avoid this peril, Hervé had to circle to the north and follow the basin of the Tambo River until it was safe to turn to the south. The detour added about an hour of flying time to the trip.

At Kiriketi, Father Adolfo received us most cordially and pledged to help the Ashaninka in any way he could. There were no refugees here, although Father Adolfo said he had heard rumors that some families had attempted the journey, but were forced to turn back. He reminded me of the rigors of crossing the Vilcabamba Range; in addition to the difficulties of following a barely visible path up and across numerous sheer cliffs, one had to negotiate a two-day trek through the narrow channel of an elongated valley that was subject to murderous flash floods. During the rainy season, the trip through this valley was suicidal.

Father Adolfo took us on a tour of his mission facilities, and I was very impressed. I was also eager to go upriver to view the native settlements.

We spoke late into the night about the future of the natives and the best way to prepare them for further clashes with progress. I was impressed with Father Adolfo's dedication to the Machiguenga—his people—and his calm, balanced ideas. It was refreshing to meet a missionary whose main interest was the welfare of the natives and not cramming the sacraments down their throats and forcing them to embrace a so-called civilized way of life. We toured the medical facilities, and I was very taken with the husband-and-wife team of doctors who worked here. They served some thirty separate communities all along the river, and to expand their effectiveness they had trained some of the natives in first-aid techniques.

Two mornings later, in the midst of a torrential rainstorm, two Machiguenga, Julian and Martín Montaro, took Mickey and me upriver to give us an idea of how their people would react to a possible influx of Ashaninka refugees. Father Adolfo allowed us to use the mission's motor, which we installed on a native boat. He supplied us with gasoline and oil and also cans of food, rice, coffee, and sugar.

Before we embarked, Father Adolfo briefed me concerning the special hazards of river travel here at lower altitudes, where the water was warmer. We were still too far upriver from the Amazon to worry about more than an occasional school of piranhas. More troublesome were the stingrays that might lash your leg with a

133

painful strike; the best defense was to splash the water prior to entering, to scare them off.

Our destination was the home of a Machiguenga named Flavio, at a place called Cuchiri. I had met Flavio some time earlier; he was a teacher, who at one time had considered entering the priesthood. The trip was lengthy, for custom dictates that one does not pass a Machiguenga hut without stopping and explaining the purpose of one's journey. It was four o'clock before we arrived at Cuchiri. Flavio was not there, but he appeared about forty-five minutes later, bearing a tapir on his shoulders; it had been a good hunt. He greeted us and immediately began chattering excitedly, waving his arms in wide gestures. The other natives listened to him intently, obviously deferring to his judgment.

In the evening, Flavio and others gathered to discuss with us what was happening to the Ashaninka, but I did not yet broach the possibility of a migration. I suffered through this meeting. A chilling, steady rain brought an ache to my bones, and I had to excuse myself several times, for I had a bad case of the grippe. I was grateful when it was time to retire to my sleeping bag.

At breakfast in the morning, Flavio presented me with the prized portion of the tapir, the liver. Gathering my courage, I slid a piece into my mouth. It was barely cooked and full of what felt like tiny, gritty bits of glass. Even after many years of living in the jungle and eating what the Indians ate, I could not stomach this particular delicacy. I picked at the pungent, dark red, membrane-filled meat, and took only a few more tentative bites.

My condition grew worse throughout the day, and I felt my fever rising, but I tried to attend to the business of inspecting the Cuchiri area. I was pleased when the Machiguenga themselves brought up the subject of an Ashaninka migration. Flavio said that he and his people had identified a portion of land where the Ashaninka could settle without disturbing Machiguenga life.

These are good, generous people, I concluded. They could teach us all a lesson in brotherhood.

Mickey and I and our guides left on the motorboat trip back downriver; as I shivered from both the discomfort of the relentless rain and the effects of fever, I reflected on what I had seen and heard. The Urubamba region was an option for the Ashaninka, I decided. A move here could be their salvation, but it would be a bittersweet solution for me. Kiriketi was a Dominican mission; there would be no place here for a Franciscan such as I.

The motor gave out three times. Each time we had to put in at the riverbank to attend to it, and each time we were assaulted by *manta blanca,* peppering our skin with bites. The only defense was to jump into the river and brave its other hazards.

By the time we arrived back at Kiriketi, I was exhausted and drenched with fever-induced perspiration. One of the doctors gave me an injection of antibiotics, and Father Adolfo put me to bed.

Three more days passed as we awaited a plane to take us back to Mazamari. Further injections brought my fever under control, and I spent much time in rewarding discussions with Father Adolfo. But it was difficult to wait patiently for transportation, for I knew that this was another three days that my people had to endure in isolation and fear.

CHAPTER NINE

March 1, 1990. I rode with Father Ferrer in his Jeep on one of his regular journeys from Mazamari to Satipo. When we arrived I headed for Bar Azul, the café that Fortunato and Yolanda owned. Fortunato greeted me with a wide, toothy smile and a bear hug. Town life appeared to agree with him. "You're getting fat," I chided, gesturing toward the paunch that had grown over his stomach muscles.

He laughed and pointed at my own ample belly. Then his dark eyes grew serious as I asked if he had any news about the Ashaninka. "No," he said sadly.

Over a few beers, we theorized about the whereabouts of the Cuti refugees. Fortunato agreed with me that the Cubeja region, which formed a natural mountain fortress, was a likely site.

When I asked if he had seen anybody around town whom he knew had connections with the terrorists, Fortunato lowered his eyes and his voice. "Be careful in this town," he warned.

I left the café, on the north side of Satipo's central plaza, and found my way to a drugstore where I made a few essential purchases. In the store, I suddenly came face-to-face with Antonio, whom I had last seen at the end of our argumentative bus ride from San Ramón to Lima, before I left for the U.S. I was in no mood to banter. Theoretical concepts had turned into practical, hideous reality. I could not prove it, but I felt certain that he had been involved with the destruction of the mission. I took a direct, combative approach. "Why did you burn the mission down? Why did you kill the natives?"

Antonio was in his late forties. His meek, weasellike exterior belied the fact that he, as well as two of his grown daughters, was committed to Sendero. He replied with what I assumed was a smooth-tongued lie: He knew nothing about this, for he had been in Lima at the time of the attack. He promised to make inquiries when he returned to the valley.

I did not believe that he had remained in Lima during all those intervening months, and I told him so. I watched my back as I walked away, muttering an old Spanish proverb to myself: *"Cuídase del agua manza."* ("Be careful of still waters.")

At a small house at the edge of Satipo, I met quietly with a woman who knew much about what was happening in the Ene River valley. In fact, she had once been a full-fledged member of the terrorist movement and was having difficulty extricating herself entirely. Sendero still demanded numerous favors from her.

One of the stories she related to me was of how Sendero held what it called judgments to deal with any of its members who were suspected of the slightest indiscretion. The accused was forced to sit on a tree stump in the jungle court, but there was no testimony and no defense—only the administration of the sentence. The victim was aware of his fate. Someone would come up from behind and slip a wire garrote around the condemned person's neck. Another would stab. Before the judgment was over, each person present was required to administer a stab wound, either to the mortally wounded body or to the corpse.

My informant had been involved in such an incident and was wrestling with her conscience. She wanted to know if she had committed a sin by stabbing a corpse. "Don't worry about it," I said. "The good Lord will understand. He's the only one who knows all the circumstances. Don't lose time worrying about what happened in the past, but look toward the future."

The woman warned me not to consider flying into Cuti, for she had heard that the terrorists had mined the airstrip. Whether or not this was true, I knew that I could not take a chance. I would have to pass the warning on to the various civilian pilots I knew, as well as to the military authorities at Mazamari.

The woman provided me with two very different versions of what the terrorists wanted from me. First, she said, according to some of the people who had escaped from the valley, the Sendero raid on Cuti had not gone according to plan. The raiding party had orders to burn my house and the mission, but not necessarily to harm the natives. The Ashaninka are not overly protective of their possessions, but if anyone sheds native blood, they must have vengeance. It was because the terrorists disobeyed orders and murdered six Indians that the Ashaninka retaliated. Now the terrorist leaders wanted to speak to me, to persuade me to intervene and calm the Ashaninka, to avert further bloodshed. They vowed that if I did so, they would return all that they stole, and they would never attack the mission again. "They say it is very urgent," my informant said to me. "They want no conflict with the natives. And the only person who can bring some agreement between the natives and the terrorists is you."

"How can I know that this is true?" I asked her.

She had been told that Sendero had a plan to convince me. The terrorists claimed that all of my personal belongings and important documents were hidden in a certain area of the school. Sendero suggested that I go to Cuti to verify this; then I would know that they were being honest with me. The terrorists assured that they would not harm me.

But the woman provided me with a second story, related to her by a settler who had once been a member of Sendero. According to this source, the terrorists wanted to entice me to return to Cuti so that they could capture me alive; they had a special torture in mind, which would serve as a lesson for all the natives. "Tell the father that he is to leave this region, and if he can, he should even leave Peru," this source had said. "There is a high order from way above that he is to die, because he is the hindrance to their cause in this region." The source warned that the terrorists would find me sooner or later, and even knew that I was staying in the parish house at Mazamari at this very moment.

138

It was all very confusing. I did not know whom to believe, or what to do.

While I was in Satipo, I visited one more important contact, a good friend connected with the military, who provided me with three hand grenades.

Captain Edward Reeder, who commanded the Green Beret detachment at Mazamari, presented a gruff and stern exterior; he reminded me of the action-movie star Chuck Norris, whom I had seen in a few taped dramas. The captain was cordial and understanding, and he quickly gained my confidence. Apparently, personnel from the American embassy had briefed him, and he pledged to help me and the Ashaninka in any way that he possibly could. He agreed to take me into the valley as soon as the helicopters returned from duty in Santa Lucía.

From our base at the mission house, Mickey and I held long discussions, speculating on the whereabouts of the natives. I argued that they were in Cubeja, because of the times I had joked with Olga about running away there—and because this was also Fortunato's guess.

Mickey agreed that Cubeja was a reasonable possibility, but he wanted to try to contact Shirampari at the settlement n ar the Parijaro falls. Shirampari was Mickey's closest friend amo g the Ashaninka. What's more, he would be a strong and fierce warrior, should the need arise. Mickey pointed out that Parijaro lay directly on the Cutivireni River, on the immediate line of Sendero's crucial escape route, and he contended that Shirampari was likely to be our best source of information.

I countered that the terrain around Parijaro was very mountainous, severed by deep gorges and the large, cascading waterfall that, although it provided great beauty, also cut across the trails. This was an extremely difficult region to navigate. Worse, I reminded Mickey, "Shirampari's sister Tsinani is married to Moisés, the traitor." Even though Moisés had taken up with Claudia, he would still have influence over Tsinani and her brother. "Is he to be trusted?" I asked.

"I know Shirampari," Mickey said. He assured me that we could rely on the man completely. "We will be much safer where Shirampari is," Mickey contended.

"Okay," I agreed with reluctance. "We will ask the helicopter pilot to take us to Parijaro."

The day before the flight, Captain Reeder asked me to describe the layout of Cuti and point out where the terrorists would most likely enter the compound. I sketched out the airstrip area for him as best I could, highlighting the storage buildings at the far end. I pointed out a pathway that led up from the Ene to the airstrip and explained, "This is the way the terrorists would come."

March 9. The day was cloudy and drizzly. Mickey and I whiled away the morning. In the afternoon, sure that the Green Berets would not attempt a flight with the visibility so limited, we headed to a bar in Mazamari. But just as we lifted beers to our lips, several American troops rushed inside, looking for us. We had to get to the airfield fast, they said. The helicopters had arrived and the flight was on!

We raced back to the mission house to gather our few supplies: food, blankets, and a two-way radio. Captain Reeder gave us a handful of emergency flares. Our secret stash of three hand grenades was hidden among our packs, along with Mickey's dismantled shotgun and my pistol.

We took off from Mazamari at 3:15 P.M. for the forty-five-minute flight. Our craft led the way east as a second helicopter flew behind and above, offering protection. The noise of the engines roared in through the open doorways. Mickey squatted on the floor in front of me, directly behind the pilot, shouting directions in his ear, leading him toward Shirampari's settlement at Parijaro.

After thirty minutes of flying time, we passed Cubeja, off to the left. I spotted an area of cleared ground. Seven or eight huts were visible, and the thatching on the roofs was still green, indicating that they were recently built. I tried to point out these huts to Victor, the Green Beret sitting next to me, but he could not hear me over the noise of the engines.

Still directed by Mickey, the helicopter moved away from the huts at Cubeja.

Minutes later we reached a high-altitude clearing, at an elevation of well over three thousand feet. Below us, the giant waterfall of Parijaro fed into the Cutivireni River. Near the clearing were a few huts, partially burned. The pilot hovered his craft just off the ground as a contingent of U.S. soldiers jumped out and, with practiced movements, formed a perimeter. They trained their eyes and their machine guns on the surrounding jungle.

With a start I realized that I was now in a war zone. The moment seemed unreal.

Mickey and I pushed our gear out of the open doors of the helicopter and dropped to the ground. The fierce downdraft created by the rotors kicked dirt and bits of grass into our faces. Debris from the roofs of the burned-out huts flew about.

Instantly the sentries hustled back aboard. The pilot shouted out a reminder that he would return to this same spot in two days to pick us up. Then he gunned the engine; the rotors whirred faster, and the helicopter lifted off the ground. Very suddenly, Mickey and I were stranded on a mountaintop in the aboriginal jungle; the decreasing noise of the retreating engines emphasized our isolation.

The area around us was grassy and treeless. We gathered our equipment and moved toward one of the nearby huts. As we entered, we shared a gaze of astonishment; here was a small propane stove and a *primos*, another type of camp stove, fueled by gasoline or kerosene, which operated much like a blowtorch.

"A propane stove here?" I muttered. "This could not belong to the Ashaninka."

The stove was almost certain confirmation that terrorists had been here. But where were they now? And would they return?

"What are we going to do?" I asked Mickey.

By now it was late in the afternoon. "There," Mickey said, pointing down into the jungle foliage that spanned the mountain cliffs from here all the way to the riverbank. "I know where Shirampari lives." He guessed that we were about a thousand feet above the crest of the Parijaro waterfall. That giant fountain splashed downward for a full thousand feet. Shirampari and his people had several camps in the area, but Mickey guessed that they were presently situated at a point more than halfway down the falls and off to the southeast. He said that the trek would take only about forty-five minutes, but the trail was steep—nearly vertical at times—so he suggested, "Why don't I go alone, because I can walk faster." When I agreed to this plan, he warned, "Be careful. If the terrorists come, it will be from the direction of the river." He left me with my pistol and two of the grenades. He took his 12-gauge shotgun and the remaining grenade and left with the promise, "I'll be back later."

I watched the Frenchman's slender frame disappear from the small meadow into the deep green overgrowth.

I busied myself by scouting the immediate area. I walked over to a ledge and strained for a view of the waterfall but could not see it. For a few moments I stood there quietly, listening to the rumble of the water as it tumbled along the rocks to the river. Then I returned to the huts, alone with my thoughts.

Idly, my hand grasped a stick. I scraped it across the ground, amusing myself by creating patterns in the dust. Then, like Don Quixote, I lurched about, wielding the stick as if it were a saber, decapitating imaginary enemies. A colony of ants caught my attention, and I watched them live the dramas of their own tiny lives, oblivious to drug traffickers and terrorists.

By the time twilight descended, my nerves were frayed. I concluded that Mickey was having difficulty locating Shirampari. If he did not return soon, I reasoned that he would surely wait until dawn to negotiate the treacherous upward path. Facing the prospect of a night alone, I decided to prepare camp while I could still see. I lugged my backpack into the partially burned house and found a charred slab of wood that could serve as a bed. I spread mosquito netting around it and then carefully positioned my hand grenades within easy reach. I started a fire, heated some water, and brewed a cup of coffee.

I realized that I was not only tense, but frustrated and angry. I berated myself for being here at Parijaro, trying to make contact with *Mickey's* friend, instead of seeking out *my* friends.

Just before total darkness encompassed me, I heard the sound of someone approaching. My first thought was that it must be Mickey, but in an instant I realized that it could be *anybody*. I grabbed for my pistol and trained its barrel at the doorway of the hut. A moral dilemma flashed through my mind: Was I willing to kill another human being in order to protect my own life? Would my convictions prevail over the basic human survival instinct? I did not know.

A face appeared, framed in the doorway of the hut, illuminated by the glow of my fire. It was a friendly Ashaninka face, and others soon joined it. I allowed the air to gasp from my lungs and I lowered my pistol.

The natives were pleased to see me, but Mickey was not with them. They indicated that in the morning they would take me to him, down at Shirampari's lower camp. We would leave very early, and Mickey had sent instructions to bring the radio and battery. This latter request perturbed me. The twelve-volt battery was very heavy, and I could see no reason to lug it all the way down the mountain and then haul it back up the following day for our scheduled rendezvous with the helicopters.

We dined on sardines from my cache of supplies, supplemented with a bit of yucca root that the Ashaninka had brought with them. Some of them spoke a few words of Spanish, and I was able to find out important pieces of information. They were well aware of what had happened to the mission, and they indicated, as I had thought, that at least some of the Ashaninka from Cuti had taken refuge at Cubeja. Yes, they believed that Shirampari could take me there.

All through a long, sleepless night, I asked myself: What am I to do? What do the natives expect of me?

In the morning I realized that I had misunderstood the plan. The natives informed me that we were to stay here this day and wait for Mickey to arrive.

Heavy rains descended upon us, and the morning passed slowly. The weather delayed Mickey's return.

When the Frenchman finally did appear, Shirampari was not with him. Mickey reported that there was a weird mood in the

Ashaninka camp. He could draw little news from Shirampari; in fact, no one seemed willing to speak openly with him. "We have to go back down the hill," Mickey said. *"You* have to talk to Shirampari."

Our tension erupted in a heated argument. I reminded Mickey that Shirampari was supposed to be *his* friend, not mine. Was the leader of Parijaro acting like a little king, demanding an audience with me? I stared off toward the edge of the precipice that led toward the falls. "That's one hell of a drop," I muttered. "In fact, it's a goddamn gorge."

"The natives will help us," Mickey pointed out. "They will carry the battery and the radio. Just make the best of it. Shirampari is down there and wants to speak to you."

"Why the hell didn't Shirampari come up here?" I asked. My nerves were worn, my frustration growing. I stifled an impulse to throttle Mickey. I grumbled, "Shirampari walks around the jungle like you walk around Grand Central Station. There's no reason he can't come here."

"No, he won't come," Mickey said.

My resentment festered as we packed our equipment. We carefully shrouded the battery and the radio in waterproof plastic, stowed both items in baskets, and, using vines, lashed these to the strong backs of two natives. I loaded my own pack with a few tins of tuna and sardines, a small supply of coffee and sugar, and a couple of bags of candy that the children loved so much.

Then we set off.

An Ashaninka led the way, moving swiftly and easily. We left the meadow and followed a tapir trail down a gentle incline and into a dense growth of trees. Soon we encountered the first in a series of slopes, some approaching the vertical. To negotiate the worst of these, we had to grasp strong jungle vines. The terrain was slippery from the rainfall, and several times I lost my footing on the slick clay surface. I told myself: Mariano, you are becoming very experienced at sliding on your ass. The roar of cascading water grew ever louder in our ears.

We had descended about five hundred feet when we encountered the most perilous portion of the trip. Here the trail ran

144

directly across the top of the Parijaro waterfall; we had to cross it from west to east. Cold spray filled the air and drenched our clothes. The deafening blast of noise from the falls drowned out my curses. My anger at Mickey and Shirampari reached a new peak.

In a single file, we began to cross the twenty-foot stream that emanated from an underground river. I stepped into the current and found myself in icy cold, knee-deep water. The stone bed beneath my feet was polished to a slippery sheen by eons of erosion; as I inched forward, I felt as if I were walking on a carpet of banana peels. The native in front of me reached back with his hand. I grabbed for support and he held firm as I jumped over a chasm in the rock.

I stopped to catch my breath. To my right was a sheer wall of stone. To my left, was an eight-hundred-foot drop straight down. The current pulled at my feet, urging me toward the edge of the precipice. Holding tightly to the hand in front of me, I moved warily ahead and across.

On the far side of the falls, we were enclosed by trees. From here, the trail sloped slightly upward as it moved east of the water.

I hoped that the rest of the trip would be easier, but I was dismayed to see the trail lead us to another series of cliffs, even steeper than those above the falls. At several points, clinging for my very life to vines, I had to lunge across fearsome chasms.

It was nearly noon when we reached a clearing and a small hut, which Mickey said was the home of Vikingo. The house was empty, for Vikingo had traveled to Sankatiaro on a sort of reconnaissance mission to see if he could learn any news concerning the terrorists. Mickey offered the welcome news that Shirampari's settlement was only a short distance beyond.

Shirampari saw us coming along the trail but remained near his hut and did not even venture forward to meet us. I was happy to recognize María, a young girl who had been with us at the mission for many years, but I was surprised to realize that she, too, was avoiding me. In fact, all of the Ashaninka were especially wary. Each time I ventured a question as to the possible whereabouts of the Cuti refugees, all eyes looked to Shirampari for his unspoken permission to speak. And I was rewarded with stony silence. Only the children greeted me warmly as I parceled out candy.

Mickey spoke with Shirampari alone for a few minutes, then came back to me in a defensive mood. "He won't talk," Mickey said. "He just doesn't know anything."

I growled, "What do you mean? He has to know something about what has gone on."

"No."

"Well, I'm going to speak to him—"

"No, don't," Mickey interrupted.

I was on the verge of explosion. Mickey had dragged me here— forcing me to risk my neck—at the whim of a man who now refused to talk to me? Mickey's attitude angered me. He claimed to have a close, warm relationship with the natives, but had he spent twenty years with them as I had? No, he was a relative newcomer. It is one thing to laugh with the Ashaninka, to wear *cushma*, to allow them to paint your face, to walk barefoot through the jungle with them, to drink their *piarinsti*, and to eat their yucca. But these things are superficial. To be sure, Mickey understood the words of the Ashaninka language far better than I, but I doubted that he had much insight into the subtleties of their personalities. He knew what was on the Ashaninka tongue, but did he know what was in the heart?

I said none of this. I merely snapped, "They don't want us here. This is just a waste of time."

Then I said to myself: Mariano, cool off. There was a small stream nearby, and I decided to do just that.

As I bathed, the cold water soothed my body, but my mind still fumed. Mickey is impetuous and imprudent, I thought. On the other hand, I had to admit to myself that he was a very sensitive person, intuitive and perceptive. I knew that his intentions were good, but, I thought, so is the pavement on the road to hell. One part of my mind concluded: He's wrong. But another conceded: I'm wrong. As my internal dialogue continued, I compromised and decided: We are both wrong. There was no choice but to calm down and reassess the situation from scratch.

By the time I emerged from the water, I had made a firm resolution: Whatever we do, this time it will be *my* decision.

I headed straight for Shirampari's hut, found Mickey at his side, and declared gruffly, "We have to talk things over."

Before I could pursue this, Mickey announced with a grin that Shirampari had gone hunting, especially for me. Once more I fumed. It was true that Shirampari had killed a monkey, but I knew damn well that he had not done so just for me.

The natives fed us a lunch of monkey and yucca that, after the sardines of the past two days, tasted like a banquet. I needed a great deal of water to wash it down, however, for a lump of anger still lodged in my throat.

After the meal, I spoke with Shirampari in Spanish. A few other natives gathered around, and I sometimes directed questions at them, but they pretended not to understand, even though I knew that some of them comprehended the thrust of my words. Even María pretended to speak only Ashaninka.

Shirampari declared that he knew nothing of what had happened at Cuti; he did not know where the people were.

Confusion assailed me. Shirampari *was* a good man. I did not know him intimately, but he had been to the mission many times, and I had always thought him to be honorable. Yet patent lies were falling from his lips. The Ashaninka *always* know what is happening to the other communities within their area. What's more, until recent years, when too many of them learned the ways of subterfuge from the settlers, the Ashaninka simply did not lie. Shirampari's evasion was a deep and dangerous mystery.

I asked if he could show us the way from here to Cubeja. I explained, "I know that the people of Cuti are at Cubeja, and I also know there is a path from this river, crossing over that little mountain range, that will lead us to Cubeja." I gestured in the general direction.

Shirampari replied, "I don't know the path."

Mickey winced.

All about, I saw fright-filled eyes. With a shudder I remembered that Shirampari's sister Tsinani was married to Moisés, the traitor.

Our conversation continued, and the level of my dissatisfaction increased. Then, suddenly, we were interrupted by a series of blasts in the distance, emanating from the direction of the mission at

Cuti. Eyes turned toward the west. Shirampari's bearing betrayed nervousness.

"Bomba! Bomba! Cuti! Bomba!" the natives shouted, pointing in the direction of the blasts. This was the sound of furious destruction, uncomfortably close to us. I realized that these Ashaninka were even learning the vocabulary of war.

Later Mickey suggested that we try to reach the Americans on the radio to redirect the helicopters to this lower camp in the morning. That way, we would not have to climb the mountain.

"No," I countered. "We made it very plain to the Green Berets that we would be up there. It would not be very easy for them to find us down here."

Mickey and I both understood that we had to get out of here— away from Shirampari and from each other. As several natives prepared to accompany us back up the mountain, Mickey suddenly "remembered" that he had left a bow and arrow off somewhere in the distance; it was an obvious pretext. He went off to search for it, and said that he would rejoin me at the top of the mountain.

Our small group set off, following the tapir path along the rocks, over boulders, across many streams, and up the series of difficult cliffs. The air was cool, but the exertion drenched us all in perspiration. Grit from the jungle caked our arms, legs and faces. Shortly before we reached the top of the Parijaro falls, we stopped to rest alongside a shallow pool. The water was inviting. I stripped quickly, laying my shirt, shorts, and sneakers on the ground. I removed my crucifix and placed it on a rock. Then I jumped into the refreshing water alongside the Ashaninka, and bathed.

After the respite, we dressed and moved easily through the meadow leading to the top of the falls. Soon I found myself once more faced with the prospect of the treacherous crossing. I worked my way gingerly through the rapid current, greatly aided by the natives.

Only when we had reached the other side did I realize that I had left my crucifix on the rock back by the jungle pool. One of the Ashaninka boys volunteered to retrieve it, and I was impressed as he scurried catlike across the top of the falls. He was back in a few minutes with a broad grin and my cross.

After a trek of two and a half hours, we reached the original camp, the spot for tomorrow's rendezvous with the helicopters. When Mickey arrived later, he was surprised to find that I had made the trip in relatively good shape. By now, Mickey and I both knew that our friendship was endangered, and we avoided speaking to one another.

That evening I reached the Americans by radio and reported what little information I had gathered. We confirmed tomorrow's flight.

We went to bed early, and Mickey pointedly used a different hut from mine. Once more the torrential rains came, and once more, although I was exhausted, I could not sleep. I drank coffee, smoked cigarettes, and found my spirits sinking ever lower, despite the adrenalin that pumped through me. Where were my people? How could I find them? What could I do to help? My thoughts returned to the clearing that I had seen from the helicopter as we flew near Cubeja. I remembered the green thatched roofs, and my resentment against Mickey built once more. Will the Americans be willing to bring us in on a second flight, this time to Cubeja? I wondered. I decided that in the morning I would ask the pilot to drop us at Cubeja instead of taking us back to Mazamari.

Eventually I drifted into a restless, troubled sleep.

About six o'clock in the morning, as only a faint glow of sunlight penetrated the clouds, I was awakened by an unexpected noise—the staccato beat of rotary propellers—emanating from the nearly total darkness.

"The helicopters!" I called out over the sound of the pouring rain, awakening Mickey in the adjacent hut.

Neither of us could believe that the American pilots were flying in the midst this storm, but we quickly packed our gear and ran into the clearing, barefoot. To my surprise, the natives scattered; this was uncharacteristic of the inquisitive Ashaninka.

Left alone, Mickey and I stared into a dense fog. The sound told us that the helicopters were *below* us, but we could not see them, and we knew that they could not see us, way up here on the mountaintop. I thought: My God, they're going to crash into the side of the cliff. Mickey pulled signal flares out of his pack and set them off. I wondered what good it would do to send flares *up* when the helicopters were *down.*

For some time the noise of the rotors teased us, alternately closing in and drifting away. After a half hour, as the morning sun began to filter through the fog, Mickey finally tried a smoke grenade, and that worked.

Once they located us, the aircraft zeroed in quickly. The pilot motioned for us to hurry. Mickey and I ran back and forth to load our gear, and in our rush, we left behind Mickey's shoes and my sneakers.

I hoped that the pilot would take the same route to Mazamari that he had used two days earlier so that I could convince him to let us off at Cubeja. Too late, I realized that he had bypassed Cubeja in order to fly over Cuti, because he wanted to show me what had happened to the airstrip only yesterday.

As we flew over my home, I felt an emptiness deep within. Below me, I saw that the airstrip was pocked with numerous large craters. The pilot told me that it was his men who had dynamited the airstrip in order to render it useless to the drug smugglers and Sendero. These were the explosions that we heard yesterday as we were in Shirampari's camp. My God, I thought, the airstrip was the only hope we had!

Grief overcame me. The aggressive American action had cut off the Ashaninka completely. Tears coursed down my cheeks, and I tried to hide my face. I thought: I'm not going to let the damn Green Berets see this stupid priest crying.

I realized that now we were totally dependent upon the Americans and their helicopters. Without them, it would be impossible to get in.

Arriving at Mazamari, Mickey and I found a hearty breakfast awaiting us. I was not hungry, but I knew that I had to keep up my strength. I sat next to Victor, the Green Beret trooper who was fast becoming my friend, and forced myself to poke at boiled eggs and toast.

As I ate, Captain Reeder approached, sat next to me, and half grumbled, "Your description sucks."

"What do you mean?" I asked in amazement.

"You never told us about the barbed-wire fence along the length of the airstrip," he said.

"We had cows at one time," I explained, thoroughly confused.

"What about the field of elephant grass between the airstrip and the mission?"

"Cows," I explained again.

The captain said, "I hope to hell we never have to depend on you for information—you really—the whole fucking airstrip has a barbed-wire defense."

I explained that I never attempted to describe the airstrip or the entire mission compound for him. I thought that he was interested in the area near the river where Sendero would most likely come from. How was I to know that he planned to destroy our airstrip?

Several minutes passed before we came to see that we had a simple misunderstanding.

Idly, the captain reported that at the far end of the airstrip his men had found two warehouses full of mechanical equipment, tools, piles of metal roofing sheets, and stacks of milled lumber—which, in the jungle, is as precious as gold—along with an electrical generator and several gas-powered motors.

Sendero was systematically stripping the mission buildings and the Ashaninka homes of everything of value. Because they could not haul off the booty all at once, they were stockpiling it and using as many boats as they could find to ferry it across the Ene.

"What did you do with all of this?" I asked.

"We blew it up."

"You just blow up anything when you don't know who it belongs to?" I asked. "That was our property."

One of the Green Berets shrugged and asked, "How were we to know who it belonged to?"

I had to swallow my anger because I needed the Green Berets and their helicopters more than ever. I chose a moment when I thought that Captain Reeder was receptive, and I said, "I think I know where my people are." I turned to Victor and asked, "Remember when we were going over in the helicopter and I pointed out the huts with green leaves?" He did not. I turned back to the captain and said, "I think that's where the people are. Would you please take me there?"

"How do you know?" the captain asked.

"I really don't. But the leaves on the roofs were green."

He seemed unconvinced.

"There's another reason," I added quickly. "I always used to fool around with Olga and tell her, 'I'm going to run away with you to Cubeja.' " I explained that Cubeja was very isolated. The group of natives who lived there were quite primitive. Some of them wore *cushmas* that were not made of cloth, but produced instead from the *kiriniroki* or *potoo* tree, in the old-fashioned manner. "Brother Pío told me, many years ago, that missionaries could not go into Cubeja because the natives had said it was too dangerous. So that makes it a good place to hide."

Captain Reeder asked a good question: "How will we know if the people there are terrorists or natives?"

CHAPTER TEN

March 15, 1990. The helicopter pilot descended slowly, warily, toward Cubeja. Above and behind us, a second helicopter maintained surveillance. I stood in the open doorway with my arms braced against the frame. Behind me, Victor grasped the belt of my pants. This was the compromise that I had worked out with Captain Reeder. If I spotted hostile faces, I would warn the pilot; if the faces were friendly, my presence would reassure them.

As we neared the ground, I spotted a few Ashaninka and waved my arms broadly in greeting. I recognized the gaunt face of Felipe. His black hair was long and unkempt; his *cushma* was ragged. Always slender, he now appeared emaciated. He gave me the first indication of how the people of Cuti would receive me when his face broke into a broad, spontaneous grin.

Green Beret troops dropped to the ground, formed a circle around the aircraft, and trained their machine guns outward; the drill was now a familiar one.

Mickey and I hopped to earth and dragged our supplies out after us. The sentries hustled back on board. The helicopter pilot shouted his assurance that he would be back for us the next day. Then he was gone.

The moment the aircraft disappeared, more natives emerged from the forest. Fourteen refugees from Cuti gathered around, embracing us, crying openly. Never had I seen the Ashaninka demonstrate so much affection. All were extremely thin; the children were coughing, wheezing, and suffering from a variety of ills.

Using his elementary Spanish, Felipe told me that Matías and the others had all been waiting for me. He sent a few of the children to find Matías and tell him that the padre had finally returned. Felipe said that Matías would arrive late in the afternoon, along with his family and one man who had been critically wounded during Sendero's attack on Tinkarini.

Mickey and I settled in. By now, we had made up. We knew that we both wanted to help the Ashaninka in any way we could, and to do that, we had to rise above our petty jealousies.

Our immediate concern was to protect our small supply of explosives—the shotgun shells—from the always-inquisitive Ashaninka. Quickly we fashioned a high bamboo platform and set it up inside one of the few huts, out of reach of the small children, and we warned everyone, *"Dinamita, dinamita!"*

At midmorning, after I was certain that the helicopters had returned to Mazamari, I reached Victor on the radio and told him that we expected the arrival of a badly wounded man—could tomorrow's flight bring a doctor? Victor promised to relay the request.

From Felipe and the others, I drew what details I could concerning the events of the past few months, but I knew that I would have to wait for Matías's arrival to get real information.

For a break, I took a swim in the chilly waters of a nearby creek.

About six o'clock Matías arrived, along with Olga and their son. Capitán was with them also, a strong, handsome yet poignant figure. At Tinkarini, the terrorists had butchered his wife and three of his four children. Now, his sole surviving daughter stood at his side, wide-eyed and fearful.

The wounded man was not with Matías, for he had died along the trail.

Matías and I spoke for hours. He filled me in on the details of the attack on Cuti, and the deaths of Mario, Roy, Alberto, and Martín. As I listened, I felt intense pain. Until now I had not realized the extent of the torture and degradation that Sendero had inflicted upon Mario. Matías also explained the treachery of

Claudia, who had betrayed her own brother-in-law to Sendero and then persuaded her lover, Moisés, to join the enemy force.

I detected a bit of pride in Matías as he recalled the Ashaninka counterattack. Matías said that when the terrorists returned to gut the mission, they took whatever they could find that might be of any use—they even tore the aluminum sheets off the roofs and stacked them on the riverbanks so that they could return for them later. Then they burned what was left, including about eighty houses in the surrounding area. They collected their spoils at one end of the airstrip and proudly surveyed their top prize—our tractor—unaware that the Ashaninka were positioning themselves for an ambush. As the terrorists hauled supplies down the trail from the airstrip to the banks of the Ene, the natives struck, some armed with shotguns, others with bows and arrows. Matías described how one of the terrorists, as he sought to escape, was shot through the throat with an arrow. Matías was not certain how many terrorists were killed, but he knew that it was at least sixteen.

He said that they had received the salt, chocolate, and candy that we had dropped by parachute at Christmastime, but he had deeply distressing news to add to this story. He had received my note suggesting that he attempt to get a letter through to me at Satipo, and acted upon it immediately. He had scrawled a letter and entrusted it to three young men—Antonio, Marcos, and the brother of Chibo. They set off from Tinkarini on a desperate attempt to make contact with me in Satipo, but they were caught by terrorists and murdered.

The litany of horror went on. Matías told me of the February 7 attack on Tinkarini, led by Moisés. The terrorists had killed fifteen Ashaninka with machetes. Most of the victims, he said in Spanish, were *niños* and *niñas*, "little boys" and "little girls." A few women were killed, trying to protect their children. This was when Capitán lost most of his family. Matías's wife Olga was also injured, taking a number of shotgun pellets in the shoulder, hand, and head as she fled into the jungle, shielding her child with her body.

After that, the families of Cuti had dispersed further, abandoning their cacao and yucca fields and their small stores of personal belongings. Matías had led a small group here to Cubeja. Nicolás and his family were holed up on the other side of the Mamiri; it was only a short distance away in kilometers, but the journey was difficult by foot.

Besides food, Matías said, what they needed most right now were shells for their small supply of shotguns. And they wanted any other type of firearms, ammunition, and explosives that they could get.

At intervals throughout the evening, a few more families straggled in, emerging from their private hideouts.

Mickey and I talked over our plans. "We just have to get some supplies here," I said, and Mickey immediately agreed. Food, medicine, and blankets were critical. At this altitude the night air was cold, and the children, in particular, were suffering from it.

"The best thing is for you to go to Lima," I said to Mickey. "I'll stay. The reason why I'm saying this is that I know damn well that the helicopters won't abandon me here. But if I go and you stay, maybe they won't come back."

I thought that Mickey would put up an argument, but he saw the logic of my reasoning. He was a civilian, of no importance to the military or to any of the politicians in Lima. I was the padre—and also a gringo. My life held a certain amount of public relations value, and the attention I had received from the American embassy underscored the point. In addition, it was clear that I was the one to whom this group of Ashaninka looked for deliverance. If I left on the helicopter, the natives would feel abandoned. "Go to Lima," I implored Mickey. "Talk to our friends. Talk to the military and the American embassy. Talk to Senator Miguel Vega Alvear. See if you can meet with my provincial. Try to get some help."

Mickey nodded in agreement.

I composed letters to friends and acquaintances in Lima, introducing Mickey and begging their assistance. I wrote to Jamie and Javier Pardo, to my British friend Graham Curtis, to my provincial Felix, and to Bishop Ojeda.

All night it rained heavily. Sleep would not come. I grieved deeply over the deaths of the three young men who had tried to get a message through to me in Satipo, and took a measure of the blame for myself. I drank coffee and smoked what I vowed would be my last pack of cigarettes, ever. Am I helping them here? I wondered. Can I help them more if I am not here? It was clear that the Ashaninka viewed my arrival as the first step in their salvation. They expected me to pull off a miracle. But, I thought, I don't know what to do. My mind raced: I could only hope that the Americans would continue to help, and that the Sinchis at Mazamari would offer assistance as well. The colonel of the Sinchis had been very kind to me, and I wondered if I could persuade him to station a few of his men here at Cubeja to teach the Ashaninka basic techniques of self-defense. I said to myself: At the least, he might give us some ammunition so that we can better protect ourselves.

In the morning, the pulsating sound of the rotors announced the return of the American helicopters. As before, one of them landed while the other hovered. Sentries scrambled to their posts.

I was surprised to see Captain Reeder emerge, along with the doctor we had requested. I asked the captain if he could send the helicopters across the Mamiri to locate Nicolás and his family and bring them here; it was important for us all to be together. The captain agreed and took Mickey along as a guide.

Meanwhile, I took the doctor to examine Olga's wounds. He reported that the injury was not serious; there was no infection. "Eventually the pellets will work their way out," he assured us.

Unfortunately the doctor did not have time to examine any of the other sick and wounded. The helicopters returned, delivering Jamie and his wife and son, and an explanation that Nicolás, somehow aware of our arrival, had already begun the overland journey to join us.

His mission accomplished, Captain Reeder was eager to leave and asked me to get on board quickly.

"No, I'm staying," I said. "You are wasting your time to try to convince me to go."

Mickey embraced me before he climbed on board. He left his shotgun with me.

The shock in Victor's eyes showed that he could not quite believe that I was staying behind.

The Ashaninka placed all of their hopes on me, I realized during yet another sleepless night. They were absolutely helpless and discouraged, and my heart ached for them. They were completely disoriented. The atmosphere was one of fear—hovering on the verge of panic. And yet here I was, more confused than they. I resolved to do everything possible to lift their spirits and renew their self-confidence. I could not permit myself to show an iota of pessimism. Or fear.

On the following day, I spoke with Matías and Capitán, trying to convince them to take necessary defensive measures. "If you stick together, you can beat Sendero," I declared. But I knew that it would require a measure of order and discipline to which they were unaccustomed. I persuaded the calm and thoughtful Matías to assume the alien position of leadership, with the more swashbuckling Capitán as his Chief of Staff. "The welfare of the natives depends on you," I told them.

I completed a census that showed that there were thirty-one Ashaninka here.

It took us a week of intense labor to clear some of the surrounding jungle terrain, to deprive any invaders of cover. We erected a few huts in the center of the compound to protect the women and children. After each day, I was exhausted.

I set up the radio in one of the huts and spoke twice daily with the Green Berets. I was always pleased when the voice on the other end was Victor; the others did not have the patience—or the interest—to tune the equipment properly, and it was often difficult to communicate. But Victor's voice always came through clearly. He signed off with a cheery *"jatajana,"* "good-bye" in Ashaninka. He is a good man, I thought. It is nice to know that there are still some people who are caring and sincere.

It remained a mystery to me how the Ashaninka managed to spread the word of my arrival so efficiently. Each day a few more families came in, serving both to strengthen our defenses and compound our living problems. I was particularly happy when old

Gregorio arrived, along with his entire clan of sons, daughters, and grandchildren. Nicolás and Teodoro had created problems for us in the past, but now we valued them as fighters.

I was greatly impressed with the affection the Ashaninka showed for me. All these months, they *knew* that I would come to their rescue. Their morale had improved since my arrival, but I could see that they had little confidence in one another.

I was awash in a sea of information. Some of the new arrivals had—at great risk—escaped from the terrorists, and as they told their stories, the climate of panic increased. From what I could gather, a large number of native families had been conscripted into the terrorist ranks. The community of Camantavesti was completely taken over, as well as other settlements along the Ene and its tributaries.

The escapees were a mine of military intelligence, and I somehow had to get their information back to the authorities. For example, several people confirmed for me the chain of command whereby Sendero issued orders to a growing number of Ashaninka renegades. The man in charge of the native forces was Alberto Quiroga, a mysterious character who was the government's supervisor of education for the entire Ene River valley. Over the years, he had visited Cuti repeatedly to inspect the operation of our schools and—I realized now—to assess our facilities. Quiroga had always treated me in a polite, professional manner, but I had wondered how a foreigner—he claimed to be Argentinean—had managed to land a high post in the Peruvian educational system. According to the reports I now received, Quiroga issued orders through two Ashaninka lieutenants, Valeriano and Antuñez, who then passed them on to a variety of field commanders, including Moisés, Rigoberto, Pochete, Adrian, and Ángel. Quiroga sometimes conducted clandestine meetings in a large safe house in Satipo; and I knew that the authorities, both in Mazamari and Satipo, would find this information very interesting.

I also learned that the terrorists had an ammunition dump in what the government had designated as Section 3, located across the Ene, almost due west of the mission, midway between Stirario-chieri and Sabibeni, high in the mountains, where three peaks

159

formed a defense perimeter. Between the first and second peaks was an isolated schoolhouse, the only building in the area with an aluminum roof. Directly behind this a storage building held massive supplies of guns, ammunition, and dynamite.

The center of operations, the terrorist Pentagon, was in a maze of caves in an area called Ucherauto, near the Quimpiri River. By light plane it would be a brief, ten-minute flight from the mission to the terrorist camp; the difficult overland journey would take at least a day and a half. Although the terrorists lived and conducted most of their business in the caves, they utilized a central facility known as Potasi, the "Big House" of Reunión, which was equipped with a printing press used for propaganda.

All these sites were in a major center of cocaine activity. At the point where the Quimpiri flows into the Ene, the drug smugglers had established a camp on the Ene side. A group of small islands was here, and the narcos had built a facility on one of these, called Malvinas, which I assumed was some sort of coca-processing laboratory. Its proximity to the terrorist base reinforced the notion that the terrorists and smugglers were in league.

I wanted to learn more, and I asked questions.

One of the Ashaninka reported that the man in charge of the terrorists was a gringo "about as tall as you, Padre," he said. He had a flowing beard. From his cave, which he rarely left, the gringo gave orders for operations throughout Peru, always surrounded by machine-gun-toting guards. No one was to reveal the location of the cave—even the generals—upon pain of death. His orders had to be obeyed without question. To object was to die. "Some of the people say that Abimael Guzmán is there, too," Nicolás reported.

Once, it was said, the gringo ventured out, accompanied by Moisés, to the stream known as Anaro, where he gave a lecture to the insurgents. One of the Ashaninka described the speech: "He told us that all who fight for the poor and the exploited would return to fight again. If we fight to liberate the poor we will return to life. We must kill all the *yanquis* and the rich people and those that exploit us. Otherwise, we will be tortured. If we do not join forces with them, our wives and our sons do not have a right to go on living; they are contaminated by the semen of the father, who

160

is a coward and an imperialist—and all the children must be killed." The gringo proclaimed to the Ashaninka that God does not exist. He is an invention of the rich and powerful, the gringo preached. "Anyone who does not accept our way of thinking has to be killed, because we have the truth, and we are the only ones who have the truth. One day all the natives and the Quechua will be millionaires."

Several of the new arrivals told me that the enemy was aware of my return and knew the exact location of our camp here at Cubeja. The terrorist line of propaganda had not changed: I was the principal obstacle to the Ashaninka's liberation; I was the one who enslaved them and kept them poor. I was a spy for the U.S. Sooner or later, the terrorists warned, the *yanqui* government would attempt to take over all of Peru and, finally, all of South America. Some of the Ashaninka claimed that they had been offered money for the delivery of my head; others said that the terrorists wanted me alive, so that all could see how an oppressor should die.

I asked some of the escapees if they believed Sendero's doctrine. They said no, and that many of the natives who were fighting with the terrorists did not believe it; they fought out of fear. The Ashaninka who were brought into the terrorist camps were subjected to systematic intimidation and brainwashing. They were given very little to eat and drink and were allowed to go nowhere—even to the bathroom—by themselves. They were instructed to keep their children quiet at night, or they would be forced to slaughter their own children. If they did not fight, the terrorists would kill not only them but their wives and children.

Hearing all this, I muttered to myself, "The sons of bitches . . ." It was clear to me that Sendero was completely repulsive. Abimael Guzmán was not interested in the poor; he was merely interested in exploiting them in order to gain power. He had proved that he was willing to kill indiscriminately, whether the victim was a military man, a business or political leader, a Quechua, or a native.

The terrorists had emphasized that the Ashaninka must beware of the helicopters that fly overhead; these really belonged to Sendero, but the *yanquis* had taken them away, and now the helicopters searched for natives in order to kill them.

161

Deep fear had spread among the Ashaninka, who were trapped by vicious forces they could not comprehend. Many prophesied: We will be attacked; we will die.

I worried that no one in the government would ever believe my reports of a secret cave, a mysterious gringo, and an enslaved population of native warriors.

I was depressed and full of anguish, but I could not afford to share these feelings and had to make a great effort to hide my concern from the natives.

How is Mickey? I wondered. What is he doing? Is help on the way?

March 27. The community of refugees grew larger every day. My latest census showed 53 men, 50 women, and 140 children; I entered every name in my diary so that there would be a record.

All of them were hungry.

All of them were afraid.

CHAPTER ELEVEN

"*Get all the natives together,*" I told Matías. "It is very important that we have a talk. No one should miss it."

Through Matías's translation, I asserted that our present state was not too bad. We were situated on a fairly high mountain in a position that would be difficult to attack from below. With six shotguns, a few hand grenades, and an arsenal of bows and arrows, we were well equipped to defend ourselves. The problem was, the Ashaninka still had difficulty with the concept of defense.

I admired Matías's patience as he labored to convey this message to his people. The majority seemed to grasp what we were saying. Máximo, the leader of the group who lived here at Cubeja before the others came, listened with special attention.

I reported that the American helicopters would return soon, and tried to allay the fears that Sendero had implanted. The helicopters were good, I said. They would frighten any terrorists who were in the area.

One of the natives said that the terrorists knew everything about the helicopters: that they were not always based in Mazamari and sometimes went off to other areas of the country and were not available. The speaker disclosed that he—and the terrorists— knew that the helicopters were gone now and would not return to Mazamari until later this month.

163

I was amazed and shocked by the accuracy of this intelligence, but I tried not to show my concern.

The listeners reacted with varying degrees of apprehension. Those who showed the most fear were ones who had escaped from the Sendero camps, and our discussion lapsed into an argument over the pros and cons of defense. One of the Ashaninka asserted that we were few in number and the terrorists were numerous and well organized. Someone else pointed out that a few of the renegade lieutenants, such as Moisés and Rigoberto, were from the Cuti area, and thus were certain to guess where we might hide. They would surely come after us. I could see that the Ashaninka were more afraid of this threat from within their own society than from Sendero itself. They declared that our only hope was to run away.

"To where?" I asked. "We cannot keep changing from place to place." I explained that if we continued to run, we would never be able to stop. It was true that the Ashaninka renegades knew the valley as well as any of them, and it was true that they would pursue us relentlessly. "But we must stand and defend ourselves, or we will run forever," I argued. "We are ready for an attack. They would have to come at us from below. All we have to do is set off one grenade, and they will run like rabbits. If we don't defend ourselves, sooner or later everyone will be massacred."

I pointed out what I thought was another natural advantage. An attacking force would probably be composed of Ashaninka, rather than other Sendero soldiers, because the natives could negotiate the terrain far better. And since so many of the Ashaninka had been recruited against their will, they would be reluctant to fight fiercely against their own people.

Someone reminded me that the terrorists would be holding the wives and children of these natives as hostages.

"If we lose faith and confidence—even before we encounter the enemy—then we are licked," I lectured.

"There is no food here," someone said. "There is hardly any yucca left."

"That is good," I replied. "If we are skinny, we will be able to move faster and defend ourselves better. And there will be less bulk for the terrorists to aim their bullets at."

The meeting decided nothing.

Over the radio, Victor asked how we were doing. "It's like we're in the Sheraton," I replied glibly. "I know people who spend a fortune to live like we are. Who can afford this type of safari?"

"Yeah," Victor said. *"Jatajana."*

March 28. I realized suddenly that I was singing the words of an old song: "Laughing on the outside, crying on the inside."

On the radio, Victor reported good news—at least one of the helicopters was expected to arrive back in Mazamari soon, earlier than either we or the terrorists had thought. The bad news was that Victor still had no word of Mickey.

It was a strange, topsy-turvy day. For some unknown reason, most of the Ashaninka were in better spirits, even those who had been the most pessimistic yesterday, but my own mood was hollow.

Facing another interminable day of waiting for news of the helicopters or for news from Mickey, I decided that we had to do *something.* I asked Matías and some of the others to come with me to survey the surrounding terrain, to see where we might find the best location to establish a new town. Matías commented that this was very good land for growing yucca—even better than the land around Cutivireni. Also, the water supply was better.

I turned this information into a wry joke. "The terrorists have done us a favor," I said. "Now the land is better for the yucca. We have never been so well-off before."

In the afternoon I went for a swim in a small nearby stream that paralleled the Cubeja River and was delighted to discover that Teodoro had created a rustic shower for me. He had wedged an open framework of bamboo sticks into the rocks at a point where the stream flowed down in a small waterfall. The result was a faucet of water, ice-cold, clear, and invigorating. He had even arranged rocks to serve as stepping stones.

But the jungle shower cheered me only briefly, and I worried that the natives would see through my optimistic facade. Never had

I felt so empty inside. Never had I felt so responsible for these people. And never had I felt so inadequate. I told myself that I must pray, but the words would not come. I wrote in my diary:

> God does not intervene. He leaves us to ourselves. *We* must find a solution to our problems. I must try to meditate to see the way out of this. I feel an immense gratitude to Almighty God for my vocation. I believe in Him like never before in my life. However, I don't feel Him. It seems like a contradiction. Even in this state that I find myself in, I am the happiest man in the world; yet I feel completely mashed.
>
> I can't quite believe in any help that God will give me. To ask Him to help me seems a bit absurd.
>
> I love God without reserve and I find myself incapable of speaking of God to the natives. I have tried, and it comes out very artificial. It is better to be quiet. I see God as a force that can do all, and yet He does nothing—an omnipotent Being who has more confidence in His creatures than we have in Him—a Father who loves us so much that he leaves us to our own choices. I am starting to understand the words of Christ, "Father, why hast thou abandoned me?"
>
> God is present like I've never felt Him before. But absent in our duress. It is for us to discover that in the creation of the universe, He is the force of His realization. If this was not so, He would have made things halfway.
>
> In Spanish, I would say *jodido pero contento,* "fucked up, but very happy."

March 29. After another night with little sleep, I woke to find the Ashaninka uneasy once more; their spirits—and mine, too—rose and fell in an unpredictable pattern.

I listened carefully as Matías told me of a place down the mountain, very close to where the Cubeja empties into the Mamiri, where we could form a good defense line. He explained that because the jungle was impassable there, the only possible route in was to wade upstream along the banks of the Mamiri. The spot that intrigued Matías was at a bend in the river guarded by a series of immense boulders—each of them almost as large as a hut—which formed a natural stockade. Sentries stationed here could easily repel an attacking force.

"I would like to go and see this," I replied. In truth, I believed that the altitude of Cubeja provided a more formidable defense, but I was pleased with Matías's initiative, and I was ready to try anything to distract the people, to give them some measure of hope and, by doing so, to infuse them with at least a minimal level of courage and confidence.

Matías, Nicolás, Eusebio—the fourteen-year-old image of his older brother, Capitán—and a few of the other natives agreed to accompany me. Jamie brought along Mickey's 12-gauge shotgun. Several young boys joined our party, looking comically grim-faced as they clutched at their undersized bows and arrows. A scrawny dog followed us into the jungle.

Initially, the path was quite good, and the route led easily downhill. After a half hour of walking we came across a *purma*, a field where someone had previously lived. The resident had cleared a hectare or two of land for a house and a yucca field. For some unknown reason, the homesite had been abandoned long ago. The hut was gone, and the land was overgrown with light brush, but the jungle trees had not yet taken over. We were walking through the *purma* when our attention was diverted by a rustling sound in the underbrush off to our left, caused by a small animal scurrying to find refuge in a hollow tree trunk. Instantly, the Ashaninka men and boys warmed to the hunt. They peered into the log from both ends, attempting to identify their prey. The men pushed aside the eager boys, but the dog took the lead. He poked his nose into one end of the log, but retreated quickly, yelping in pain. This brought much laughter from the hunters.

For several minutes they attempted to flush the animal out of its lair, without success. Finally they killed it with a well-aimed arrow, and one of the boys retrieved it. The victim was a small, rodentlike creature, about the size of a groundhog. The hunters tied it to the limb of a tree to keep scavengers away; we would retrieve it on the return trip.

Then we continued on. From here, the path grew steep and

difficult, leading us, in about another fifteen minutes, to a native hut, situated at the edge of an immense wall of solid rock. Far below were the waters of the Mamiri. The hut was the home of Isario, the son of Horacio. Another young man was with him. We accepted Isario's invitation to drink *piarinsti,* and Eusebio decided to stay there for the day while the rest of us continued on our way down the mountain.

After an additional forty-five minutes of rigorous hiking, we reached the Mamiri and moved upstream toward our destination.

When I surveyed the location, I thought: It is true—this place is quite appropriate for a defense. There appeared to be only one path leading from the river up to Isario's house at the top of the cliff, and a series of steep, rugged rocks framed the pathway. And at the river, a perimeter of huge boulders provided a vantage point where sentries could easily note an enemy's approach, even from a great distance.

We relaxed with a swim. Then Matías and some of the others tried their hands at fishing.

"I will start back," I told Matías. "The climb back is quite steep, and I will take it slowly." Matías agreed. He, Nicolás, and the others would continue with their fishing and rejoin me later at our base camp.

The upward climb was, indeed, rigorous, but the path was clear. I made my way back slowly and quietly, my mind distracted by the continuing attempt to plan a future for the people. As I passed Isario's house, I waved and called out a greeting, but did not stop. I was glad to arrive back at camp to find that everything was calm.

I had been back for about a half hour when I heard someone scream, *"Terruco! Terruco!"* The terrorists were here? Where? Men, women, and children scattered in panic.

I managed to grab the arm of one man as he scurried past me. I stared into his wild eyes and asked, "What happened?"

He threw his arms up and yelled, *"Terruco! Terruco!"*

"Yes, but where are the terrorists?" I demanded.

In an excited voice he told me that someone had run up from Isario's hut with the news that Rigoberto, along with other terrorists, had attacked the site where, earlier, we had drunk *piarinsti.*

"Now they will come and kill us!" the frightened man cried.

A tremor of fear swept across me, and I had to force it out of my mind. Teodoro and Nicolás—my best fighters—were away with Matías. We were forced to make a stand on our own. Somebody had to organize a defense quickly.

"Quiet down!" I bellowed. "If anything happens, you will only have yourselves to blame."

Get them to do something, I commanded myself, or there will be more panic. Everyone will scatter, and who knows how long it will take to regroup them? Quickly I designated a few young men to rush down to Isario's house to verify whether the report was true, and if it was, to provide reinforcements for Matías and the others.

I saw that Olga was shivering with fear for Matías. "Olga, get all the women and kids together and get them to the houses we built in back," I said. "Keep them quiet and wait to see what happens." She composed herself and marched the other women and small children to the huts at the rear of the camp.

I divided the men into two groups. I sent one group forward to the entrance of the camp; if the terrorists were coming, they would have to approach from here. Some melted into the brush, their bows and arrows at the ready; others hid behind tree trunks that we had felled in strategic positions. I sent the second, smaller group of men to the rear to take up posts in front of the women's huts. Finally, I stationed myself and two older boys—one of them was Nicolás's scrappy son, Jorge Luis—in the middle of the encampment. I kept a pistol and hand grenades ready, taking grim solace in the fact that I had finally managed to get the Ashaninka to make a stand.

We waited in silence.

My eyes met those of the two boys at my side. Their faces showed determination and not an inkling of fear. They said nothing.

Many minutes passed. I thought: If something has happened to Matías, Nicolás, and Teodoro, I'm up shit creek.

More than a half hour elapsed as we continued to train our eyes forward. We saw only jungle. The men stationed ahead of us blended in completely. I knew that each man had his bow and arrow ready, and each would shoot only if the target was close enough to kill; these men knew how to hunt.

After some time, Jorge Luis pointed forward to the path, and said, "Matías is here."

The others were with him. Matías told us that the danger was over. Our sentries regrouped in the middle of the camp. Someone ran off to spread the all-clear signal to Olga and the rest of the women. Then Matías, while sipping from a bowl of *piarinsti*, told us what had happened. It was true that the Sendero lieutenant Rigoberto had suddenly appeared at Isario's house with a small band of renegade Ashaninka. Rigoberto demanded to know where the padre, Matías, and Nicolás were.

The interrogation was underway—the terrorists had already tied up Eusebio—when Matías and his group, returning from their fishing trip at the base of the mountain, surprised them. Rigoberto was sitting on a log. Jamie fired his shotgun at Rigoberto's feet in an attempt to scare him. A brief, fierce battle ensued. The terrorists tried to escape, but Matías and his men killed Rigoberto and an Ashaninka rebel known as Jodas (a derivative of a common profane verb). One other terrorist, Ángel, fled across a narrow ledge, flung himself into space, tumbled down the sheer cliffs, and fell to his death on the rocks at the bank of the Mamiri, far below. Eusebio was rescued, and all of our people returned safely. They even remembered to retrieve the carcass of the animal they had killed earlier in the day.

Listening to the details of this account, I realized that the Ashaninka had much to learn about fighting. In front of everyone, I grabbed the shotgun from Jamie's arms and lectured, "We are not at play. If you shoot, you shoot to kill. If you cannot act as a man, you cannot have the rifle." Jamie was very embarrassed, but my point was made. I wanted the Ashaninka to understand that this was a very serious situation; we were not playing games. Heads nodded in agreement with me.

As I replayed Matías's account in my mind, I theorized that Rigoberto had planned to use the young Eusebio as bait. He surely had to regard Capitán as a fearsome enemy, and I wondered if he thought he could lure Capitán out in search of his brother. There was no way to know. It was impossible to read the twisted minds of the terrorists.

That evening I reached the Green Beret base by radio. The connection was poor, but I managed to convey an account of the day's events, including the deaths of the three terrorists, and assured the Americans that we had suffered no casualties. I wondered if, over the static, they could hear the desperation in my voice.

After that, I called the Ashaninka into a meeting. "This yelling and screaming is not to be tolerated in the future," I lectured. "If we are attacked, there is to be complete silence. The women and children will retreat, and the men will stand and fight." I assigned the men into groups and made sure that they understood where each squad was to station itself should another emergency arise.

Thunderstorms plagued us throughout the night. The bolts of lightning were so spectacular that it seemed as if you could reach out and pluck them from the air. To the Ashaninka, this was a sign, for they believe that God uses lightning to purify the world. They could hear the desperate wails of the three dead terrorists from within the thunder, especially those of Rigoberto.

March 30. The radio transmission was much better this morning. Victor told me that the Green Berets were finally able to send a helicopter for me. I knew that I had to go out in order to report my intelligence information to Captain Reeder and the Sinchi commander at Mazamari and to find more substantial help for the people, but I worried about what might happen in my absence. So far, we were operating in a very haphazard manner, and I knew that we needed a more comprehensive plan.

"Matías," I said, "you have to come out with me. We will go see the *comandante* of the Sinchis and give him our information about the terrorists." I hoped that in return the *comandante* would bring in a detachment of troops. "With this information, the army will be able to blow the terrorist headquarters to hell," I said.

He agreed.

On the morning when the helicopter was scheduled to arrive, I celebrated mass, using the opportunity to assure the Ashaninka that everything would be okay. "Matías and I are going to leave, but we will come right back," I promised.

We waited all day but the helicopter did not arrive. Finally, about seven o'clock that night, Victor reported by radio that one of the helicopters had crashed near Santa Lucía. "I am very sorry," I said. "Was anyone hurt?" Victor said that five men were seriously injured. Obviously, today's flight was off, and when the people heard this, I could see their spirits deflate.

On the heels of this news, yet another family of refugees arrived—Julio and Elena along with their three children—warning us in excited voices that the terrorists were set to attack us at any moment.

Nicolás, Teodoro, and some of the other men spent the entire night on guard duty. Few of us got any sleep; many frequently arose and paced restlessly. At four in the morning, the natives had gathered themselves in small clusters, talking and glancing nervously into the darkness. I thought: They are their own worst enemies. They believe everything they hear, and they work themselves into a frenzy.

At seven o'clock, an American voice told me over the radio that the helicopter would not be coming in today, and he did not know when they would be able to send a flight. "How are things going?" the voice asked.

"There is a lot of disquiet," I reported. I arranged a 1:00 P.M. radio call, and told the voice that I would have more information for him then. Finally I asked, "Where the hell is Mickey?" But there was still no news of the Frenchman.

That day, more Ashaninka families arrived in camp, refugees from Sendero. In all, nearly seventy of the people in our camp had escaped from the terrorists. I pointed out to Matías, "Most likely, some of these people who are escaping from Sendero are spies."

"No," he countered. "If they were spies, Sendero would not let them bring their children." He said that he had spoken with them and believed that they were sincere. "They want to be with you," he said. "They say that what the terrorists say about the padre are pure lies. They are convinced that the padre is the only one who can save them."

"The only ones who can save them are themselves," I replied. "They must find sufficient faith within themselves, and not put their hopes in anyone else. They must convince themselves that they can make a stand and defend themselves. They should not have any hopes of receiving help from others. Not the Americans. Not the military. Not the politicians. Not the Church."

Matías, Teodoro, Nicolás, Jamie, old Gregorio, and some of the others cornered me. Máximo, the leader of the original Cubeja group, was with them.

"It is urgent that we leave this place," Matías said. "We will be attacked. It is certain. And if this happens, most of the people will abandon us. Only a few will stay to defend."

"With just a few good natives we can make the attackers run," I argued.

We spoke for an extended period of time, but I made no headway with them.

Slowly, as other Ashaninka realized that a serious discussion was under way, they gathered, the men joining us, the women and children remaining at the outskirts of the circle, their ears attuned to our words.

"There is no food," Máximo interjected in a realistic tone. "There are too many people. The fields of yucca have been depleted. Now the women have to go far away to get yucca. It is a big risk. With so many coming and going, we are afraid that the terrorists will grab the women." It was obvious that Máximo and his Cubeja clan were weary of sharing the land, the danger, and, most of all, the yucca.

He was a good man, and I understood his point. Mickey was fond of pointing out: "The natives cannot live without yucca. They will kill for it." And I knew that all the Ashaninka understood and accepted the fact that this was Máximo's land and Máximo's yucca.

But the yucca was gone, and even Máximo was ready to abandon this sanctuary. He said that as soon as the main group of

Ashaninka left here, he would take his smaller group farther up into the mountains. "We want no more stake in this place," he said. "If we stay, we are doomed to be killed. All of us."

Once more, I tried to point out the defensive advantages of this location, but no one would listen.

"We have to leave," Matías declared with finality. He said that Nicolás's brother Pablo was "in a very good situation" at a high-altitude location known as Tzibokiroato ("the Place of Ants"), where the yucca was plentiful. After the attack on Cuti, Pablo had fled there with his family and a few others as guests of Julio. "It would be fine if we would all go there," Matías assured. "The families will be well hidden."

"What is the true reason that the people want to go?" I asked. "Is it because there is no yucca? Or is it because they are afraid of the terrorists?"

Matías admitted that it was for both reasons.

Again I attempted, with all my force, to convince them that we should stay where we were. I argued, "Any day now the helicopters will arrive, and if we leave this place, they will have difficulty finding us. The Americans will say that we are cowards, that the natives don't have the balls to defend their land." But I could see that my reasoning was futile, and reluctantly, I asked, "How many days will it take us to get to Tzibokiroato?"

"At least five," Matías answered. "We will have to cross the Mamiri to the Cuti."

I knew that the route was divided by a rugged mountain range. "This will present quite a problem," I said. "We will not be able to carry the battery and the radio." I tried to convince them that it was better to stay here at Cubeja *with* the radio. "Because of the weight, we will not be able to take the battery with us."

This argument had no effect.

Finally, I tried the only plan I could devise at the moment. I declared, "Matías, I am going to stay just where I am. Please tell all the natives this."

As Matías relayed this message in the Ashaninka tongue, many of the women began to cry. The children picked up the cue and tears rolled down their cheeks.

"They say they will not leave you behind," Matías said softly.

I could not remember a moment of my life when my heart felt heavier in my chest. I succumbed to the tears and the will of the majority. Who was I to impose my own course of action upon all of them? I could not bear that responsibility. What's more, I thought, maybe they are right and I am wrong. Swallowing my misgivings, I told Matías that I would go with them to Julio's house at Tzibokiroato, but I sought to buy time. "We must stay at least one more day," I said. Already, it was too late in the day to begin the arduous journey, and it was nearly time for my afternoon radio call to the Americans. I told Matías that after I spoke with the Americans, we would use the remainder of the afternoon to make plans.

He agreed to this.

"Things are a bit complicated," I reported over the radio. "Very possibly, we will have to abandon this place."

The voice from Mazamari asked, "Are your lives in danger?"

I did not know how to answer this question. It is difficult to describe fear and panic over the crackling static of a poor radio connection. "The natives believe that we will be attacked, and should leave where we are," I explained. "Don't worry. We'll find some solution to the problem." Then I asked, "Is there any news of the helicopter? How are the men who were injured in the crash?"

"Some are in serious condition."

This saddened me. I felt terrible about trying to describe our problems. There was not much the Americans could do to help, so why should I add to their worries?

All that afternoon, the Ashaninka spoke with certainty about the coming attack. And that night, as if to underscore our anxiety, sleep was interrupted by a violent electrical storm and sheets of cold rain.

CHAPTER TWELVE

April 1, 1990. By 5:00 A.M., when I emerged from my hut, the Ashaninka were ready. They had packed their meager possessions and were eager to leave on the extended journey. Some of the women had their precious pots and pans lashed to their bodies.

I stalled. I had promised to call the Americans on the radio at seven o'clock, so I told Matías that we had to wait until then. Silently I prayed for more rain so that we might have to delay our departure further.

At seven, I reported to the Americans that we were ready to evacuate and that we would be out of contact for at least five days. I added that I was not sure that we could take the radio with us.

"If you leave the radio, you are to destroy it so that the terrorists don't get it," the American voice warned me.

I asked if there was any news about a helicopter flight.

"No," came the curt reply.

I sensed that the Americans were growing impatient with me and the natives, and I could understand their frustration. The Ashaninka were of very little concern to them, and I was surely a thorn in the American backside. "I will call you back at ten o'clock to report," I promised.

When I told Matías that we had to wait around until ten, I read frustration in his eyes. He knew that I was stalling, and I knew that the ten o'clock call was my last chance. I busied myself recording yet another census. My count reached 323.

"There is nothing I can do," I reported to the Americans at 10:00 A.M. "They want to go. Don't worry about us. We will be able to take care of ourselves."

One of the natives offered to carry the radio, to lug it over the sharp terrain that lay in our path. I wrapped the equipment in plastic to protect it from rain and from the waters of the various rivers and streams that we would have to cross. I recruited a young boy to carry the cumbersome battery, promising that I would reward him with a new pair of shorts and a knife.

I pulled off my blue jeans in order to assume my traditional hiking garb. I was most comfortable in shorts; scratches on my legs did not bother me. I slung the jeans over my shoulder and tied the legs across my chest, using my pants as padding for the burden of my heavy backpack—stuffed with a change of clothes, an extra pair of sneakers, aspirin, antibiotics, iodine, Band-Aids, mosquito netting, twine, a light nylon blanket, copybooks, pens, a fish line, hooks, and what was left of my supply of hard candy for the children. I strapped on my military-style Sam Browne belt and tucked my canteen and hunting knife into the appropriate pockets. I asked Nicolás if he wanted to carry my pistol; he accepted with a broad grin. Others toted my supplies of ammunition and hand grenades. I cut a strong, straight branch to use as a walking stick, useful for balancing myself, for vaulting across small chasms, and for warding off snakes.

Our procession of desperate people trudged off, embarking in small groups that thinned out to a single file. Within each group, the men took the lead, hacking away with machetes, and the women and children followed. The youngsters toddled forward with determination, getting only an occasional lift from an adult. A few stragglers, as always, brought up the rear.

Walking on the hardened soles of their bare feet, the Ashaninka handled the terrain easily—even the fields of stones leading to the hillside ledges. Energies were focused forward. There was no trail, but the smallest child could follow the signs of passage—broken twigs, trampled leaves, and branches slashed by machetes. The forest floor was made slippery by a persistent light rain.

No one spoke; even the babies, riding on their mothers' hips, did not whimper or cry.

All day long we trudged forward, alternately climbing up and sliding down the slopes of various mountains under the darkened canopy of the rain forest. We worked our way east and generally lower, toward the Mamiri. The banks of the streams and small rivers were welcome respite. Here, one could jump from boulder to boulder, and at times, the mood was almost playful.

On their own, small groups stopped to rest, leaning their heavy backpacks against immense tree trunks. Several times I paused, resting my weight against my walking stick, so that Gregorio and Vieja could catch up to me.

By five o'clock, as dusk approached, we assembled in a loose colony to establish ourselves for the night. The Ashaninka gathered large palm fronds and spread them out on the forest floor for bedding. The only available food was a tiny supply of berries, and these did not go far. I did not eat any of them, for I was too tired to get anything into my stomach. A few children ran up to tease me for candy. I was so exhausted that I did not even bother to put up mosquito netting.

All night long it rained steadily, soaking everything except the radio and battery, still encased in plastic. Even at this lesser altitude, the night air was extremely cold.

We set off about seven o'clock the next morning, April 2, and hiked farther east. Initially, the terrain was similar to what we had already encountered, but by midmorning we approached a series of steep ledges, each of them dropping ten feet or more. The natives hacked down small trees, stripped the branches, and used them as poles. We slid down these, fireman-style, one ledge at a time.

The route backtracked, and we were forced to move upward. We searched for crevices in the ledges and wedged our bodies into them, inching our way up. My body was bruised and scratched.

All day steady rains soaked us to the bone; the monsoon season was an extended one this year.

Late that afternoon we arrived at the house of Elario, at a place called Ocheroato, on a high cliff overlooking the Mamiri. The hut was abandoned, and the natives told me that Elario and his family had been abducted by the terrorists to be indoctrinated. We made camp here for the night and were pleased to see the late sun emerge from the rain clouds. We spread out all of our gear to dry.

In the twilight, Matías took me to the edge of the cliff and pointed east. Far below us was the Mamiri, and directly across from our position was the point where the Tancari River emptied into the Mamiri. Tomorrow, Matías said, we would descend to the Mamiri, cross it, and begin to work our way southeast and upward toward a nameless, north-south ridge rising at least six thousand feet high, which bisected the Mamiri and Cutivireni rivers. It was a watershed. Tzibokiroato was on the far side of that ridge, near— but well above—the Cutivireni River. We still faced at least three more days of hiking.

Someone reported to me that one of the young women had suffered a miscarriage during the day's journey. I used what little energy I had left to tend to her. She was too weak to stand, and her eyes begged me for help. I bathed her brow with a cool, damp cloth and gave her some antibiotic pills to guard against infection, but there was little else that I could do. Her relatives said they would stay with her for a few days at Elario's house, and join us later at Tzibokiroato.

The natives helped themselves to some of Elario's yucca. There was also a bit of corn, but I was once more too tired to eat.

We left Ocheroato the following morning, heading for what Matías described as "the house of Julio." The descent down the face of the cliff toward the banks of the Mamiri was not too difficult; there were only a few ledges so precipitous as to require poles. At this juncture, the mountainside featured large boulders fashioned by nature into a convenient staircase.

As I reached the near bank of the Mamiri I was surprised to encounter César, his brother Lucio, and a small party of other natives. César greeted me warmly, and I returned the greeting, but I was wary. César had been the patriarch of the Tinkarini community until Sendero sent them on the run. He had heard of our migration and had brought his people to join us. Some time earlier he had argued bitterly with Mickey and banned the Frenchman from his area. There was something strange about César. I knew that he was an enemy of Sendero, but I was not quite sure that he was our friend. Nevertheless, Matías and the others welcomed him into our group.

We crossed the Mamiri, and Matías led the way south, along the far bank. Our elongated procession snaked forward in this direction for some time before it unaccountably stopped. We waited for some time in confusion until Matías sought me out and announced that he had lost the trail. We would have to backtrack, he said, in order to locate the Tancari River.

A flash of anger and suspicion took hold of me. I wondered if this was true, or if César had filled Matías's head with warnings of a terrorist presence here on the riverbank. Were the Ashaninka running away once more?

But we were lost in the wilderness, and there was no pillar of cloud to lead us. I could not argue with Matías; we had to go back.

After several wasted hours we were back at the point where we had first crossed the Mamiri this morning. Now we began to work our way upstream along the Tancari, edging our way past the sides of a deep gorge. We scrambled up and down slippery rocks. I knew that a fall would not kill me here, but I wondered what would happen if I broke an arm or a leg. What good is a crippled padre in the jungle?

Shortly before nightfall, we made camp in the foothills approaching the watershed.

April 4. At 6:00 A.M., we headed for the ridge, working our way up a mountainside that was steeper and more foreboding than any previous terrain we had crossed. The face of the mountain was covered with dense forestland; here and there white seams of limestone broke through the dark green pattern. We moved with relative ease through the forested areas, although the limestone ledges were formidable. Our procession edged crabwise, back and forth across the ledges, seeking tenuous handholds and footholds. Some

180

of the cliffs were smoothed by the erosion of waterfalls; to negotiate these, we used jungle vines as ropes.

Progress was slow. Many of the Ashaninka lagged behind, particularly the women with small children. Some of the younger men moved on well in front of us, and Matías told me that they would press on ahead of the main group. They would reach Tzibokiroato before us and would begin to prepare the area.

When we stopped to rest, I ate a few wild berries. Someone offered me a handful of worms, boiled in a common pot because they are poisonous if eaten raw. Fried jungle worms are acceptable, with a consistency similar to bacon, but this was a variety I had never eaten before, rather greenish and covered with hairs; they looked more like caterpillars than worms. I managed to down only a few of them before I was hit with an explosive case of diarrhea. This was difficult to understand, since I had almost nothing in my stomach. Perhaps, I thought, the natives did not boil them long enough. Or perhaps God multiplied the worms in my belly like the loaves and fishes. I could only hope that we were not too far away from Julio's house.

We resumed our trek along the wet, slick limestone ledges. I had to exert incredible effort merely to reach out for a boulder or a vine in order to drag myself forward a few feet at a time. One had to be extremely careful not to grasp at the trunk of chonta trees, which were loaded with sharp spikes that could pierce the flesh like a spear. Another hazard was the bees and hornets that nested on the undersides of leaves.

Whenever I began to feel sorry for myself, I glanced at the young boy moving with resolve at my side, carrying the heavy radio battery on his back. And I looked at the women pulling themselves along on vines, with their own packs on their backs and babies nursing at their breasts. These people are really admirable, I thought. Even in this situation, through all this hardship, I heard no one complain. One had to witness this silent heroism in order to believe it. I realized that only one who has lived with the Ashaninka can truly appreciate them. There was not a politician, a military man, or a religious brother who could understand the natives from a distance. It was necessary to share their hardship, to feel it in one's own flesh. At this moment, there was no doubt in my mind that they were the chosen people of God.

By nightfall we had nearly reached the top of the watershed. All night long I was plagued by diarrhea.

April 25. By midmorning, we were on the elongated crest of the ridge. Teodoro, in the group ahead of us, had shot a monkey. Some of the women prepared it and cooked it, then Teodoro offered me the very best portion, heavy with meat cut from the leg. I felt suddenly ashamed. There were many hundreds of Ashaninka and only one monkey. But Teodoro insisted that I eat my portion, and I was easily persuaded. I was famished and seriously weakened by the rigors of the journey as well as by relentless diarrhea. Monkey meat is very dark, and similar to beef jerky. If cooked well, it is quite tasty. This was undercooked and tough but, under the circumstances, very good. As I ate, my conscience got the better of me, and I shared my portion with the boy who carried the radio battery.

We changed direction, veering due south along the top of the ridge. The land was relatively flat and the walk was refreshingly easy. We encountered several natural clearings. Some of the natives commented that here, more than a mile high, the land was good for yucca.

When we reached a point on the ridge where we were due west of Tzibokiroato, we cut ninety degrees left, plunging down the eastern slope. For several hundred feet we had to go almost straight down. Rainfall and subterranean streams had eaten away at the limestone, forming chasms and tunnels in the rock. Some of these were narrow enough so that we could brace ourselves and descend slowly; it was like crawling down a series of chimneys. But at other points, the bare rock offered no support. Even the youngest and strongest men needed the aid of vines and the vise-like grip of helping hands.

I clung to the side of the slope, moving gingerly, testing each step on the slippery rocks before daring to shift my weight. One misstep and I would plunge into the abyss below. I realized that if we were attacked now, we would be totally vulnerable.

Finally we reached a plateau where we walked with relative ease for about a half hour until we encountered a friendly Ashaninka face. It was Timoteo, who lived at Tzibokiroato. The advance party had alerted him to our arrival, and he had come forward to meet us. He offered a gourd full of *piarinsti* to quench our thirst.

After a brief respite we continued on for another hour. On this final stage of the journey, the heavens opened and a deluge poured down. Fearsome forks of lightning blinded us, and deafening thunder echoed through the canyons.

It was late in the afternoon when we reached the tiny settlement known as Tzibokiroato. Timoteo's wife Lucía threw her arms around me and sobbed on my neck.

A meal was ready. Several of us sat together and dined on fish and yucca. We ate the poorly cooked fish whole, entrails and all.

I could not believe my eyes. The young men who had gone ahead of us had already built a small hut for me, about nine by twelve foot, with an elevated sleeping platform, so that I would be off the cold, wet ground. Already, half the thatching was in place on the roof. Some of the men were hauling large leaves quite a distance to the house, and women were weaving the thatching together.

I set up the radio and immediately informed the Americans of our safe arrival at this new location.

How wonderful, I thought. Finally there is a climate of happiness and security. Julio had three enormous yucca fields here, which would provide a plentiful, if temporary, supply for our large group until they could clear fields and plant their own crops.

Over the next few days, I had a chance to reflect, and I was very pleased. This plateau was well defended on three sides. To the east a very high cliff overlooked the Cutivireni River by several hundred feet. From here, because the cliff was treeless, one had a vista of almost the entire Ene River valley. The north and south sides of the encampment were enclosed by solid walls of stone, one above the Tzibokiroato River and the other facing the Stiteta—both small tributaries of the Cutivireni.

I could see only two possible routes onto the plateau. An attacking force could attempt a frontal assault from the Cutivireni; however, this would be like climbing the Alps, and they would probably need ropes. The only other path was the way we had come, across the watershed and through the tunnel-like formations of limestone. It was far too laborious a route for anyone to be able to mount a surprise attack. If we kept a force of sentinels at the western edge of the plateau, we could spot terrorists long before they reached us.

The soil was inferior to that of the Cubeja region, but it was not bad.

I took an afternoon walk with Timoteo and Jamie to search for a favorable spot to establish a village. I chose Jamie for a special reason; I had embarrassed him in front of his people when I took Mickey's shotgun away from him, and now I wanted to help him rebuild his image as a leader. We walked for an hour, staying within the safe confines of the plateau, to a place called Tsetaroato. Two crystal-clear streams insured adequate water. One of them fed a fall that produced a 150-foot cascade of rushing white froth. The land was very rocky. This was good as a base for a village, but the yucca would have to be planted at a distance.

As we scouted through the forestland, I felt a sudden stab in the back of my neck. I cried out in pain and swatted at the attacking hornet, but he had already done his damage. Timoteo spit into his palm and applied saliva to the wound. A node formed on my neck, but the pain quickly subsided to a dull ache.

Upon reflection I realized that Tzibokiroato's isolated location was a mixed blessing. It was great for defense, but inaccessible to our friends as well as to our enemies.

"Is there a possibility of making an airstrip here?" I asked Matías. We studied carefully. One of Julio's yucca fields lay on a flat, narrow mesa, just barely long enough for a runway. It jutted out on the projection of a cliff, overlooking the Cutivireni, sort of like a huge tongue, I thought, taunting the terrorists. Matías and I agreed that an airstrip was possible here, but it would take an expert pilot to negotiate a landing under the best of conditions. The area was plagued by low-lying clouds and crosswinds.

***

Very quickly the natives built temporary shelters and tested the land for hunting. Each day, more families straggled in to join us, looking to Matías and me to save them from incomprehensible threats. We were pleased with the arrival of the young woman who had suffered a miscarriage along the way. By the time she and her family entered the camp, she was feeling much better.

Morale was high, but I expected that to be a temporary phenomenon. Many of the children were coughing, ill with bronchitis from the cold and damp conditions of the past week. Already, one of them had died, and more were close to death. The night was punctuated with the sounds of coughing and hacking. I also knew that the Ashaninka were unused to living in such a large community. There would be tension before too long. And inevitably, the lingering fear of Sendero would be heightened by an energetic rumor mill.

The Ashaninka had to make their own decisions, and they had to make them quickly. They had to get to work soon if they were going to put in an adequate yucca crop.

Matías called a *reunión*. The men gathered around him. On the perimeter of the group, the women strained to listen, as children played at their feet. Antonia, Roy's widow, breast-fed her new, fatherless daughter. Matías spoke for an extended time, reviewing the problems that they all faced: The acute issue was the threat of a terrorist attack, but the basic task was the job of establishing life here. These seemed to be mutually exclusive concerns; the only way to offer protection was to band together in a settlement—but this was not their preferred way of life. Matías said that he had consulted with Julio—for this was Julio's land. Julio was gracious, allowing that the plateau offered plenty of room for all. Until the new arrivals could plant yucca, they could use his. Matías concluded, "The only problem is that we have very few shotguns."

Everyone listened solemnly to this. Their eyes revealed their thoughts: Even after the torturous journey from Cubeja, many were not sure that they had found a permanent home. Some talked about traveling farther east, across the Vilcabamba Range to the Urubamba, to the land of their cousins, the Machiguenga. I did not tell them of the scouting trip that Mickey and I had already made, for I believed that Tzibokiroato offered long-term hope. Matías achieved a consensus: They would remain here, build a new mission, and form a settlement around it.

A few stragglers brought news. Apparently, we had left Cubeja just in time. Shortly after we pulled out, Moisés had arrived with an attacking force of about 150 terrorists and was furious to realize that he had missed us.

I saw the fearful reaction this news produced, and I wondered whether their resolve would hold. What good would it do to build huts and clear fields for yucca if, before long, the Ashaninka panicked and demanded another retreat?

My latest census showed a total of 465 Ashaninka. Matías said that many more families were hiding in the jungle, anxious to be with us, but wary of the terrorists. He predicted that our numbers would swell.

Shirampari and his group from the Parijaro region joined us at Tzibokiroato, and it was now that I learned, for the first time, why he had been so cold and distant to Mickey and me: The terrorists had captured his son and used his life as leverage in an attempt to recruit Shirampari and his people to their cause. They had warned Shirampari that helicopters would come in, carrying soldiers who were under orders to kill them. They said that I, the padre, was in on the secret plan, because the time had come when the Americans were intending to take over the entire country. Shirampari, frantic for his son, did not know what to do. He trusted Mickey and me, but the terrorist propaganda rang in his ears. When he and his people heard the American helicopters coming, they were terrified. "I was ordered to kill you and Mickey," Shirampari said to me. "We were supposed to kill everyone on the helicopters, and if we did not, Sendero would kill us."

"I am glad you didn't," I said.

He smiled weakly. A pained, faraway look in his eyes reminded me that he had left a son behind.

CHAPTER THIRTEEN

April 9, 1990. Victor said on the radio, "I have a surprise for you."

"What?"

After a moment of static, Mickey's voice came over the air. He had much to tell me about his conversations in Lima, but the details would have to wait. For now, he had more immediate news. When he learned of the crash of the American helicopter, he realized that help would be delayed from that sector, so he had returned to the Peruvian military authorities, seeking help. He had arranged for a Peruvian Air Force helicopter, under the command of an army general, to come into Tzibokiroato. He suggested that it was time for us to switch roles; now he would stay with the Ashaninka, and I could come out to muster assistance.

After I finished speaking with Mickey, Victor said that he had a second surprise for me.

I was amazed to hear Lucas's voice on the radio. He had returned from Belgium, and he, too, wanted to come to Tzibokiroato to see what he could do to help the Ashaninka. This was difficult to fathom. Colonel Froude of the American embassy had been very concerned about Lucas's safety, and Fred Hamilton had asked me not even to mention his name to anyone. So what was Lucas doing back in Peru, in Mazamari? I could not figure this out, and a small, inner voice told me that I still needed to learn more about Lucas.

I had seen the helicopters in action, and I knew that the pilots would risk little time on the ground. They would drop off Mickey and Lucas and whisk me away instantly.

"Lucas," I said suddenly. "This is very important. I do not want you and Mickey to come in on the flight. I must have a chance to speak with you both, first."

"All right," Lucas agreed, sounding puzzled.

With Victor, I set the details of the helicopter rendezvous. Then, after the transmission ended, I found my spirits high. Now we had the active support of the Peruvian military as well as the Americans. We had the best of both worlds!

April 10. The helicopter landed in a mountaintop clearing near one of Julio's yucca fields. I was surprised to see that it carried both the Peruvian colonel who commanded the Sinchis and Captain Reeder, the Green Beret commander. Obviously, the military brass wanted a firsthand look at the natives' situation, but they also seemed genuinely pleased to find me safe and sound. The *comandante* greeted me with a characteristic hug, and I was surprised when the hard-boiled Reeder did, too.

Mickey and Lucas were waiting for me at the military base in Mazamari. Lucas had put on some weight; he was still thin, but the muscle tone had returned. Mickey had gained a few gray hairs, undoubtedly produced by his conversations in Lima.

After I had a brief chance to relax in the Green Beret quarters, Captain Reeder told me that the Sinchi colonel was holding a letter for me. As I walked over to the colonel's office to retrieve it, I reasoned that the message was probably from my provincial, Felix, written in response to the note I had sent out with Mickey. I expected words of caution, for Felix simply did not understand—or share—my concern for the Ashaninka. When I obtained the note from the *comandante* and began to read it, my suspicions were confirmed, but I was astounded at the tactic that Felix had chosen. The letter was dated March 20. Felix wrote:

I have received your letter and I have learned of your situation. I ask you, under the merit of Holy Obedience, that you come to Lima as soon as possible. I can do nothing else but order you to come out immediately and come to Lima. Afterwards, we will talk.

This was not the first time I had been a cause of concern to Felix, but it was the only time he had resorted to the vow of obedience to compel my actions. This was a power play straight out of the Middle Ages.

Anger took hold of me.

Felix was treating me as if I were a recalcitrant child. He did not know what was going on in the Ene River valley; we had not had a chance to discuss the situation. Why could he not trust my judgment to do the right and necessary things?

With the letter in hand, I trudged to the Franciscan mission house at Mazamari. There, in one of the side rooms, Mickey, Lucas, and I discussed this latest dilemma.

"Did you speak with my provincial?" I asked Mickey.

"Yes," Mickey replied, stating that Felix had not exhibited much concern for the plight of the Ashaninka, nor had he offered any assistance.

"He didn't give you any message for me?" I asked.

"No."

I was shocked. I knew that Felix had funds at his disposal. Only the previous year, the province had received a generous grant from the Banco Mercantile, amounting to about two hundred thousand dollars. Felix knew as well as I that my friendship with several of the members of the bank's board—including Patricio de Almenara, Juan Pardo, and the bank president himself, Francisco Pardo—was instrumental in securing the donation. But Felix was apparently unwilling to provide a single peso to help the Ashaninka. Why?

Although it was clearly important for me to speak with Felix, could I rush off to Lima now?

Mickey, Lucas, and I concluded that our primary task was to get help to the Ashaninka as soon as possible. In Lima, Mickey had purchased critical supplies. He had attempted to have them shipped here to Mazamari by the Americans, but he had run into a series of bureaucratic snafus. Frustrated, he had persuaded Jamie

189

Pardo to hire a private plane to ferry the vitally needed materials; they were due to arrive here shortly.

We all knew that we must get those supplies onto helicopters and into Tzibokiroato as fast as possible. The people were desperate for food and medicine. The children were in critical need of blankets. Lucas was prepared to set up a small clinic in one of the huts and dispense basic medical care. There were just too many things for me to do to concern myself with Felix. "And if I go to Lima, it may not be that easy to get a flight back to Mazamari," I pointed out. I was very confused. Should I follow my desire to return to help the natives, or should I comply with Felix's summons?

Captain Reeder told me that the Americans were ready to fly us back in and would be able to return for us in one week's time. It seemed vital that I go along. Based on this information, Mickey, Lucas, and I agreed that all three of us would go into Tzibokiroato and stay for the full week. Then Lucas and I would return to Mazamari while Mickey remained with the Ashaninka to help them plan a defense for any attack by Sendero. After that, I would find a way to get to Lima to see my provincial. Surely Felix could wait one week.

I reasoned that once he learned of the circumstances of my people, Felix would understand why I was tardy in following his instructions. It was not my intention to go against my vow of obedience or to cause Felix any grief, but I had to consider the priorities. While Felix was my superior and I owed him respect, the needs of the Ashaninka were critical, and I could not afford to lose the opportunity to arrange assistance while the helicopters were available.

Mickey had a possible explanation for Felix's concern. He informed me that by chance I had become a big story in Lima. During his visit, he had fallen into a casual conversation with his friend Marcos Zileri, the son of the publisher of *Caretas*, Peru's most prominent newsweekly. He had told Zileri of our desperate efforts to locate the Cuti refugees and, strictly as a sidebar to the conversation, mentioned that we carried arms with us—a pistol, shotguns, and a few hand grenades. The next thing Mickey knew, the March 26 issue of *Caretas* had sensationalized the story, reporting in lurid prose about the gringo padre who was helping the Ashaninka wage an armed conflict in the Ene River valley. The title of the magazine piece translated as "Pistol Packin' Padre" and the subtitle blared: "With the Bible in one hand and a revolver in the other, Mariano Gagnon the missionary comes to the defense of his Campas." The piece featured a caricature of me. I was bare-chested, my face painted with two dark horizontal stripes. A pistol was thrust into the belt of my shorts.

I chuckled when I saw this and thought: Well, at least here's an image of a priest going around with something other than his rosary. But Mickey cautioned me that some people wondered openly what business a gringo priest had in fighting a Peruvian jungle war. We guessed that as a result of this coverage, Felix had come under pressure to get me out of the area—and keep me out.

I tabled this topic. I had already decided that Felix's concerns would have to wait. Our conversation moved on to other issues. Lucas offered the intriguing news that he had spoken with Hamilton at the American embassy about the possibility of working for the CIA. He claimed that he was not personally interested in such a job, but he saw opportunity here. If he had official connections, he would have access to more resources that could be used to help the natives. In particular, he could call in an American helicopter whenever necessary.

Mickey exploded upon hearing this, claiming that it would cause us much trouble. He wanted no connection between the Ashaninka and the CIA.

But I did not think there would necessarily be a conflict, and I agreed with Lucas that such an arrangement might be beneficial. The Americans seemed committed to helping us, and this might deepen their resolve.

Mickey suddenly suggested that he and I go off to a sidewalk café for a glass of orange juice. I accepted the invitation; clearly, he wanted to speak with me privately.

"I don't like the idea of Lucas going back in," he told me when we were alone. "And I don't like this CIA talk. There is too much going on."

I felt that Mickey was overreacting, but I asked him what he

191

meant—what was "going on"?—and I listened patiently to his explanation.

Mickey reported that our original plan—for me to remain with the Ashaninka as he sought support in Lima—had worked beautifully. Jamie Pardo was sympathetic to the natives' plight and had responded with a generous donation. All in all, our private contacts had provided enough money to purchase more than a ton of supplies. Our political contact, Senator Miguel Vega, had put Mickey in touch with others who could help. One of these contacts, an admiral in the Peruvian Navy, promised to give us shotguns. He would also call Colonel Froude to arrange to bring the guns into Mazamari on a U.S. flight due in tomorrow.

"I will believe this when I see it," I replied. I admitted to Mickey that I had very strong doubts that the Peruvian Navy would actually provide the promised shotguns and equally strong doubts that the Americans would bring them in on one of their own aircraft. "Let's hope that you are right and I am wrong," I said.

Finally, Mickey disclosed that he had devised a battle plan, and he sketched it out for me. The Peruvian Army would move south from Puerto Ocopa. The Sinchis would attack from the west, crossing the Anapati River, and the Peruvian Navy would approach north from Luisiana. Together, they would squeeze the Sendero forces out of their hideout on the western banks of the Ene.

This three-pronged attack had been considered before, and it was all right, as far as it went, but it failed to account for the back door. The terrorists would simply flee east along the Cutivireni into the remote rain forest where no one could corner them.

But Mickey was not finished. There was a fourth, vital element to his plan. He calculated that it would take the natives only a day to construct three or four rafts. "If we could persuade the Sinchis to send fifteen or so men to Tzibokiroato," he said, "then they could float down the river with the natives under cover of darkness, starting at about three in the morning, and arrive at Camantavesti approximately two and one half hours later."

I listened carefully. If this four-pronged attack was coordinated properly, it would effectively block the terrorists' only escape route, which lay along the Cuti a few kilometers east of the mission site.

The surrounding terrain was nearly impassable. The mountains formed a chasm that would funnel the entire Sendero force toward Camantavesti; the ambushing party of Sinchis and their Ashaninka guides could easily vanquish them.

After our return to the mission house, Mickey drew detailed maps, and I typed a step-by-step itinerary of the proposed battle plan.

"It's good," I agreed. "It could work."

The support of the Americans, and of Captain Reeder in particular, was very important to me. The American helicopters were my most reliable pipeline to the people. By now I was aware of friction between the Green Berets and the Sinchis. First of all, they had differing objectives. The Americans were here to squelch the cocaine trade; the Peruvians were after Sendero. Second, it was obvious that Reeder did not wish to share his plans with the Sinchis. Because there were too many security leaks in and about the Peruvian camp, the Americans tended to act unilaterally. Often, their helicopters took off at the first hint of morning light, heading to undisclosed locations for unspecified missions. Understandably, the *comandante* saw this as undermining his authority, and he bristled.

I had no desire to become enmeshed in this power struggle. This plan needed Peruvian help, but I did not wish to do anything that might make me appear to be keeping secrets from the Americans. I decided that the most prudent course of action was to bounce this new strategy off of Captain Reeder first, and Mickey agreed.

When the DEA airplane arrived the next day, it brought in supplies for the military base, but it also carried Colonel Froude and Fred Hamilton. The colonel stepped off the plane in full fatigue uniform, with a pistol strapped on his hip.

John Wayne has arrived, I thought.

Mickey gestured toward Froude and whispered to me, "Ask him if they brought the shotguns."

But I did not see an opportunity to raise this delicate subject at the moment. As the group headed off down the grass surface of the runway, Froude suddenly turned to Hamilton and, in an exaggerated tone, ordered him to carry his bag, as if he were a fuzzy-cheeked busboy. This ruse, obviously designed to convince us of Hamilton's supposedly subservient position, was very puzzling. Then, as we walked toward the military offices, Froude said over his shoulder to Hamilton, "I think it would be really nice if you see the mission here at Mazamari. They've got a beautiful setup. Why don't you go there with the padre?"

Accompanied by Mickey and Lucas, Hamilton and I set off on the half-mile walk through town to the Franciscan mission house.

Hamilton asked me, in an innocent tone, "Are you coming back to Lima with us?"

"Yes," I lied. "Is it all right with you?"

"I am nobody," he said, continuing the charade.

At the mission house, Father Mario and two mission workers, Juan and Rafael, greeted us and brought out a supply of beer and Cokes. We sat at a large, round table in the receiving room. Hamilton placed his elbows on the table, leaned forward in an aggressive posture and, suddenly and unaccountably, attacked Mickey. Their animated argument concerned Mickey's efforts to ship supplies from Lima. Hamilton said that the Frenchman's delivery of boxes and crates to the airport for transport by the Americans had created a bureaucratic nightmare. He complained that the crates were not properly marked and weighed; the boxes were not secure; the paperwork was in disarray. "You just don't do things this way," Hamilton counseled. "Everything should be done in an orderly manner." Using a practiced, glib tongue, Hamilton piled ridicule on Mickey, claiming that he was not really interested in helping the Ashaninka but in building up his own image as a cavalier adventurer. I was surprised that the normally impetuous and volatile Frenchman maintained his composure.

The tirade continued for more than ten minutes. What is Hamilton trying to accomplish? I wondered. Was he trying to undermine my confidence in Mickey? And if so, why? Did he want to drive a wedge between Mickey and me so that I would be more reliant upon Lucas?

It was Lucas who finally changed the subject, asking Hamilton, "How are things coming along as far as me working for the CIA?"

This seemed like an imprudent question, and one that was totally out of character for the always-discreet Belgian to ask in front of everyone. I held my tongue, and listened carefully. I observed the expressions on the faces of Hamilton and Lucas, particularly Hamilton, who puffed himself up like a peacock and retorted, "It's impossible!" He launched into an involved explanation, the gist of which was that one had to be an American to be a CIA agent. He asserted that under no circumstances would the agency recruit a Belgian citizen.

Aha! I thought suddenly. This is a show, for our benefit. I reasoned that Lucas must have reported to Hamilton that he had told Mickey and me about the possibility of working for the CIA. Hamilton must have programmed Lucas with this ridiculous question so that he could make it clear that Lucas was not an agent. Did this mean that he *was*? Hamilton was no fool. He would have not offered Lucas a CIA job in the first place if such a thing was impossible.

My impression of Hamilton was changing quickly. For someone who was supposed to be little more than an errand boy at the American embassy, he seemed to possess a great deal of authority. I wondered: What is his position at the embassy, *really*? He certainly was not a peon.

I wanted out of this strange discussion, and I said, "I'm going to go up and pack my bag for the flight to Lima."

My mind reeled from the sense of intrigue as we walked back to the airstrip. Hamilton, Froude, and Lucas were playing some sort of game, but so was I. At the airstrip, I deposited my bag next to the aircraft, for all to see. Hamilton and Froude showed no obvious interest in the sight of my suitcase, but I knew that they had noticed it.

Mickey again urged me to find out whether or not the DEA plane had brought the shotguns. When we managed to catch Colonel Froude by himself near the cargo plane, I asked.

The colonel claimed that he knew absolutely nothing about a shipment of guns and that he had not been contacted by anyone from the Ministry of the Navy. "This would not be allowed," he said.

"But we need the guns," Mickey protested. "Time is going by. The natives have no way to defend themselves."

The colonel drew me aside and suggested an alternate plan: Perhaps I could have the Sinchis request the shotguns. Then the next DEA plane could bring them in, and the Americans could turn them over to the Peruvian authorities. Whatever the Sinchis did with the shotguns would be their decision.

I was unsure that any of this mattered. I still doubted whether the Peruvian Navy would ever provide the weapons.

A few minutes later, a sudden wave of nausea encompassed me. I walked quickly to one side of the airstrip and vomited my lunch. Perhaps this was the legacy of my time in the jungle, or perhaps it was the effect of Hamilton and Froude's presence. But most likely it was the tension of my own deception, for I knew that I was about to annoy Hamilton and the colonel very much.

Returning to the side of the airplane, I picked up my bag, suddenly thrust out my hand toward the two American officials and said, "Good-bye. I hope you have a nice flight back to Lima."

Hamilton's face fell. He asked in a shocked tone, "Aren't you coming with us?"

As I had suspected, the colonel knew about the letter from Father Felix, for he asked me, "Didn't you receive a letter from your superior, ordering you back to Lima?"

I gave him a cold look and answered yes. I then added, "Colonel, am I becoming a pain in the embassy's ass?"

"No," he replied, "just in mine."

The Green Berets told me that the U.S. helicopters would not arrive to take us and our supplies into Tzibokiroato until April 20. We had to cool our heels for more than a week.

During that time, Mickey and I approached Captain Reeder. It was our first opportunity to acquaint him with our plan. With enthusiasm, Mickey explained the coordinated attack that would squeeze Sendero toward an ambushing force at Camantavesti. He pulled out a map and showed the captain how it would work.

Captain Reeder's expression grew tense, and he seemed very

agitated. The plan did not include American forces, but I could see that he wanted no part of a discussion concerning Peruvian military actions. "Has anybody else seen this?" he asked.

"No."

"Don't let anybody see this," he cautioned. "Do you have any other copies? You should burn this map."

Mickey and I exchanged puzzled glances. Captain Reeder's vehement reaction was a mystery.

Lucas secured some videotaping equipment, presumably from the Americans. He busied himself documenting, as best he could, the effects of Sendero's February attack on the nearby village of San Martín, where the terrorists had killed thirty-four people, some Ashaninka, and some Quechua, hacking the victims to pieces with machetes.

As the days passed, I found it nearly impossible to sleep at night. The evening of Tuesday, April 17, I was alone in the mission chapel. I spent the entire night there, but I was unable to pray. Over and over I asked: What can I do to help the people?

I reviewed my feelings concerning my vows. Most of my religious brothers considered these to be etched in tablets of stone, unalterable facts of the monastic life, but I viewed them as open to interpretation. It was never my intention or desire to subvert my life to the wills and whims of my superiors. God gave me a mind, and He expected me to use it.

In my view, taking a vow does not make you a puppet or mean that you should surrender your talents. Each vow was a contract, wherein one gave up a certain right in order to gain other advantages. For example, the vow of poverty did not sentence a padre to a life filled with sackcloth and ashes. In fact, most of the religious brothers I knew lived quite well. They resided in comfortable monasteries and ate good meals. They drove modern cars. They took exciting vacations. They never had to worry about the costs of illness or old age. Their poverty was of a rich variety.

Similarly, although the vow of chastity prevented a religious man from enjoying the God-given blessings of family life, it allowed him to devote his time and energy to his special calling. Such enforced bachelorhood resulted in a freedom that, at times, could be almost selfish.

What, then, was the purpose of this vow of obedience? One is not a peon in the hands of his superiors; rather, the superiors are placed in their positions as servants to facilitate—to enable a member of a religious order to fulfill the high ideals for which he joined that order. I could never sacrifice my mind—and my conscience—on an altar of blind obedience.

April 18. Two Green Berets came to tell me that Captain Reeder wished to see me in his office. I walked up to the base and presented myself, wondering what was to come now.

"We've got news," the captain said. "A DEA plane is coming in from Lima today, and you're expected to return with it. The order comes from your superior, and it's been passed through the embassy."

I replied, "At this moment, I'm not sure whether I'm going."

"Aren't you supposed to obey?" he asked.

Captain Reeder was a nice fellow. But I thought: This is none of your friggin' business.

I looked him in the eye and replied curtly, "I need a few minutes to think about it."

I could not believe that Felix had such little trust in my judgment. The helicopters would be here in two or three days to take me back to the Ashaninka. How could I go to Lima now? I could only conclude that Hamilton and Froude were pressuring Felix to pressure me, and now they had enmeshed Captain Reeder in the plot. Why? Why did they want to keep me away from the people?

I worried that if I did not take flight to Lima, the embassy would conclude that I was an incorrigible rebel and might even issue orders to cancel the helicopter flights altogether. Then even Mickey and Lucas would be stranded. I decided that going back to Lima was the safest thing to do to ensure the welfare of the natives, but I was concerned that I would be unable to return in time to take the promised helicopter flight into Tzibokiroato.

I was in a confused, despondent state of mind when one of the

Green Beret troops beckoned me to the side. He lowered his voice to a conspiratorial whisper and informed me, "There will be additional DEA flights back here from Lima in the next two days." So it was possible that I could go to Lima, do my best to assuage Felix, and return to Mazamari quickly.

Mickey's face looked as if I had thrown ice water on him when I announced, "I have to go. I have no alternative. If I stay, there is too much risk that we will never be able to bring supplies to the natives." I tried to explain that the provincial must have received a lot of pressure from the embassy—"especially the two assholes, Froude and Hamilton," I said. "Only God knows what they have told Felix." I added quickly, "Don't worry. I will be back by Friday, and I *will* go into Tzibokiroato with the helicopters."

My morale was very low when I prepared to board the DEA plane.

"I'm very sorry for what has happened," Captain Reeder said, as he shook my hand.

"You should not worry about it," I replied. "By Friday I will be back to go in with the helicopter."

The right side of the captain's lip turned upward in what I had come to know as his characteristic, sardonic grin. His eyes narrowed, as if to say: You are the most stubborn bastard I have ever known.

My own eyes answered: You are right.

In Lima, I headed straight from the airport to the monastery, determined to have it out with Felix as quickly as possible. But the provincial was not in.

I felt the need for contact with friends, so I called Javier Pardo. His wife, Christina, answered. I announced that I was in Lima and assured her that I was all right.

"You must come over," she declared. She said that they already had an engagement for the evening, but on the following night, I was to be their guest at a dinner party at their home.

I also called Colonel Froude at the embassy and asked anxiously, "Are you going to have any flights into Mazamari?"

"I don't know," he replied, "but I'll do everything I can to get you back there. Why don't you call me back tomorrow afternoon? I'll see what I can do for you.''

I located Felix's secretary, Father Vicente Pérez Gereñu, and vented my frustrations. "Why has the provincial proceeded in this manner?" I asked. "Instead of giving me a hand, he has confused the situation and really messed up the possibility of helping these natives. Why did he have to get mixed up with the American embassy? Does he have so little trust in me? Does he think I am completely out of my mind? Does he think I'm an imbecile? He does not understand the predicament of the natives at all, and he does not give a damn!"

In an attempt to calm me down, Father Gereñu offered me a beer. I brightened at this idea and allowed him to lead me off to a small side room. He ushered me to a seat, located a couple of cold beers, and treated me with such gentle kindness and respect that I was able to restrain my temper. We were able to discuss the situation in a more rational manner.

Father Gereñu assured me that everyone here was concerned with my situation, especially Felix.

"I wish he was a bit more concerned about the natives," I answered. "They are completely abandoned."

In response, Father Gereñu handed me a copy of the *Caretas* article that had caused so much uproar, the one featuring the caricature of the "Pistol Packin' Padre." I could see from his expression that he was genuinely perplexed. He knew that the Church must care for all of its people. But did the Church have the right to help them wage war? This was a thorny theological issue, and in Father Gereñu's eyes I saw, for the first time, the depths of the problem faced by the hierarchy.

CHAPTER FOURTEEN

On the day of his arrival in the New World, Christopher Columbus reported in his diary that the natives were friendly. By the very next day, he was referring to them, ominously, as "servants."

According to some estimates, in the seventy years following Columbus's voyage, as many as ninety million Americans died from enslavement, illness, war, and murder; the total number of deaths was nearly twice the population of Europe at the time. These victims were the true Americans, the natives who were already here when Columbus "discovered" the land.

Very few of my Spanish colleagues have ever been willing to recognize the role that the Church played in this tragedy.

In Peru, the alliance between the conquistadores and the Church began when Francisco Pizarro and a Dominican priest known as Father Valverde sought out Atahualpa, the Inca. Father Valverde presented Atahualpa with a Bible and demanded that the Inca declare himself "servant of the Pope and vassal of the King of Spain." When the uncomprehending Atahualpa let the Bible fall to the ground, Pizarro's men attacked and took the "blasphemous" Inca prisoner. Atahualpa offered to buy his freedom with a roomful of gold; Pizarro accepted the booty and then ordered his prisoner garroted.

This set the tone for Spanish rule.

The royal councillor Palacios Rubios was entrusted with the task

201

of producing a document that would provide theological justification for war against the natives. According to this thesis, Christ entrusted to Peter

> the whole world for his [Peter's] reign, lordship and jurisdiction. Peter's successors gave these new discovered lands to the king, hence the natives are the king's subjects and must submit to his rules. Should any resist, the *Conquistadore* was to say to them: "I will wage war against you everywhere; I will subject you to the yoke and obedience of the Church and their Majesties. I will take your persons, your women and children and enslave them, and I affirm that the consequent deaths and destruction will be your fault."

The Church endorsed and defended this theology. The Jesuit provincial Manuel de Nóbrega suggested that by subjecting the pagans the Christian conquerors "will have legitimate slaves, taken in a just war, and they will thus have the service . . . of the indians. . . . Our Lord will gain many souls," wrote Nóbrega, who added, as a none-too-subtle afterthought, "and your Highness will obtain great wealth."

Thus justified by the Church, the conquest of the New World was accomplished with complete disregard for the natives and the most obvious truths of the gospel were prostituted by the very persons who claimed divine guidance.

That the Catholic conquistadores did more to conceal the face of the true God than to reveal it was illustrated by the story of one Carib Indian who was sentenced to be burned to death for participating in an uprising. Prior to his execution, he was offered the sacrament of baptism and, thus, the promise of heaven. He refused, reasoning that if heaven was populated by Christians, he did not wish to spend eternity there.

A royal decree gave Spanish colonizers the right to levy upon the native populace a tribute to be paid by forced labor over three generations. Once a father, son, and grandson had slaved for the patron, the family was free—to live in poverty. The patron enforced the system by using imported tracking dogs to hunt fleeing

Here we were: a ragtag defensive force of poorly armed Ashaninka and a simple gringo padre. Somehow, we had to stave off a determined five-thousand-strong army of Shining Path guerrillas.

ARMANDA VELARDE TORRES

Discussing security with a Peruvian soldier, after the mission was burned in 1984

Caretas/VICTOR CH. VARGAS

Conducting an interview with members of the Peruvian press, after the mission was burned in 1984

Caretas/VICTOR CH. VARGAS

Mario Zumáeta's widow, Cecilia, with her baby. Cecilia has shorn her hair as a sign of mourning.

The soft-spoken, considerate Matías Miranda necessarily assumed the mantle of leadership.

Teodoro and Capitán, prepared for defense; Capitán lost his wife and three daughters in one of the Shining Path's early attacks.

With a precious few shotguns, the Ashaninka were forced to defend themselves. No one, it seemed, was willing to help us.

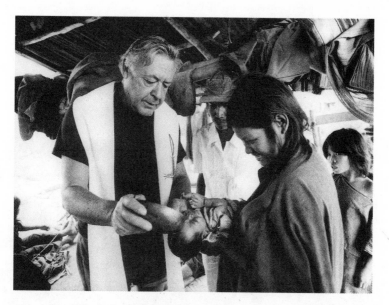

An Ashaninka baby is baptized, even as we were on the run from
the Shining Path.

In rare moment, I allowed an Ashaninka woman to beautify me
with the traditional red face painting.

Celebrating mass after the 1984 fire, when many of the
Ashaninka were ready to seek revenge

Caretas/VICTOR CH. VARGAS

Nicolás stands guard.

Bush pilot Armando Velarde Torres,
the hero of this story

The fiery Nicolás with his wife and their
children

Grim-faced Ashaninka men and boys, armed with
our precious shotguns, wait for the next assault.

Caretas/VICTOR CH. VARGAS

The Passage

Indians and by force-feeding his subjects Catholicism, to save their souls and, not coincidentally, to instill a sense of obedience and respect for authority.

Throughout centuries, the Church blessed the feudal system and happily accepted the donations of the rich. Only in recent times has the hierarchy of the Church taken a different tack. Now, the Church leaders seem willing to blame the rich for all of Peru's woes. In truth, if any group is to blame, the Church stands in the forefront of candidates.

One cannot examine the history of Peru without considering the role played by the Franciscans. I had studied for the priesthood at the huge, fortresslike, adobe-walled sixteenth-century Monastery of Santa Rosa de Ocopa, located about an eight-hour drive to the east of Lima in the immense Montaro Valley. This historic structure had once been the base of Franciscan mission activities throughout South America, and it was proud of its heritage. As you descended a stairway into the sacristy, you were confronted with an exhibit of the portraits of seventy-three missionaries slain by the Ashaninka; there were blank spaces on the wall, giving the impression that additional martyrs might be forthcoming.

The patron of our province was Saint Francis Solano. His memory was venerated in our classes, where we learned how he walked from Panama to Argentina, preaching the gospel, baptizing thousands of heathens, and administering the sacraments. We were taught to imitate him. What we were not taught was that Saint Solano left a legacy of racism. For example:

Solano talked the Indians into accepting a statue of the child Jesus as the mayor of the town of La Rioja. Duly named to office, this statue of the white child in warrior's robes has ever since been the center of an annual ritual reaffirming the Indians' submission.*

Missionaries such as Saint Francis Solano were the first to cross the Andes to the inland jungle of Peru. They established towns and

*See Penny Lernoux, *Cry of the People* (New York: Doubleday, 1980), p. 347.

211

carved out remote roads. They explored the rivers extensively. In fact, they named the great river, which was later to be known as the Amazon, the Río de San Francisco, after Saint Francis himself. From a "civilized" point of view, their accomplishments were enormous—but at what cost to the natives? Their goal was the spread of Christianity, and this, in their minds, required them to impose Iberian culture upon the indigenous people. To them, the Indians had no culture.

One could make the case that the missionary had probably been the Ashaninka's worst enemy. The historical record clearly indicates that the early missionaries coveted their rich lands.

And when the missionaries did turn their attention to spreading the gospel, their tactics were heavy-handed. The first catechism drawn up in the Western Hemisphere, begun by the Dominican Pedro Córdova and his Santo Domingo community in 1510, promised to reveal to the natives "a great secret that they never knew before." Thus gaining their rapt attention, he proclaimed, "All your ancestors, fathers, mothers, grandparents and relatives who have died are in hell, and you will go to hell also unless you are baptized and become Christians, for all those who are not Christian are God's enemies." This was not evangelization; this was terrorism.

On the credit side of the ledger, from the beginning, there were a few voices within the Church calling for justice. The Dominican friar Bartolomé de las Casas was perhaps the most vocal early critic. In his work *A Very Brief Report on the Destruction of the Indies*, he declared, "The natives have acquired the right to wage a most just war against us and wipe us off the face of the earth, and this right will be theirs until the day of judgment."

In 1511, the Dominican friar Antonio de Montesinos, O.P., delivered a homily to the conquistadores. In it, he asked basic questions:

By what right and by what title do you hold these indians in such cruel and horrible slavery? By what authority do you carry on such detestable wars against a people who are meek and peaceful in their own lands? You slaughtered countless numbers of them. The obsessive work you impose on them makes them ill and brings death to them. More precisely, you killed them, as every day you piled up more and more gold. And these people, are they not human beings? Do they not have rational souls? Are you not obliged to love them as you do yourselves?

When the message of that sermon was reported in Spain, Ferdinand, the Catholic king, sent a letter to the provincial of the Dominican order, affirming his "God-given" right to exploit the natives:

When I and the queen, my wife, sent letters ordering that the indians should serve the Christians, we called a meeting of our council, and then the other learned men, theologians and canonists. In view of the gifts and grants that our very holy father, Alexander VI, gave us, of all the island and lands already discovered and yet to be discovered, we agreed in their presence, and with the consent of the Archbishop of Seville, that this servitude was in agreement with both Divine and human law.

Upon receiving this, the provincial immediately sent a letter to Father de Montesinos and all the friars working with him. He accused them of inciting the Indians to rebellion and declared, "To put an end to the harm done and to stop this grave scandal, I order all of you, each and every one of you, by the power of the Holy Spirit and under Holy Obedience, and under penalty of automatic excommunication, that you not dare to preach on this topic [exploitation of the Indians] again."

Thus was criticism squelched.* However, history has shown us that it is easier to silence a theologian than to answer the questions he raises. Nearly five hundred years after Father de Montesinos

---

*For more information on the historic tensions among the conquistadores, the Church, and the native populations of South America, see Charles Finnegan, O.F.M., *Towards 1992: A New Evangelization* (Silver Spring, MD.: Franciscan Mission Service of North America, 1990).

spoke out so boldly, those questions remained.

In the wake of Vatican II, the worldwide council of bishops that brought sweeping changes to Catholicism, it became permissible, even fashionable, to criticize the Church's traditions and authorities. Several of my colleagues were quite willing to do so; still, the majority—especially those of a Spanish, rather than Peruvian, heritage—were of a conservative bent and tended to agree with the sentiment expressed in a book by Father Olarte, who, at the time he wrote, held the title of religious superior of our Franciscan missions in Peru. He was a decent but misguided fellow who was still alive at the time I began my mission work. Father Olarte suggested that the best solution was to put the Ashaninka into "something like concentration camps," with the men under the guidance of priests and the women under the guidance of nuns. Over time, perhaps they could be encouraged to intermarry with other elements of Peruvian society so that, eventually, the native race would disappear altogether.

This viewpoint was underscored in 1969—just before I headed off to work with the Ashaninka—in a conversation I had with the man who was then my provincial. Father Odorico Saiz was a benevolent man with a paternalistic attitude toward the younger priests. He was a doctor of history with, I regrettably concluded, a one-sided view that tended to excuse any excesses in Church actions. He pointed out that the natives themselves—in their conflicts with various tribes—had been guilty of exploitation, slavery, and torture, and had practiced human sacrifices.

"It is true," I conceded. "But we did the very same thing and justified it with theological principles!"

"Ay, gringo, gringo," the provincial muttered. "The only thing you can do is talk. If you knew history, if you knew all the circumstances, you would know that I am right. Remember that at one time, all Europe was made up of tribes, and they were conquered." By being conquered, he said, they were civilized. And along with civilization came Christianity. Turning his attention to the Ashaninka and other indigenous South American tribes, he contended, "We *must* learn the lessons of history."

"Precisely!" I responded. "We must learns the lessons of history

214

so that we do not make the same mistakes."

At this point of the discussion, Father Saiz reminded me of a principle of my training: that a good member of a holy order must be like a dead body; if his superior places him on his right side, he should stay there. The inference was that I should *think* like him.

I am not an intellectual; however, over the years I did enough of my own thinking to sympathize with a group of scholars who came to be called liberation theologians, who contended that the Church in Peru, which was still very strong, could bring about a social revolution without bloodshed. This clearly could not happen until we learned from history. Perhaps the Church's most glaring defect is its inability to admit error. And by not acknowledging her faults, she continues to fall into the same traps, even in this present age.*

The message of Christ is liberation; how could we continue to preach this when so many of the people of Peru were enslaved, in one form or another?

We have come a long way since the days when Father de Montesinos and his colleagues were silenced by the threat of excommunication, but we still have much farther to go. I wondered if we were paying sufficient attention to the words of Pope Paul VI, who reminded us that our task is to proclaim the good news of salvation. This great gift of God liberates everyone.

At the heart of the debate between the liberation theologians and the old-liners is the very substance of the missionary calling. Many conceive of the missionary as an itinerant dispenser of the sacraments, who should trudge from village to village to baptize the populace and then administer the Eucharist. But to others, myself included, the missionary's spiritual role must have an impact upon all of life. Theology should be the basis for social and political action. Any religious vision should produce a healing power that binds human beings together and seeks to help them rejoice in the gifts that God has given.

*It was refreshing to hear Pope John Paul II, in 1987, confess to a Native American audience: "The cultural oppression, the injustices and the destruction of your life and traditional societies need to be recognized. . . . We are called to learn a lesson from the mistakes of the past."

In sum, by the time I responded to Felix's invoking the vow of obedience, I was still convinced that it was possible to bring Christianity and the good news of the gospel to the Ashaninka without forcing them to abandon their own unique culture.

At noon, I met Felix in the monastery's dining room. He embraced me and appeared genuinely happy to see me.

Despite my own concerns, as I looked at Felix, I could hardly suppress a smile. The short, pudgy, pasty-white face beneath balding blond hair reminded me of the little plastic friar that had so intrigued Sister Primitiva. Felix had tremendous energy and walked with a bouncing gait. He was an intelligent man, a doctor in canon law, and a tireless worker. We were often at cross-purposes, but I admired much about him. He bore his nickname of Little Caesar with good humor, and I knew that he was incapable of holding a grudge.

Felix appeared nervous, but our conversation was marked with sincerity. He seemed very sympathetic about my situation and about the plight of the Ashaninka, and I suspected that Father Gereñu had mentioned something about my mood. Still, he grilled me about my role in the past and current tensions between the Ashaninka and their neighbors.

It soon became clear that as I suspected, Hamilton and Froude had been pressuring Felix to rein me in. They had told him that the ambassador was quite upset with me because I had cost the Americans a lot of money. They charged that I had authorized the Green Berets to dynamite the airstrip at Cuti, and they were concerned that I was trying to involve the Americans in the conflict between Sendero and the Ashaninka.

I protested that this was ridiculous. I explained to Felix that when I returned from my visit to the U.S. and had heard about the attacks upon the Ashaninka, I had first gone to the Peruvian Air Force seeking support. I had only switched my attention to the Americans because Hamilton and Froude had encouraged me to do so. "They offered to help, and now they are bitching about it," I moaned.

"You can't buck the American embassy," Felix cautioned.

"I'm not trying to buck the American embassy. But I'm certainly trying to defend what I believe in. And I'm not going to give up. If the American people knew what the hell is going on down here—that they are willing to expose the natives to all kinds of risk, that they are willing to send twenty thousand natives down the drain, that they are willing to destroy whatever facilities we have, that they are willing to tell open lies, all in order to fight the drug trade—don't you think they would protest?"

Felix continued, unimpressed with my defense. He said that the embassy was concerned that under the influence of Mickey I was trying to provide the Ashaninka with shotguns in order to start a guerrilla war.

"I am not trying to start a war," I assured him. "There already is a war. I simply want the natives to be able to defend themselves."

On the basis of secondhand information, Felix appeared to blame Mickey more than me. "You should have nothing to do with Mickey," he advised. "He should not be welcome in any of our Franciscan houses."

"Mickey should not carry the blame," I declared. "I realize that Mickey is impetuous and outspoken. However, he has the natives' cause very much at heart. What Mickey did, I agree with." I assured Felix that I was quite willing to bear the responsibility for the furor caused by the *Caretas* article.

The conversation grew more heated. "The Church must not resort to violence," Felix insisted.

"The Church must not be hypocritical," I countered. "The Church has employed violence throughout history. My God, Felix, more blood has been spilled over religious contentions than for any other reason; we have cast more shadows than light."

His face reddened, and he tried to silence me, repeating, "The Church must not assist—the people must do it on their own."

I was enraged. "Domination is violence, Felix. Silencing the liberation theologians is violence. Violence is the Church trying to become the universal conscience." I contended that the Church's ultimate weapon, excommunication, was violence in the extreme, since it was no less than a condemnation to hellfire.

Felix tried a different approach. In a quiet, sincere tone, he asked, "Do you think your presence is good or bad for the natives?"

I replied, "If I thought it was detrimental, there is no way I would stay there. Many times I have talked to the natives about this. If they wanted me to go, I would go. But they want me to stay." I saw a twinge of doubt in Felix's eyes, and I wondered if he thought that my motives were selfish, so I told him of my vague plan: If Sendero's attacks continued, we would move the Ashaninka east to the Urubamba region, out of the Ene River valley. That would save them, but there would be no place for me in their new lives.

"Would it be better if they go to Puerto Ocopa or Cheni?" Felix asked.

"In this case, more or less, they would be in the same situation," I replied. "Sendero is busy in those places, too."

Felix was a faithful disciple of Father Odorico, and as the earlier provincial had done twenty years ago, he tried to get me to view all this from the historical angle. He reminded me that Rome had crushed the heathens—our own ancestors—in order to Christianize them. Perhaps the process was painful, but, Felix seemed to say, look at us now. His implication was that Ashaninka culture was godless and worthless, and that the only way to salvage something from it was to let it disintegrate so that the few survivors would be forced to emerge into modern—Christian—life. He suggested, "Might it not be better to leave them as they are and abandon the mission altogether?"

"If we leave them, they will be killed or forced to join the terrorists."

I waited for Felix to answer, but he said nothing. Moments passed. His silence spoke volumes.

"You are a fascist," I hissed. "No one gives a damn about the natives. No one is concerned with the plight of the Ashaninka; the Indians have always been considered expendable, even by the Church."

We were at an impasse, and Felix declared that the only person responsible for the vicariate was Bishop Ojeda. This was obviously a stalling tactic, for we all knew that the bishop and Felix always rubber-stamped one another's views. "I will not make my decision until we speak with the bishop," Felix said. He explained that the

218

bishop was away at a meeting, so we were unable to meet with him now.

I spent the afternoon pacing nervously in and about the monastery.

At 3:00 P.M. I called Colonel Froude, as directed. To my surprise, Fred Hamilton answered the phone and informed me that the colonel was, at this moment, speaking to Washington on another line. He assured me that the call would be short, because connections to the States were very expensive, and the embassy did not have the budget for many of these calls.

It was all I could do to restrain myself from laughing at this unbelievable explanation.

Hamilton promised to have Froude return my call shortly. I waited one hour before, in frustration, I called him back myself. This time I reached him and immediately asked about a flight to Mazamari.

The colonel said that he was very sorry, but all flights to Mazamari had been grounded for about a week. What's more, there were problems in Santa Lucía—he said he could not give me the details, for "security reasons"—and the helicopters had to remain there; they would not arrive in Mazamari in the next day or so, as planned.

Abruptly switching gears, the colonel said that Ambassador Quainton insisted on meeting me and wanted to set a date. He suggested that I attend an upcoming dinner where both the ambassador and the embassy's second-in-command would be present.

"Fine," I growled.

The colonel said that he would call me the next day with details. Then he added that it would be a good idea if the two of us spoke before I met the ambassador, and he suggested that I stop by his home for drinks.

"I'll call you back," I said.

That evening, I was early for my dinner engagement with the Pardos, and as I sipped a drink, I described to Christina the details of my frustrating day. With the news that the flights had been canceled, I did not know when I could get back to the Ashaninka. Christina listened attentively, but I worried that I might be boring her.

When Jamie Pardo and his wife, Anna, arrived, I repeated my story for them. Jamie was unusually reserved. He told me that while I was in the jungle, he was worried about my welfare, and on various occasions he had called the American embassy to try to get news concerning me.

I made a joke of this. "I have never lived such a clean life," I said. "In the jungle, I had no drinks and no cigarettes. I even lost a bit of weight."

Jamie brushed this aside and spoke to me of his impressions of Mickey's visit to Lima. The Frenchman's stories about the terrorist attacks and the hopeless plight of the Ashaninka were alarming. Yet Jamie appeared upset with Mickey.

Did Mickey exaggerate? I wondered. No, it would be impossible to overplay the dangers of the situation. So what was bothering Jamie? Mickey had brought with him my letter declaring my total trust in the Frenchman. Had Mickey said or done something to offend?

"Did the supplies come in to Mazamari?" Jamie asked.

I assured him that everything arrived—food, medicine, and blankets—but explained that we had still been unable to get them in to the natives. Jamie said that he was very impressed with Mickey on this point. The Frenchman, unasked, had provided receipts to document all the purchases he had made with the Pardos' generous donations.

Finally, Jamie disclosed the source of his reticence. He said that Mickey had mentioned to him the possibility of getting firearms for the Indians.

This was not wise on Mickey's part, I realized. He had put my best friend in Lima in a difficult spot. On the subject of firearms, Mickey should have been more discreet.

We adjourned for dinner in Javier and Christina's aristocratic dining hall. A servant attended us, bearing exquisite food on silver platters, but as always, the atmosphere was not stuffy. It was after dinner, when we had moved into the drawing room for drinks, that

Jamie dropped a bombshell. He told me that a member of the American embassy had charged that I was responsible for the loss of a helicopter and serious injury to five men.

I froze. Momentarily, I was too stunned to speak. "Who said this?" I asked.

"I must keep the name in reserve," Jamie answered.

"Well, it is completely false," I raged. "The very sad accident with the helicopter had absolutely nothing to do with me. The damn helicopter crashed in Santa Lucía." Hearing this accusation from my friend brought a sudden and terrible pain to my stomach. How was it possible that someone from the American embassy—and I could pretty well narrow the possible sources to two—could make the charge that I was responsible for the tragedy?

It was very late, after one o'clock, when our British friend Graham Curtis arrived to drive me to his home for the night, and I was freshly shocked to hear him repeat the same rumor, which he had heard during dinner this very evening with several ambassadors. The American ambassador, Anthony Quainton, had declared, "Yeah, we know of this priest. He's the cause of the loss of a helicopter and five men."

"Graham, that is bullshit," I said.

"Well, tomorrow you must call and get this cleared up," he suggested. "It is obviously a misunderstanding." The others echoed his advice.

When we arrived at Graham's home, he suggested, in the manner befitting an English gentleman, "Let's have a Scotch." Over our late drink, Graham agreed with my contention that Froude and Hamilton were feeding false information to the ambassador. He suggested that I bypass them and attempt to deal directly with the ambassador, immediately.

I had a great deal of difficulty getting to sleep that night. Here I was in Lima, waiting impatiently to meet with Felix and Bishop Ojeda, and worrying about what Quainton thought about me. If the reasoning behind Froude and Hamilton's backbiting was to delay me, they were accomplishing their objective. The hours and days were passing, and my people were scared and starving. Morning light would bring Friday, the day that the helicopters were originally scheduled to arrive back in Mazamari. Colonel Froude had told me they were delayed indefinitely, but what did *his* word mean? Any day now, the helicopters might arrive unannounced, and I knew that my friends in the Green Berets would seek to load them immediately and fly the supplies into the jungle. Mickey and Lucas were there and could certainly attend to the details. I knew that they would want to go in and remain with the Ashaninka. And I knew that the natives would welcome them. But I was vain enough to believe that my presence was critical also.

I rose very late in the morning with the thought: This is all screwed up. How can I possibly sort out everything? How can I hope to please Felix, Bishop Ojeda, Froude, Hamilton, Ambassador Quainton, the Pardos, Graham, the Peruvian press, and all the others who insisted upon venturing an opinion? Everyone was drawing me into a controversy, but the important issue was not me; it was the Ashaninka. I muttered, "Fuck everybody! I'm going back to my people."

I was quiet and preoccupied as Graham drove me to the monastery. I barely listened as he mentioned that his secretary's husband had obtained a box of medicine for the natives; he had brought the box along in the trunk of his car. It took me a moment to respond to Graham's invitation to join him and some of our other friends at the Phoenix Club for lunch; it was a going-away party for James Blunt, one of the officials of the British embassy.

"I'm not going," I snapped.

"Look, it will do you good."

"No. I'm going back to Cuti."

Graham's face tightened, but he said nothing.

"There's something fishy going on," I continued. "I'm going to try like hell to get back to Cuti."

CHAPTER FIFTEEN

From the monastery, I called my friend Felipe Valiriestra, manager of one of the airlines that flew out of the Lima airport, and asked, "How much would you charge me for a chartered flight from Lima to Mazamari?"

"You lucky bastard," Felipe said. "I think we've got a flight going out for Banco de Crédito, so it won't cost you anything. It's not to Mazamari, but to Satipo."

"Close enough," I agreed.

"Can you be at the airport at one-fifteen?" he asked.

"I will definitely be there," I said.

I stuffed a few necessities into my bag and raced out of my room, hoping to find Felix. I had no intention of sneaking out on him. I would tell him that I was quite willing to return to Lima to meet with him and Bishop Ojeda at their convenience. But unfortunately, neither Felix nor his secretary, Father Gereñu, was around. I encountered Father Marcos and begged him to drive me to the airport immediately. He agreed to do so; Brother Roque joined us for the ride.

"Please explain to the provincial, or to anyone else who has questions, that I am not running out," I said to Father Marcos. "If I can get back to Mazamari soon, I expect to be able to get into Tzibokiroato to see my people. I will soon be back here to explain the whole situation."

Father Marcos agreed to relay my message.

We encountered a traffic jam, and I was worried that we would be late. My nerves were on edge. It was precisely 1:15 P.M. when I rushed onto the airplane and we took off for Satipo. The hour-long flight on the modern turbojet aircraft took us across the Andes to what seemed like another world.

The moment I stepped off the airplane at Satipo, I encountered my friend Tommy Simonich, a bush pilot of Yugoslav heritage. He was one of several pilots who had kept the mission supplied over the years.

"Gringo," Tommy asked, "where the hell are you going?"

"Mazamari," I answered.

"I'll take you," Tommy volunteered. "Jump in."

It was only a short hop in Tommy's Cessna, and by two-thirty I was in Mazamari. I decided to go straight to the parish house to see if Mickey and Lucas were there, but they had gone off somewhere. Overcome by exhaustion, I lay down on my bed, seeking a bit of rest. There was nothing else to do until my friends arrived with, I hoped, news of when the helicopters would were due.

I had just dozed off when the pulsating sound of rotors echoed overhead. Here were the phantom helicopters, which were not supposed to arrive today! I leaped from the bed, pounded my head in frustration at my own naïveté, and mumbled, "The son of a bitch!" It was clear that Colonel Froude had lied to me about the helicopters.

I rushed on foot through town toward the Green Beret base camp and arrived in time to see Captain Reeder and a few of his men greeting the crews of two helicopters that had just arrived with DEA personnel. The captain's face registered shock when I approached, as if he had seen a ghost. But he, as well as his men, was pleased to see me. "How the hell did you get back to Mazamari?" Victor and several others asked.

Mickey and Lucas arrived on the scene and greeted me with warmth. They, too, were amazed at my sudden appearance.

They explained that two American military planes had arrived from Lima that very day. Since I had not come in on either of those flights, they had assumed that I was staying in Lima and would not be available to go into Tzibokiroato with the helicopters.

Another blatant lie, I thought. Colonel Froude told me that all flights from Lima to Mazamari were canceled. "It doesn't matter how I got here," I answered. "The important thing is, I'm here. I told you I'd be back."

Captain Reeder explained that these were not his helicopters; these were DEA equipment. He introduced me to the commander of the DEA team, a towheaded, muscle-bound fellow named Frank Stacey. We adjourned to a briefing room, where Stacey peppered me with questions concerning the situation in the Ene River valley. He agreed to take me in to Tzibokiroato. We set a plan to begin shuttling the supplies early the next morning; it would take several round trips. Between the first and last flights, a few of the Green Berets and a doctor would stay with the Ashaninka, to provide what help they could. We were all to meet here at the Green Beret base at five-thirty the next morning.

For one more night I had difficulty sleeping. The adrenalin was pumping, and my mind kept repeating: At last, I will be with the people!

April 21. Mickey and I arrived at the airstrip a bit after five o'clock. Sleep lay heavily upon my eyes, but I could barely contain my excitement. Our spirits were high, for we anticipated a happy reunion with the Ashaninka.

A contingent of troops was already busy loading the helicopters for the first trip. I overheard one of them mutter, "Lotta tension in the air this morning."

Captain Reeder appeared, and I greeted him with a hearty "Good morning."

He did not respond. Rather, he attended to his business in a surly mood. He glanced at the boxes of supplies and snapped loudly, "Too much weight. Can't take all that stuff in. We have to leave some of these supplies here." I was tempted to remind him that this was a DEA mission and that it was none of his business, but I kept quiet. Captain Reeder stalked off in the direction of the Sinchi camp.

Within minutes, the helicopter pilot appeared and asked one of the soldiers, "Why are you leaving these supplies?"

"There is too much weight," the man replied.

"Nah," the pilot said. "We can take all that, and a lot more."
The pilot directed the men to load everything. Then he explained
to us that he was going to fly the helicopter a few hundred feet up
to the Sinchi camp to take on fuel. Mickey and Lucas climbed
aboard, but I set off on foot in an attempt to catch up with Captain
Reeder, to see if I could discern the reason for his bad temper.

A sudden loud explosion broke the peace of the morning. All
eyes turned to see a dust cloud above the site of a land mine
guarding the American section of the living quarters. Apparently
a bird had landed on the trip wire and blown himself away. The
timing was unfortunate, for it put us all further on edge.

When I finally reached Captain Reeder, he looked at me pointedly and asked gruffly, "Where are you going?"

"Over there," I responded in a tone that matched his. I pointed
to the Sinchi base.

He grinned sarcastically, but said nothing. Then he stalked over
toward the training field, where a contingent of Peruvian *policía*
was waiting for the class he taught.

The helicopter arrived at the Sinchi base, but experienced some
sort of problem with its fuel pump. A mechanic fiddled, removed
a part, and drove it back to the American headquarters. Within
fifteen minutes he returned and reinstalled the mechanism. By
now, Mickey, Lucas, and I were terribly eager to be on our way.

Then, when everything was ready for takeoff, when I was just
about to climb on board, a Green Beret named David came up to
us and announced, "You and Mickey cannot go. Only Lucas. I'm
sorry, those are orders."

I felt my body stiffen. "What do you mean, I can't go?" I asked.

"I'm sorry," he repeated.

Why not Mickey and me? I wondered. Why the hell just Lucas?

But I did not have an opportunity to ask these questions, for
Stacey arrived and took over the conversation. He declared, "You
cannot go on the aircraft because it is overloaded."

I had expended so much energy to get to this point. I had
overcome so many obstacles. These past few days I had scurried

around—like a busy ant—from Mazamari to Lima to Satipo and finally back to Mazamari and now—also like an ant—they were squashing me. I stared straight into the DEA commander's eye and replied, "You know as well as I do that that is a fucking lie!"

Stacey held my gaze, but said nothing.

I turned away in disgust and strode back toward my quarters at the mission house. Behind me I heard the helicopters roar to life. I turned and watched them soar off toward the jungle, taking the supplies—and Lucas—with them. I realized that my body was shaking beyond control. I thought: I'll be damned if I'm going to let them get the best of me.

As my gaze settled upon the facilities at the Sinchi base, suddenly a crazy plan came to mind, spawned by a twenty-year-old memory.

When I reached my room at the mission, I changed quickly into my most rugged clothes and pulled on boots. Then I marched over to the Sinchi headquarters, confronted the colonel, and announced, "I want to do a few practice falls."

"You thinking of making a jump?" he asked. He knew that it had been twenty years since I had made a parachute jump, and back then I was already forty years old.

I nodded. I reasoned that with a few practice falls under my belt I could find a bush pilot who would fly me over Tzibokiroato. This seemed to be the only way I could get to my people.

When I told my plan to the colonel, he asked about the terrain around Tzibokiroato. After I explained that it was a high, isolated plateau with a very limited landing area, he muttered, "This is very foolish." Seeing that this did not deter me, he suggested that I use a special type of parachute that would provide maximum maneuverability. Then he assigned me his best instructor for the practice falls.

I knew that I was extremely rusty and had to reacquaint myself with the proper way to land. There are several points on your body that must accept, in succession, the shock of hitting the ground. The technique is a simple by-the-numbers process known as the drop and roll.

After my first fall from the small platform, as I dusted off my clothes, I lectured myself: Mariano, if you don't land in the small clearing, you better make damn sure that you fall into one of the yucca patches; that's the only thing that's going to save you. I realized that my body was shaking, and I thought: Now wait a minute. I'm not going to be jumping scared. I've *got* to make up my mind not to be scared.

I heard the helicopters return from their flight to Tzibokiroato. A few minutes later, as I was climbing the platform for another fall, Captain Reeder and his men walked past, returning to their quarters. I saw wonder in their faces, and I returned their gazes with a cool stare of my own, as if to say: Look what the hell you're putting me through. After they were gone, one of the Green Beret troops approached and asked, "What are you doing?"

I raged, "What does it look like, asshole?"

Soon the Peruvian colonel reappeared, with an expression of sincere concern on his face. He declared that it would be suicide to attempt to jump into Tzibokiroato. "Aside from the fact that there is very little space, there is a strong crosswind," he told me. "I cannot authorize the jump. I cannot give you a parachute. It is out of the question. You are putting me in a very delicate situation. If something should happen to you, I would consider myself responsible."

I responded with a gaze of utter frustration. But I thought: Mariano, be honest with yourself. As much as you want to make the jump, you are scared. I said weakly, "I'm still gonna get in there."

"Do not give up hope," the *comandante* said gently. "General Delgado will be arriving any day from Huancayo in a helicopter. You might be able to go in with the Peruvian Army."

Mickey raged at me for storming away from the helicopters just before takeoff. "If you would have stayed, I'm sure they would have taken you in," he contended. He explained that no one on the helicopter crew knew where Tzibokiroato was. Nor did Lucas. So they had taken Mickey along as a guide, and he was sure they would have taken me, too, as long as I agreed to remain on board.

"You went *in*? I asked incredulously. "Why the hell didn't you stay? Why didn't you just jump off and give them the finger? They're not going to shoot you."

"I did not want to leave you alone."

Once more, the pressures of the situation brought me an argument with my good friend. "Well, you left the natives alone," I growled.

"You should have come," Mickey retorted. "Then we could have both jumped off. If you weren't such an impetuous Canadian cow, you would be there now."

After noon, we managed to corner Captain Reeder along with Stacey and his assistant. I could not remember a moment in my life when I was more angry, and my language reflected my mood. Out of control, I screamed, "As far as I am concerned, Colonel Robert Froude, Fred Hamilton, and the ambassador—and all the rest of them—are a bunch of goddamn fucking hypocrites and liars!" Addressing Stacey, I said, "I only met you yesterday, and I thought you were a pretty nice fellow, but from what you told me at the airport this morning, you are also a liar like the rest of them. You told me there was too much weight on the helicopter, and you knew this was a lie."

Captain Reeder interrupted. He explained that he had suggested this to Stacey as the reason that Mickey and I could not go on the flight. "It was my doing," he admitted. "I told him to tell you that."

I turned back to Stacey and immediately apologized on that point. But I had more to discuss. I asked him why the DEA had bombed the airstrip at Cuti.

"Because flights for the narcos are landing there," he answered.

"Why did you not do the same thing at Uchiza?" I asked. Uchiza was in north central Peru, near the Huallaga River, strategically located between the eastern ridges of the Andes and the coca-growing plantations of the northeastern jungles. It was only a small village, yet its main street was lined with establishments of money changers. Everyone in Peru knew that the airstrip at Uchiza was the main base for drug flights to Colombia. It was rumored to cost twenty-five thousand dollars in bribes to fly out of the town.

Somewhat apologetically, Stacey explained that they could not destroy the Uchiza airstrip because the police and the Peruvian Army were stationed there, and also because there were many civilians in the area.

"Ah, civilians," I said in a tone of deep irony. "But it is very sad that you never took into consideration that the airstrip at Cuti served families of civilians. Right now, there are at least five thousand natives in that immediate area who are completely abandoned. No one can get into the region because of what your people did to the airstrip. The natives are completely isolated, with no hope of receiving help." My anger was back, in full force. My voice rose in pitch and volume as I bellowed, "You killed all the natives in the States, so then you came down here to kill more! Why the hell don't you bomb Miami?" To end my tirade, I chose a careful word. I said, "You have absolutely no consideration for the . . . savages—"

Stacey's face registered shock. He interrupted me and asked with quiet cunning, "Did you use the word *savages*?"

"Yes, because that is exactly what you think of the natives." I thought: You friggin' Pharisee.

"We have a mission to fulfill," he argued.

"Yeah, tell me about it," I responded. "And you have done everything in your power to stop me from fulfilling mine—including degrading yourself by using open lies."

"That was done for your security."

"This is another lie," I charged. "And a pretext. And a lot of bullshit. Why was it that Lucas, a Belgian, who had nothing to do with the natives, was permitted to go in while we were not?"

"He is going on a special mission."

At this point, I was too emotionally exhausted to pursue the subject further. I had vented my rage, and had nothing more to say. I turned to leave, but Stacey stopped me with a quiet, polite request. He said that he would like to speak with me alone, later. His tone calmed me, and I agreed to a 3:00 P.M. meeting.

"I feel very sorry for what has happened," Captain Reeder said. "But there is nothing I can do."

Why was the American embassy doing everything it could to

keep me from my people? I wondered. Are they afraid that I will be some kind of embarrassment to them? Or do they think that I am mixed up with the drugs? To my surprise, I discovered that I had sufficient energy left for one final insult. I spat out the words, "Please call Hamilton back and tell him that I wouldn't even give him the sweat off my balls."

In quiet conversations with several people, I learned much more. Others assured me that Captain Reeder was firmly on my side, but had received a direct order from the American embassy to keep me off the flight. He had double-checked this with his immediate superiors and could not get the order rescinded. In his own way, he was furious, too, but he could not reveal his anger to me.

My 3:00 P.M. meeting with Stacey and his aide turned out to be more of an interrogation than a conversation. The two men picked my brain for whatever information I could give them regarding drug trafficking in the Ene River valley. I responded as honestly as I could and was able to pinpoint on a map the location of a cocaine-processing laboratory, where the Quimpiri River empties into the Ene. On this we agreed: We all wanted the narcos out of the valley.

Stacey assumed that my cooperation indicated that my anger had abated, but he was wrong. As our conversation ended, he offered to walk with me back to the mission house.

"I don't wish to walk with you," I snapped. "I want absolutely nothing to do with you. The only one here whom I consider to be my friend is the captain."

Stacey's face grew as red as the juice of the achiote berry.

I added, "As far as I am concerned, I would not even give you the privilege of kissing my ass."

What were the Americans doing here, anyway? I wondered. No one could ignore the terrible effects that cocaine has upon the American population. But I could not accept the proposition that their actions were the way to combat drug trafficking in the U.S.

The Americans could not solve the drug problem at home, so they came to the sovereign country of Peru and put the lives of innocent people on the line. What did the Peruvians know, or care, about America's drug problem? Peru's main problem was not drug trafficking, but terrorism. Thus the American effort backfired, for the terrorists proclaimed that the Americans used the drug war as a pretext for enslaving the Peruvians. Instead of the DEA stopping the drug trade, they had aided the terrorists in fomenting revolt.

Their lack of concern for the natives also hurt the effort. By not supporting the Ashaninka, they drove more of them into the arms of the terrorists, who, in turn, persuaded the natives to grow coca to help finance the revolution.

The economic help that the Americans offered to Peru had doubtless been of great benefit in persuading the government to allow the DEA to operate here. But that foreign aid had produced much bloodshed. Perhaps international collaboration can get all nations to eradicate the evils of drugs and drug traffickers, but we cannot permit the lives of innocent people to be lost in the process. What trust can the people have in their political authorities when they see the politicians accept a handful of dollars and then allow the lives of their people to be endangered?

All of this became even more absurd when I learned that Colonel Froude had passed on to Captain Reeder an order emanating directly from Ambassador Quainton. The ambassador instructed the Green Berets to add a new course to its curriculum of instruction for Peruvian police cadets. The subject was to be human rights.

April 22. The Sinchi colonel informed me that General Delgado would be arriving soon in Satipo from Huancayo and would send a helicopter for me; he wished to speak with me.

With my hopes renewed, I waited at the airstrip for more than three hours. When the helicopter finally arrived, my first question to the pilot was whether or not he could take me in to Tzibokiroato, instead of Satipo. Of course, he could not disobey his orders, so he told me that this would be impossible since he only had sufficient fuel to take me to see the general in Satipo.

Once I arrived, I cooled my heels further, waiting for General Delgado to finish a meeting with town officials. When he finally did see me, I tried to impress upon him the sad situation of the Ashaninka. The general was a heavyset man with a clean-cut face that seemed to bear traces of Quechua heritage—this was unusual among Peru's military elite. He listened politely to my intelligence information concerning Sendero's operations in the Ene, but I was not sure that he trusted my sources. I also tried to explain the details of Mickey's proposed plan of attack, but the general clearly did not wish to hear a civilian lecture him on military strategy. Beyond that, he had to concern himself with a far larger area of eastern Peru, where terrorist activity was rampant.

He seemed sincere when he explained that he had only a single helicopter and did not see how he could spare it to help the Ashaninka. From one day to the next, he could not predict what trouble might arise, or where. Seeing dejection in my face, he offered a bit of hope. He mentioned that a detachment of his men staying in Satipo sometimes had the helicopter at their disposal. In my presence, he called the detachment *comandante* and authorized him to use the helicopter to take me into Tzibokiroato, once the unit had fulfilled its military obligations.

"Can Mickey go in as well?" I asked.

"This is not possible," the general replied, and I decided not to press my luck.

I stayed in Satipo that night and, very early the following morning, met with the local *comandante*. As I had with the general the day before, I described graphically the desperate situation of the Ashaninka and pleaded with him to fly me in as soon as possible. He, too, reacted coolly when I tried to detail Mickey's plan for an ambush at Camantavesti.

Obviously taking his cue from the general, the *comandante* tentatively agreed to fly me in on Sunday, April 29, but said that he could not take Mickey. "These days we have many missions to comply with," he explained.

It was a typical Peruvian response. He did not want to say no, so he made a vague promise, and set up an excuse to defer action on the basis of "military obligations." I thought: It is obvious that the welfare of the Ashaninka is not one of his many missions.

CHAPTER SIXTEEN

April 27, 1990. I was back in Mazamari. It was shortly after five in the morning on Friday, two days before the Peruvians had said that they might take me in. The American helicopters prepared to take off on an early-morning flight to Tzibokiroato, in order to bring Lucas back out after his "special mission." They were also supposed to deliver medical supplies and take certain civic actions, which meant that they would leave a doctor and four Sinchis there for the day. As the doctor tended to the Ashaninka and surveyed their needs, the Sinchis would look over the natives' defenses.

I held a quiet meeting with Captain Reeder. With a touch of reticence in his voice, he said, "I'll let you go in to see the people. But you've got to come out on the same helicopter."

I liked this American captain. He had been good to me. The only time he thwarted me was when he had direct orders to do so, and I did not want to lose his allegiance. I sensed that he was sticking his neck out and wondered whether or not he had the authorization to do this. "It will put you in one hell of a situation," I observed. I felt that I should level with him. "If I go in, I'm not coming back out. I'll simply jump off the helicopter and join the natives. Neither hell nor high water nor the American embassy will get me back on that aircraft."

He sighed and said, "Then you can't go in."

Seeing my frustration, Captain Reeder agreed to have his troops carry a letter from me. I scrawled a note quickly:

To Matías, Nicolás or César:
Dear Paisanos,
They don't allow me to go in with the helicopter. If the situation continues badly and you feel that it is necessary to leave the area of Tzibokiroato, the captain has agreed that three of you may come to Mazamari.

From here we could leave on Saturday with a plane from Armando and go to Kiriketi to talk with the Machiguenga about the possibility of establishing yourselves there. We would make the crossing with Mickey.

If you wish to stay where you are, build the airstrip. I will make a flight a month from now to see about the possibility of landing.

In this interval of time that you build the airstrip, should you have to escape, I will try to locate you coming in from the Urubamba. If you decide to come out on this helicopter, it would be ideal if Matías, Nicolás, and Shirampari come. Should this not be possible, decide amongst yourselves who to send. Hopefully we will soon be together again.
Un abrazo para todas. ["An embrace to all of you."]
May the good Lord accompany you.
Mariano

I specifically requested Nicolás because of his fluency in Spanish, and his knowledge of the terrorist activities. He could even guide the authorities through the jungle to point out the location of the terrorists' caves.

The American helicopter took off about five o'clock. Since the flight time to Tzibokiroato was less than twenty-five minutes, I expected them back in about an hour. But I paced the airstrip for more than three hours before they returned.

I was delighted to see Jamie, Capitán, and Teodoro emerge. They greeted me with broad grins, but returned my hugs with characteristic Ashaninka reserve. Jamie rocked from side to side, awkwardly communicating embarrassment. They were dressed only in tattered shorts.

"Where are your clothes?" I asked. They explained that they had shed their *cushmas* to help unload the helicopters and had no time to dress before they scrambled aboard.

But if the helicopters were at Tzibokiroato only briefly, why had the trip taken such a long time? I asked myself. What did they dynamite this time?

Lucas had come out with them, too, and he confirmed that the turnaround time had been brief. No civic actions were attempted.

Teodoro explained to me that Matías was not in the camp when the helicopter arrived, so there had been no opportunity to deliver my note and no time to search for Nicolás. The three men had jumped aboard at the urging of the Green Berets.

When I asked Captain Reeder why they did not carry out any civic actions, he explained that it was for the security of the natives. They did not wish to linger at Tzibokiroato, nor return in the afternoon, lest they draw attention from Sendero. This is another lie, I thought. Helicopters operated in various regions of the valley every day. One more flight was not going to entice Sendero to Tzibokiroato.

But I forgot about all this and turned my attention to Jamie, Capitán, and Teodoro. As we walked away from the airstrip to go to the parish house to get something to eat, the helicopters took off once more, heading in the direction of Cutivireni. There they go again, I thought. Where is the consideration for the security of the natives now? A bit of help surfaced from an unexpected quarter. Three Swiss Red Cross officials were here to learn what they could of the situation, and I had graphic evidence for them. "Look at the natives," I said, pointing to the three barefoot men clad only in shorts. The Red Cross people took them to a store in Mazamari and bought each of the three a shirt, a pair of pants, and a blanket. Later in the day, I learned details of the Green Berets' latest mission. Some of the Sinchis told me that the Americans had flown off to dynamite the airstrip at Quimpiri, but in the process they had mistakenly blown off the door of one of their helicopters and had nearly caused the deaths of several men. I thought ruefully: And they accuse me of starting a war! I wondered if Ambassador Quainton would inform Washington that I was the cause of this latest foul-up.

I regarded Lucas with a new sense of bemusement, if not downright suspicion, but I could see that he still retained an interest in helping the Ashaninka. "The Americans do not realize that they need to do something for the betterment of the natives," he complained.

Lucas, to me, had become the biggest question mark in this entire mess. He was very insistent when he said to me, "Tell the natives, in case the Americans ask them what I did in the interior, to say that after I got the small medical post set up, I disappeared into the jungle for several days." At first, I did not pay too much attention to this, but Lucas kept repeating the request.

What is this all about? I wondered. What "secret mission" did Lucas have in Tzibokiroato?

I muttered to myself, "*¿Qué cosa están cocinando estos gringos?*" ("What are these gringos cooking up?")

I was beginning to believe that Lucas told me what I wanted to hear and added other information only when he was sure I would learn it elsewhere. In an unguarded moment, he reminisced about how well he was looked after by Fred Hamilton of the American embassy. When he had returned to Lima from Belgium, the embassy had a car waiting for him at the airport. A room was reserved for him at the Caesar Hotel—the most exclusive in Lima—and all of his expenses were covered.

Why all this special treatment? I wondered. What did Lucas have to offer the Americans?

"You can be very sure that the three of us, Mickey, you, and I, have been thoroughly investigated by the Americans," Lucas said.

"I have no doubt," I answered.

Lucas warned me to be more restrained in my discussions with all the Americans—the Green Berets, the DEA agents, and the embassy personnel. "You should be more diplomatic," he instructed.

I acknowledged, "One of my capital sins is talking too much. I admit, I have the mouth of a whale."

Meanwhile, I received a message from Felix. He noted that on April 28 the Green Berets were staging a commencement service at Mazamari for the Sinchi men who had completed their training course. The British and American ambassadors would attend, along with Colonel Froude and Fred Hamilton from the American embassy. I was sure that this would be a typical gringo show of deference to the Peruvians, a three-ring circus. Felix wrote: "Please make every effort within your power to go to the graduation. Colonel Froude and Mr. Hamilton are very, very, very sorry for any trouble they have caused you, and they want to befriend you."

April 28. Determined to avoid the commencement ceremony in Mazamari, I went to Satipo with Jamie, Capitán, and Teodoro and had them present their story in person to the *comandante* of the Peruvian Army unit. Poring over maps, we pinpointed the location of Sendero facilities. I shared all the intelligence information I had learned from those Ashaninka who had escaped from the terrorists. The *comandante* was very interested in the chain of command by which Sendero controlled the activities of the Ashaninka renegades and was not surprised to learn that Alberto Quiroga, the government education official, was a Sendero operative who conducted clandestine meetings at a house right here in Satipo.

The *comandante* seemed willing to pay us back for our information by finally providing the promised helicopter flight. Once again I stressed how important it was that Mickey be allowed to go back to Tzibokiroato with us. "You should talk with Mickey, too," I suggested. I wanted the *comandante* to feel beholden to the Frenchman also. "He has much information about the terrorists, and he is staying here in Satipo."

The *comandante* agreed with me, and he put his Jeep and driver at my service to fetch Mickey.

When we returned for our second session, the *comandante* listened intently. Then he said, "I will inform the general in Huancayo so the necessary operation can be authorized." He agreed now that it was important for Mickey to join us on tomorrow's flight to Tzibokiroato. "Be here very early in the morning," he advised.

Mickey and I were in a good mood the rest of the day, eager to see the people. And now that I knew that Mickey was going in, I changed my own strategy. "Maybe it is better that you stay with the natives and that I return with the helicopter in order to go to Lima and clear things up," I said to Mickey. "I don't see much necessity for the two of us to be there at the same time." Mickey agreed. He realized how important it was for me to talk things over with Felix and Bishop Ojeda and to counter the obvious misinformation that had been provided to Ambassador Quainton concerning my role in the crash of the helicopters and the destruction of the airstrip at Cuti.

We also decided on the most important job for Mickey. "We cannot keep depending on helicopters," I said. Mickey would muster the natives and set them to work clearing an airstrip so that we could get in and out on light aircraft. I acknowledged, "We'll have to sacrifice one of the yucca fields." The key tasks would be to clear out the yucca plants and level the land as much as possible. "I am quite sure that it can be done within a month," I said. "And I'm sure that in that time I will be able to settle things in Lima, and if I can't get a helicopter, I'll be able to fly in on a Cessna." We arranged a signal. First, I would direct the pilot to do a low-level flyover. If it was not safe to land, Mickey and the natives should wave their hands. If it was safe, they were to take *cushmas* and arrange them on the airstrip in the sign of the cross.

That day, Jamie went into town to visit Fortunato at his café, and he returned with the news that he had seen two of the terrorists who had attacked Cuti.

Very carefully, I journeyed into Satipo to scout the area. I tried to keep myself out of view as I checked the places where the terrorists might congregate, and I saw three of them myself. I slipped quietly into the shadows and muttered, *"Hijos de putas"* ("Sons of bitches").

April 29. Finally the long-awaited Sunday morning arrived. Mickey, Jamie, Capitán, Teodoro, and I were all at the airstrip by six o'clock, disappointed to find that the day was very overcast. The Peruvians told us that we would have to wait until the sky cleared.

By ten, as the sun began to fight its way through the cloud cover, another snag arose. A mechanic told us that there was a problem with the helicopter and we could not possibly fly into Tzibokiroato until the following morning.

Angry, frustrated, and highly suspicious, I stalked off to find the *comandante,* and the mechanic followed at my heels. Now he informed the *comandante* that he would have to order a part from Lima, and he doubted that the helicopter would be able to take off until at least Wednesday.

I can't believe this is true, I thought, but for once I kept my mouth shut. I could not change the situation by making everyone angry with me. My only chance was to play the game and hope and pray that by Wednesday the flight would come to pass. In the meantime, I was grounded in Satipo.

The *comandante* advised me to be very careful in this town; he had heard rumors that the terrorists were looking for me. Then, within minutes, he asked me to accompany one of his intelligence officers into Satipo so that I could point out the location of Quiroga's secret meetinghouse.

I felt like laughing in his face. First, he told me to stay away from the fire; then, he asked me to hop into the frying pan. This was as bad as the Americans, who said that they could not take me into Tzibokiroato out of fear for my safety, then squeezed me for all of my information concerning the terrorists, seemingly oblivious to the fact that this was quite likely to bring me a death sentence from Sendero.

"Don't go," Mickey advised. "If you go, you are crazy."

"I am crazy, of course," I admitted. At least, I was crazy enough to do *anything* that might put the military authorities in my debt.

Late in the afternoon, near dusk, I felt very foolish as I sat in Fortunato's café on the north side of Satipo's plaza, making nervous conversation with my old friend. At the appointed time, a man dressed in civilian clothes walked past. Our eyes met. I said good-bye to Fortunato and stepped out onto the street.

Wordlessly, the agent and I walked south along one edge of the plaza. To our right was the parish church of San Francisco and its mission house, where I was staying. We continued on for several blocks past the plaza. At my direction we turned left, then right.

On the left side of this street, in the center of the block, was a modest, two-story, flat-roofed house. The lower portion was brick; the upper half was whitewashed wood. "There," I said softly, "is where Quiroga holds his meetings."

As we strode past, I thought I saw shadowy figures at the window.

May 2. It was Wednesday, and the helicopter flight still had not materialized. Knowing how the minds of the Peruvian military worked, I theorized that the general in Huancayo, after studying my intelligence reports, did not wish it to appear that a gringo priest knew more about the situation than he did. The only way for him to save face was to ignore my information, and ignore me. He may have passed the word to his subordinate in Satipo that I was *not* to be flown in, and the local *comandante,* unwilling to confront me with the truth, was evading the issue with a series of excuses. This was all speculation on my part, but in the context of Peruvian society, it was highly possible.

Whatever the truth, the delay spurred me. "We just cannot continue relying on these false promises," I said to Mickey. "We're not getting anywhere. If we can't get the helicopter, there is only one other way to go in, and that is by foot."

Mickey agreed. We calculated carefully. To attempt the trip from Satipo or Mazamari was suicide—the land was completely infested by Senderistas. The only other possible route was the back door, from the east, where the enemy was not the terrorists, but merely the terrain. "I don't think I could make it," I admitted. "But if you feel that you want to try, it may be our only hope."

Mickey needed little persuading.

I spoke with Enrique, a pilot from the Wings of Hope, who agreed to contact the Dominican mission at Kiriketi to discuss our plan for flying in Mickey and the natives; we hoped that Father Adolfo would put them in contact with guides who could start them on their hazardous journey.

"We've got to get that airstrip built at Tzibokiroato," I said to

Mickey. "I'll keep in contact with you by radio, and as soon as you can get it ready, I'll come in."

That evening Captain Reeder called us to his room for a very strange discussion. With him were two of his most trusted men. "I will do all I can to help you," the captain vowed. Mickey and I told him about the plan to go in on foot, and Captain Reeder promised that if we could find some way—any way—to get into Tzibokiroato, he would get us out by helicopter whenever necessary.

At one point, the captain warned me, "You should be very careful. Do not attempt to get any help from the narcos."

This surprised and angered me. I would never ally myself with the drug smugglers, and I resented the implication. I shoved my hands into my pockets to restrain an impulse to confront him with an obscene gesture.

Enrique reported back to us. Father Adolfo was not at Kiriketi at the moment, but Enrique had spoken with his assistant, Brother Máximo. For some unaccountable reason, Brother Máximo was a bit churlish; he was quite willing to accept a visit from me, but he made it known that Mickey and the three Ashaninka were not welcome.

"No problem," I said. "I'll just have to come along and straighten things out." I knew that I would have to persuade Brother Máximo to loan us a boat for the trip to Cuchiri, the jumping-off point for the journey. If I could get Mickey, Jamie, Capitán, and Teodoro to Cuchiri, I was certain that Flavio, the Machiguenga teacher, would receive them cordially and offer his help.

On the following day, we piled into Enrique's plane and took off for Kiriketi. We had gone about halfway when, near Atalaya, we encountered an angry-looking storm front. Ahead of us were lightning, thunder, and black sky. Winds were already buffeting us by the time we turned back.

I was beginning to feel like Job.

***

So many bizarre things were happening around me. The Americans and the Peruvians appeared confused about who was friend and who was foe. For example, the Peruvian Army utilized a tactic of conscripting and arming private citizens in order to defend threatened towns. To me, this was a dangerous practice, for many of the conscripts, known as Ronderos, were members of, or sympathizers with, Sendero, and the Peruvian Army did not seem to realize that it was arming the very terrorists who were out to kill them!

At the Mazamari airstrip I encountered three men whom I recognized immediately as characters involved with both the drug dealers and terrorists. I knew one of them personally, for he had passed through Cuti on several occasions. He spotted me and, with a broad grin, asked if I would speak to the DEA men to see if I could get them on the next flight to Lima.

"Impossible," I growled.

Security here was a joke. By radio, I sent messages from Mazamari to both Mickey in Satipo and to Senator Vega in Lima. Neither of the men received the messages, but two days later, an informant told me that the terrorists knew all about the transmissions. I suspected that some of the leaks came from a former Sinchi named Aspajo, who was always hanging around. He knew everything that happened in Mazamari and Satipo, and I believed that he peddled the information back and forth among the DEA, the Peruvian military, and the narcos. The Green Berets told me that they did not trust Aspajo, but admitted that the embassy seems to confide in him.

Intrigue ran deep here. I encountered a man whom I remembered as one of the drug smugglers who used to operate in and around the mission. Two years ago, he had moved to Mazamari. Upon seeing me, he asked, with a transparent show of innocence, "How are things in Cuti?" The man insisted that I join him for a drink in a bar located in a very secluded corner of town so that, he said, "we can talk in confidence." I found some pretext to back off, and as soon as I returned to the mission house, I gave his name and description to Father Fernández and warned, "In case something happens to me, you will be able to identify this man."

***

Taking advantage of a break in the weather, Enrique flew Mickey, Jamie, Teodoro, and Capitán to Kiriketi without bothering to include me. I was furious that they had left me behind but glad that they were on their way. As they flew over Tzibokiroato, Mickey dropped a letter to Matías, announcing that the four men were en route. That was the good news. The bad news was that during the course of their flight they saw many communities that had been destroyed. Cachingari and Chichireni were among the settlements that had been burned to the ground. The copilot reported that he had seen many charred corpses.

Soon after their arrival at Kiriketi, Mickey and the others set out on the one-day boat journey due south along the Pagoreni River to the Cuchiri River. They were armed with three shotguns, two boxes of 12-gauge shells, and a single box of 16-gauge shells.

At the Cuchiri settlement, they received a cordial reception from Flavio, who cautioned that they could not embark upon their trek "until the yellow flowers fall from the big trees." This was the Machiguenga signal of the end of the rainy season. To leave earlier would be suicide, Flavio said, for the intermediate stage of the journey upstream along the Cuchiri would take the group through an elongated, narrow, highland canyon. If a rainstorm occurred while they were in the canyon, flash floods would wash them away for certain. The Cuchiri, he said, would be "blown up like a stomach."

The group remained in place for a full week, during which time, in Mickey's words, it rained "like a pissing cow."

Finally the yellow flowers fell from the big trees, and the men readied themselves. In addition to their shotguns and ammunition, each carried a backpack containing eight 3-foot stalks of yucca and eight tins of tuna fish.

Flavio and a few other Machiguenga accompanied them on the first leg, a two-day trek, to the area known as Alta ("Upper") Cuchiri. Once they reached this point, at the base of the Vilcabamba Range, the Machiguenga returned home quickly, concerned that they had encroached too closely upon Sendero-held territory.

Mickey and the three Ashaninka forged ahead through the narrow canyon of the Alta Cuchiri. Aware of the flood danger, the natives set a brutal pace. For two full days they raced forward until they reached the relative safety of the canyon mouth.

Once they emerged at the far end, they faced an even more strenuous task. Above them, directly to the west, was a series of nearly vertical cliffs more than thirteen thousand feet high. The sheer face of the Vilcabamba Range was overgrown with thick vegetation. The men fashioned rope ladders out of vines, then searched until they found an animal path that led upward.

At times the path disappeared, washed away by the pounding punishment of the rainy season. On at least a dozen occasions they lost the trail completely and had to fan out, four abreast. Plunging through the dense growth, they whistled out loud in order to maintain contact with one another. Mickey feared that he might become disoriented and lose his way, and he knew that the Ashaninka would simply abandon him to his fate. Out here, one had to be capable enough to keep up. An Ashaninka would not turn back even to search for his own brother. It was destiny; it was the law of the jungle. Mickey tried to station himself in the middle rather than at either end of the group.

At one point, Jamie fearfully implored them all to turn back; he was certain that they would die.

But they pressed on and up, for three torturous days. When finally they reached the crest of the Vilcabamba Range, the Ashaninka demanded total silence, lest they disturb the bad spirits who might make it rain.

Looking back from the top of the ridge, Mickey could see all the way to the Urubamba River, which he knew was more than eighty kilometers distant. To the north, ahead of him, was a fantastic plateau, decorated with two gigantic cascading waterfalls, which he believed were the origin of the Cutivireni River.

Since there was no sign of a trail, the men decided to make camp and strike out first thing in the morning. The high-altitude night air was freezing, yet heavy with humidity. For food, they had only two yucca roots remaining. The tins of tuna were gone. There was no sign of game to hunt.

The next morning they managed to locate the path that led downward on the far side of the ridge. After a day's steady march west, they reached the Cocajal River, which empties into the Vacamaria, a tributary of the Cutivireni. From here, it was a one-day journey to the outskirts of the Cuti area.

One more day of hiking, always at a rapid pace, brought them in late afternoon to the house of Chia, Julio's brother. They were in terrorist territory by now, and on alert.

Chia's home was paradise. They feasted on papayas and fresh yucca. They sucked on sugarcane. They shared *piarinsti* with Chia—the first they had tasted in ten days. The good news from Chia was that he had seen no signs of Sendero. From this point, they would travel more cautiously, moving between well-known havens, spending each night at the home of a friend.

The next day's journey brought them to Gomeshi's home at Marioventi, where they found a group of natives fishing.

From there, they moved on toward Parijaro. Along the way, Mickey took a sudden fall. As he braced himself against a rock, he felt pain flash through his index finger. It was bent backward at a ninety-degree angle. Jamie rushed to him and forced it back into place.

When they reached Parijaro, they were welcomed by Shirampari, who had returned with his people to this position halfway down the waterfall, where they could spot any terrorists approaching along the river. From there, they were within a day's climb of Tzibokiroato.

On the final leg of the expedition, as the men worked their way up the sharp limestone ledges toward their goal, Mickey's finger throbbed. Perspiration poured from him. He knew that he was suffering from a bout of malaria.

At Tzibokiroato, he found the natives in a state of high panic. They were paranoid, convinced that Sendero was watching them from the other side of the gorge across the Cutivireni. Any minute of the night or day, they were expecting the final assault.

Mariano, I said to myself, Mickey's doing his part, now it's time to get your own butt moving. My plan was to move among my contacts in Mazamari, Satipo, and Lima, keeping my eyes and ears open.

One day, Captain Reeder told me that he had tried several times to get authorization to take me into Tzibokiroato by helicopter and had been continually rebuffed and told to comply with the orders of the embassy. He asked why the embassy people were so concerned about keeping me away from the Ashaninka.

I told him that I had heard various versions of the story. One held that I was somehow mixed up in the drug trafficking, but, I said, "They know as well as I do that is a damn lie."

The captain nodded.

I said that another explanation was that I—a gringo priest—could be an embarrassment to the embassy if I was able to let the Peruvians or the American public know that the DEA was blowing up airstrips and endangering civilians. "As far as being an embarrassment to the embassy, that is right, for damn sure," I said sullenly. "The Americans talk a lot about human rights, but this is to be applied only to the ones they see fit. Apparently, the natives do not fall into this group."

Captain Reeder was genuinely concerned about me. He said very solemnly, "You are in danger. Why do you insist on going into that region? You must realize that sooner or later they will get you."

"I'd rather take a bullet than slip on the bathroom floor and split my head open against the shit bowl," I declared.

Captain Reeder muttered, "With the kind of head you have, it is more likely that you would split open the shit bowl and nothing would happen to your head."

I drew a grin from him when I said, "Yes, Captain, we do have some things in common."

As I walked away from the captain's office, I wondered: Why is everyone so insistent that my life is in danger? I can't believe that they are that worried about my own welfare. There is something weird and mysterious about the whole thing. The truth is, they couldn't give a good shit about me. They just don't want me in there. *Hay un gato encerrado* ("There's a cat hidden somewhere"), I thought.

Later, as I chatted with some of my friends among the Green

Beret troops and complained about my difficulties, one of them commented, "Politics is very dirty."

"Affirmative," I responded.

"Have you seen *The Mission?*" the soldier asked, referring to a movie about Church and State intrigue in Paraguay.

I nodded.

"In that film, you can see how very dirty religious politics is."

I laughed in agreement at this and acknowledged, "After all, we do have twenty centuries of practice in the art."

CHAPTER SEVENTEEN

*A*t *Tzibokiroato,* Mickey fought the weakness and discomfort caused by his malarial fever. His broken finger ached from the damp, freezing cold of the nights. Food was in short supply, and his already lean, wiry body withered.

But he had no time for self-indulgence. Paranoia was rampant. He organized the Ashaninka men into teams of sentinels to stand guard in shifts throughout the long days and tense nights. He inspected booby traps set by the natives along the approaching trails. Most of these were simply pits dug into the path, implanted with sharp spears and camouflaged. One special trap, set no more than five minutes outside the camp, was a shotgun, wedged into the notch of a tree, its trigger hooked to a trip line spread across the trail.

As quickly as he could, Mickey mustered a group of men to clear an airstrip. Surveying the yucca field that jutted out on the spit of land overlooking the Cutivireni, he experienced misgivings. The flat area was short, and the only possible route for an airstrip would encompass a treacherous curve. The plateau was narrow, too, with deep ravines on either side. Even if the yucca was cleared and the land smoothed, the strip would still present a formidable challenge to even the most daring bush pilot.

There was nothing to do but begin. Each morning, Mickey

pulled his protesting body from beneath the mosquito netting, assembled his crew, and set to work.

They were laboring one day, slashing at the precious yucca with determined machete strokes, when Mario's widow Cecilia spread the alarm that the terrorists were approaching. Women and children scurried to the relative safety of the huts on the highest ground. Men and boys dropped their machetes and grabbed bows and arrows, as well as the few precious shotguns.

Minutes passed in quiet tension.

Then the word filtered about that Cecilia had merely seen a *cintori*—a possumlike animal—waddling through the fields, and had panicked.

Day after day the labor continued.

Some of the women treated Mickey's fever with their version of a sauna bath. They heated stones over a fire until they were red-hot, then threw them into water. Mickey stood over the steaming pot as a woman grabbed the front hem of his *cushma* and flapped it so that the vapors encompassed his body.

Mickey developed a plan to bolster the defense. He heard that some two hundred Ashaninka had gathered at Sankatiaro under the leadership of the local teacher. Mickey decided to journey there with a contingent of natives in an attempt to persuade the teacher to organize his people to build a series of barricades to deter Sendero's access to Tzibokiroato. On the morning when the group was to leave on this task, Mickey was too ill and weak to travel, so Nicolás, Shirampari, and about a dozen other men went, all armed with shotguns. Matías, more of a thinker than a fighter, remained behind with Mickey.

Two days later the men returned, accompanied by two families from Sankatiaro. Shirampari reported that they had received a surprised but warm reception, for the natives at Sankatiaro had heard, via Sendero, that the padre, Mickey, Matías, and Nicolás had all been killed. Nicolás's appearance belied the propaganda, and now, most of the natives from Sankatiaro wanted to cast their lot with the group at Tzibokiroato. Over the next few days they filtered in steadily until all had come, with the exception of the teacher.

Mickey thought: Here are two hundred natives who are not with Sendero, but here are two hundred more mouths to feed.

Lucas returned to Belgium on some vague errand. To me, his activities were more mysterious than ever.

I continued to cool my heels on the outside as I awaited word from Mickey concerning progress on the airstrip.

Growing impatient, I decided to make another attempt to get in by helicopter.

In Lima on May 17, I had an audience with Admiral Paniso, who was the current Chief of Staff of the triumvirate of Peruvian military leaders. The top army general was also there. After hearing my desperate plea, the two men promised to get me in to the natives within a week's time. First, I would fly on a Peruvian Army plane from Lima to Jauja, due east of Lima across the main ridges of the Andes. From there, an army jeep would take me on a forty-five minute drive southeast to Huancayo, where antiterrorist operations were coordinated by a General Delgado. The army chief said that he would tell General Delgado to allow me onto one of the many military helicopter flights that patrolled the Ene River valley. "When they go in, be ready to go with them," he said.

When I raised the subject of shotguns, to my surprise and delight Admiral Paniso said that the navy was finally ready to make good on its promise to Mickey to furnish us with ten, brand-new, Peruvian-made 12-gauge shotguns, and I sought to supplement that supply. "I have a little money left over from the contributions," I said. "I would like to buy some more." We haggled over price until the admiral agreed that I could purchase an additional ten shotguns for the price of eight.

I spent a day trudging from one ministry office to another, gathering the paperwork that would allow me to transport guns across Peru. Although my permission came from the top, each petty bureaucrat made me wait and then sought the proper deference before he would add his precious stamp of approval to my papers.

When everything was finally in order, I had twenty new shotguns, packed in two burlap parcels. There was no way I could store these

at the monastery under Felix's disapproving nose, so Alfredo
Paino, the attorney who had worked with Mickey and Diego on
their development plans, agreed to keep them in his apartment.
We were nervous as we drove through Lima with the cargo. Even
though I possessed all the necessary permissions, we knew that the
Peruvian police would give us a difficult time if they stopped us.

Realizing that I would also encounter problems when I tried to
load the guns onto an army plane, Alfredo arranged for one of
Admiral Paniso's aides to meet us at the airport.

As I waited, I busied myself by composing a carefully worded
letter to U.S. ambassador Anthony Quainton. Out of feistiness, I
wrote it in Spanish rather than English, and I employed considerable sarcasm. I detailed my efforts to meet with him personally and
then addressed the charges that he had leveled against me—and
forwarded to Washington: 1) that I had cost the embassy a great
deal of money; 2) that I was responsible for the loss of a helicopter
and several men; and 3) that I had authorized the destruction of
the Cuti airstrip. Consulting my diaries, I cited dates and facts to
refute all three charges. Then I stated that the ambassador's actions were "denying me the possibility of helping the native communities. . . ." I brashly signed the letter "Father Mariano Gagnon,
Pastor and Superior of the Mission at Cutivireni."

May 21. Quite early in the morning, Alfredo and I struggled to
load the two burlap bags full of shotguns into the trunk of a taxi.
The driver stared at the mysterious parcels and gave us a dubious
glance. At the airport, the navy aide was on hand as promised, but
army personnel refused to take orders from him. The aide had to
phone his headquarters and have the admiral call a general, who
relayed permission. Finally, my guns and I were allowed to board.

When we reached Jauja, and I hauled my cargo off the plane, yet
another army officer asked, "What have you got there?"

Within minutes I was locked into a small room, along with my
shotguns, as local authorities tried to determine what to do with
me. I flashed my paperwork, but they were unimpressed.

"Wherever the guns go, I go," I vowed.

"We have no orders about the guns," an officer growled at me.

"Why don't you call Huancayo and speak to General Delgado?"

The officer called, but the general was out to lunch.

Several frustrating hours later, they reached the general, who authorized me to bring the guns and said that he was sending his personal Jeep for me. The officers in Jauja were suitably impressed.

When we finally arrived in Huancayo, a sentry greeted us. He eyed the general's Jeep with deference, but then he saw the two large bundles. "What's in there?" he demanded.

"Shotguns," I replied. But I added quickly, "They're really not mine. They're for the general." This lie achieved the desired effect, and I was soon in General Delgado's office.

"How did you get these guns?" he asked.

Here we go again, I thought. I explained, and I showed him my sheaves of approving paperwork.

The general asked, "And what if the Campas use these guns against the military?"

"The natives *need* the military," I said. I offered an alternate suggestion: "If you wish to send your men in to protect the natives, you can have the guns."

That argument persuaded the general to allow me to keep them. He even agreed to let me leave them at his headquarters for the time being so that I would not encounter further problems in Huancayo.

The general introduced me to a Colonel Espinoza, his chief aide, who questioned me for several hours about the activities of the drug smugglers and terrorists in the region. We pored over maps, and I showed him the locations of key sites. By now, I was an expert in presenting this information, although it never seemed to result in action. When we were finished with the briefing, the colonel said that he would be happy to fly me into the jungle, adding that this was *his* decision. "We don't like orders from Lima," he grumbled.

It is a wonder that *anything* ever gets done in this country, I said to myself. This is so typical!

I had no choice but to bide my time.

I stayed at the Franciscan parish house in Huancayo, making daily calls to check on the availability of a helicopter flight. The

Peruvian military brass conjured one excuse after another as to why the helicopters could not take me in. After two weeks, I could only conclude that the Peruvian military was full of words and promises, nothing more. In frustration I announced to the military staff in Huancayo that I was leaving, but that I would stay in contact and return immediately if and when a flight was ready.

Along with what I now referred to as "the damn guns," I took a bumpy Jeep ride back to Jauja and caught a flight to Mazamari. From then on, when I tried to telephone Huancayo from Mazamari, I was told that the lines had been cut.

I attempted to contact Armando to see if he had any news of Mickey and progress on the airstrip. But it was not possible to raise him on the radio.

Lucas, having returned from Belgium, journeyed back and forth between Lima and Mazamari. He was cordial to me, and I tried to be friendly, although I remained wary. I could not figure out his game.

The Green Berets made a helicopter flight into Tzibokiroato to ferry in additional supplies to the natives. I hoped to get word about Mickey, but the Americans would say nothing to me. Lucas told me, "They are under strict orders to have nothing to do with you."

I ached to see the people. In the late, sleepless hours of the night, I determined: Once I can get back in there, I will just stay there—and the hell with everybody else!

Once more I was in Lima, trying to make *something* happen, when I received a call from NBC reporter Anabeli Rodrigo, who was very interested in the plight of the natives. She met me in the hall of the Franciscan monastery and told me that she was ready to take a camera crew to Tzibokiroato to report firsthand on the situation. She had already obtained approval from her editor in Miami. The problem, she said, was that renting a private helicopter was too costly. I told her that Mickey had the Ashaninka working on an airstrip, and I believed that it would be ready soon.

We placed a call to Armando at the Satipo airport, and he agreed to take us in on a flight paid for by NBC. First, of course, he had to determine whether or not he could land his Cessna at Tzibokiroato. He was able to contact Mickey by radio, and reported back that the airstrip was ready. Armando wanted to assess it himself, so he took off from Satipo for an aerial reconnaissance.

His first impression of the landing strip filled him with concern. The approach was good. A pilot would come in toward the high-altitude cliff from the Cutivireni side, through a wide chasm that offered plenty of maneuvering room. But this same positioning caused strong crosswinds and a natural downdraft. The 180-meter-long strip itself was primitive and bumpy—extremely dangerous—and complicated by a curve just past the midway point. To use the strip at all, Armando would have to utilize the special short-takeoff-and-landing procedures that every pilot referred to as STOL. Fortunately, his Cessna was specially modified to allow him to use the ailerons as additional flap surfaces, which would provide greater lift and enable him to land at a slower-than-normal speed. Under normal conditions the aircraft needed a landing field at least 600 meters long; STOL would permit him to cut that requirement in half. Still, the airstrip was perilously short, no more than 250 meters in length.

From the air, Armando radioed instructions to Mickey, asking him to assemble a team of Ashaninka to clear away clusters of bushes at the end of the strip to give him a bit of additional landing space.

The extra work took a few days. Then, Armando made a second reconnaissance flight and reported back to me that he was willing to take the chance.

July 6. A chartered flight landed at Satipo at 10:40 A.M. this Friday, carrying Anabeli, her cameraman Carlos Valdéz, an assistant named Victor, a Spanish reporter named Quim Amor, and me. As the crew transferred its equipment to Armando's small Cessna, I ran to the mission house to pack a few belongings and retrieve the two heavy, burlap-covered bundles that carried the shotguns.

On a sudden inspiration, I rushed over to Fortunato's café and borrowed his Peruvian flag. I wanted to display it at Tzibokiroato for the benefit of the NBC cameras and in a show of respect for the memory of Mario, who died because he refused to fly Sendero's banner.

Surveying the cargo and the passenger load, Armando determined that he would have to make three flights. The aircraft was a five-seater. Without passengers, and under optimum conditions, he could carry up to five hundred kilograms of cargo. Because of the limitations of the landing strip, he had to cut that figure in half. After some discussion, Anabeli persuaded me to wait for the final flight; she wanted her film crew set up to record my arrival. She also talked me into wearing my brown robe and cowl and white cincture, the full regalia of the Franciscan habit.

Workmen transported wheelbarrows full of cargo out to the aircraft. The cardboard boxes contained tins of tuna fish, supplies of pasta, and jars of bouillon cubes—all easily transportable sources of protein. Anabeli and a cameraman climbed aboard, and airport workers, grabbing leading edges of the wings, pushed the airplane around into takeoff position. Armando flashed a grin from beneath his black mustache, revved the engine, and disengaged the brakes. Cessna OB-1044 rolled down the runway. With its heavy load, it rose at only a moderate angle into a sky filled with billowing, gray-white clouds. Armando, with the touch of a showman, banked into a sharper-than-necessary portside turn and climbed above the mountains.

Thirty-five minutes later, as he approached Tzibokiroato, Armando realized that he was suddenly frightened. But there was no turning back. He had no time to waste. The perilous, makeshift airstrip was minutes away. He took solace in the sincere belief that God would guide his airplane. The NBC cameraman, busy recording the scene, looked up at the last moment and could not believe that he would attempt to land on such a tiny slip of the plateau.

The landing *had* to be perfect. If Armando came in too long, he would be unable to stop the airplane before it crashed into the trees at the end of the strip. If he came in too short, the Cessna would plow into the face of the cliff. He inched back on the throttle, bringing down the speed. Under normal conditions, the craft would slow to a stall speed of sixty-five knots and settle onto the runway. With the STOL procedures, the stall speed was a mere thirty-eight knots. Just as the airplane cleared the edge of the cliff, the airspeed indicator registered thirty-eight knots. The Cessna stalled and dropped to the ground.

The plane smacked onto the earth. Armando jammed his feet against the brake pedals and struggled with the rudder to negotiate the treacherous curve two thirds of the way down the strip. The wheels bumped over the uneven surface with deep ravines on either side of the narrow pathway. Finally, Armando brought the craft to a stop just short of the pile of trees, bushes, and yucca debris at the far end of the field.

There was only a moment to savor the achievement. Quickly, Armando unloaded his passengers and cargo and climbed back into the cockpit for the return to Satipo. For takeoff, he aimed the Cessna toward the edge of the cliff. Like an aircraft carrier pilot, he had to launch his plane into a void. He revved the engine, disengaged the brakes and started his roll. The end of the runway came far too soon, and he knew that he did not have sufficient airspeed. The Cessna plunged off the edge of the cliff and nosed into a sharp dive. That dive provided the necessary speed so that in moments, he was able to level off and begin his climb across the mountain peaks.

I waited impatiently for Armando to complete the first two round-trips, which took more than an hour each. Then, finally, it was my turn. We loaded the last of the cargo, including my burlap bundles full of shotguns. A second bush pilot, Tommy Simonich, who had helped me out before, wanted to come along so that he, too, would know the way; he scrambled into the back seat.

Armando leaned out of the cockpit, beckoned, and announced, "Padre, we're all set."

A sharp wind blew the cowl of my habit into my face, and I vowed to strip to my shorts at the earliest opportunity. I crawled in, secured my seat belt, then joked to one of Armando's assistants, "Take care of the nuns for me."

We were off, and my spirits rose along with the altimeter needle. A euphoric buzz came over me.

The route took us over the mission site at Cutivireni. From the air I could still make out the ugly black bomb craters, nearly spanning the width of our airstrip, but the landing surface itself was overgrown with weeds. The wreckage of the buildings was visible, although the jungle was encroaching upon these, too. Before long, I thought, Cuti will be only a memory. I lectured myself: Don't worry about the mission; worry about the people.

We flew over the brown waters of the Ene and spotted four boats below. "Narcos," I muttered. They were unconcerned about our presence, for they had radios and informants to tell them whenever the military was flying over.

After a thirty-five-minute flight, we reached the area of Tzibokiroato. Armando circled so that Tommy and I could take a look. The threshold of the airstrip, at the edge of a dramatic gorge, was a truly frightening sight. I felt a stab of fear: If we go down in a blaze of glory, so be it.

Tommy's body stiffened in apprehension. At my side, I saw lines of concentration crease Armando's face. He brought the small craft down as close as possible to the leading edge of the cliff. At the last instant, he gunned the engine to adjust his flight path; the wings dipped and then righted themselves. The tricycle landing gear hit and jolted us; the seatbelt bit into my belly. Armando strained at the rudder controls as the plane bounced wildly through ruts and over clumps of dirt. Then, suddenly, we were still.

After all the weeks of frustration, I was back at Tzibokiroato.

Cecilia was the first to greet me. As I stepped out of the plane she blessed me with a bear hug. *"Hola, padre!"* she cried.

I was surprised by an embrace from Timoteo, who clasped me so hard that the weight of his shotgun pressed against my shoulder. A hug from an Ashaninka woman is rare; from an Ashaninka man it is nearly unbelievable.

Timoteo's wife, Lucilla, followed suit. Then Pablo.

There was Gregorio's wife, with her arms about me. "Vieja," I chided.

Gregorio was next. The old man was wearing a strange-looking, multicolored hat that he had obtained from who knew where. He pulled a cigarette from his browned teeth and patted me on the back.

His son Teodoro was next in line.

"César!" I said, beaming as the leader of the Tinkarini clan came up. I scuffed him playfully on the back of the neck.

Then there was Capitán—pain etched into his strong, chiseled features. Of all these people, he had suffered perhaps the greatest loss. Yet now his face—and that of his lovely seven-year-old daughter, Gladys—beamed. He started to hug me, but as I returned the embrace, he turned his head, suddenly shy.

A voice roared, "You old Canadian cow!"

"Mickey!" We shared an almost violent clinch. He was even thinner than before, and his long hair was a bit more gray. "How've you been?" I asked.

"Good," he lied.

Shirampari grinned from ear to ear, looking slightly ridiculous in a red baseball cap.

Finally there was Matías. The pensive one was more reserved than some of the others, but he was clearly glad that I was here to assume leadership—or at least share that role with Mickey and him.

Unasked, a group of natives formed a line to unload supplies. The last boxes of foodstuffs came off the plane, then two teenage boys pulled off the heavy, elongated, burlap-wrapped parcels.

"Take them right away to that little house," I instructed, pointing to the makeshift clinic that César had built and Lucas had outfitted.

The boys grinned knowingly and did as I instructed. Matías and several of the men followed to look at the packages, but they did not touch them.

Meanwhile, the NBC cameras rolled, and some of the natives became playful. Paulino, in the Ashaninka custom of warding off evil spirits, blew cigarette smoke into the face of a little girl, a fuzzy-headed toddler clad in a bright blue *cushma*. She flinched in surprise, and her serious expression brought affectionate laughter from Paulino.

A baby, suckling at its mother's breast, turned wide brown eyes toward the camera crew.

259

I saw Roy's widow, Antonia, standing off to one side, clutching her fatherless daughter, and I reached into my bag and produced a stuffed toy monkey for the child.

In many respects, the day proceeded as usual. Men went off to hunt. Women processed the yucca. Children romped and squealed and slapped at horseflies. Babies wailed. The insect population serenaded us with a background hum. A group of about fifteen natives ate their meal from a common pot, dipping in spoons to ladle out fish soup. On occasion, Lucilla's distinctive laugh pierced the calm. I was disturbed and worried by the constant coughing and wheezing of most of the children.

Matías and I smoked cigarettes and tried to assess the situation.

That night, as a spectacular full moon rose in the east above the Vilcabamba Range, I said to Anabeli and her film crew, "I'm going to get the guns out now. Please don't take any pictures of this." They assured me that they would not.

I gathered some of the men and took them into the clinic hut. We unpacked the burlap bundles and slipped the shotguns out of their crumpled newspaper wrapping. Mickey clasped one, popped it open, and stared down the shiny new barrel. "Thanks to our friends in Lima, we were able to get these," I announced.

Mickey and I handed the shotguns to the most capable fighters. Nicolás, steely-eyed and determined, grasped one eagerly. Capitán accepted his wordlessly; he was also armed with a powerful, professionally made bow, which Mickey had brought from France.

As he watched all this, Gregorio puffed stoically upon an ancient pipe.

Suddenly I realized that the film crew was recording this scene. I reminded Anabeli that she had promised not to do this, and she assured me that they would not air this portion of the report.

Tommy, the visiting bush pilot, made a big show of teaching Nicolás how to work the pump-action mechanism on one of the shotguns, and Nicolás cooperated by pretending to listen. I thought: He knows damn well how to use it. Both men had a great time, drinking *piarinsti* and ejecting shells from the chamber. Then Nicolás took over and instructed Jamie.

We stayed up late that night, allowing the winds of happiness to blow freely.

On Saturday morning, we formulated plans. Armando and Tommy had to return to Satipo, but Armando could come back tomorrow for the film crew and whoever else was leaving. This was an easy decision. By now I realized that Mickey needed medical attention—I had never seen him so emaciated and weak—and he also faced a legal problem. His visa would expire soon, and he would be forced to return to Venezuela. Once more it was my turn to stay with the Ashaninka.

By midmorning the natives had returned three of the shotguns to me. They had attempted to hunt, but the firing pins were faulty. I suggested to Mickey that he take these to Father Ferrer, the Sinchi chaplain at Mazamari, and ask him to repair them, and I thought: so much for Peruvian craftsmanship.

Anabeli spoke at length with several of the Ashaninka. She asked Cecilia how her husband had died.

"Mario had gone to play *fútbol* at Sankatiaro," Cecilia said. "He came back on Sunday about five o'clock in the afternoon. The terrorists had arrived at Cutivireni at nine o'clock in the morning. They were asking, 'Where's the teacher Mario?' " Cecilia explained that throughout the region many of the teachers are allied with the terrorists. They are more concerned with teaching the children about Mao than with teaching them how to read and write. "That's why Mario was killed," she said. "The terrorists asked Mario to enter their group. He answered, 'Why should I? I don't want to have anything to do with you people.' But they said, 'If you don't want to enter, then it's better if we kill you.' Mario said, 'If you want to kill me, go ahead and kill me. I prefer dying, rather than joining you.' " Cecilia ended her narrative at this point. She did not detail the torture and humiliation inflicted upon her husband in the interminable moments before he died.

Anabeli moved on to another topic, asking, "So what do you want to do now?"

"I don't want to stay here," Cecilia replied. "I want to go somewhere else. If I stay here, maybe they are going to come back and kill us. They say they want to kill the wife of Mario and all her family because she speaks Spanish, and if the military comes here, then she will inform on us. She'll tell them everything."

Anabeli asked about the food supply.

"We hardly have any yucca left," Cecilia said.

"And what are you going to do?"

"We'll have to go where there is yucca," Cecilia explained.

"And now that Father Mariano is here . . . ?"

Cecilia replied, "Wherever the padre goes, I want to go."

Capitán spoke to Anabeli with quiet resolve, with his hands clasped in front of him. "We want to be here in peace," he said. "And for that we need armament."

Anabeli asked if Capitán had suffered personally from Sendero's attacks.

He replied, "I lost my wife and my three daughters, February seventh."

"Why did Sendero kill them?"

"Because we wouldn't join them."

"Are you afraid of Sendero?"

"Yes."

"Has Sendero come close to here?"

"Yes, to spy on us. When we hunt or go to get yucca, we find their tracks."

At Capitán's side, his daughter Gladys glanced up toward the reporter, staring with deep, wide, dark eyes. Anabeli asked Capitán, "And your little girl?"

"She will stay with me," Capitán vowed.

Then Anabeli spoke with Matías, asking, "What is the situation with the natives?"

Matías thought before he responded. He spoke in a low tone, with one hand resting pensively on his chin. His mouth curled upward, giving the impression of a slight, self-conscious smile. He said, "Before, we had a nice community. We were living at peace and were developing nicely. Unfortunately, then we had a problem with these bad people who came and disrupted all of our intentions. Now, we are in a difficult situation. When we came here, we were well received, thanks to the paisanos who lived here. But now, we're finishing their yucca."

Anabeli asked what Sendero's intentions were, and Matías answered, "They threaten us to join them. They abuse the innocent. That's why we're suffering. A lot of the natives who are with Sendero are suffering much more than we are." As he spoke, Matías made deliberate, emphatic gestures to punctuate his words. His toddling daughter, Lupe, approached from behind, threw her arms about her father's neck, and attempted to crawl up onto his shoulders. He cuffed her away, firmly but gently. Then he said to Anabeli, "If we don't join Sendero, they say, 'You are not worth living,' and they kill all the family."

"What are you trying to do now?" Anabeli asked.

"We're trying to organize ourselves because we don't want to work with the terrorists. We don't want to get involved in politics. We don't want to change our customs."

Anabeli asked what effect my presence would have.

Matías said, "We're happy he's here. We've known him for a long time. We get along well together."

That afternoon Matías called for a *reunión*. By the time more than three hundred Ashaninka assembled at the lower end of the airstrip, I had discarded my habit for my regular jungle attire of shorts and a T-shirt. I warned the natives, "Neither the Americans nor the Peruvians nor the Church is going to help you. You are going to have to depend on yourselves."

Glancing about, my eyes fell upon Nicolás. He sat cross-legged, with his shotgun pointed into the air.

I spelled out for the Ashaninka how I felt about this desperate siege. "If anyone comes to us as a friend, he will be treated well," I decreed. "But if they come to kill your wives and your children, you have every right to defend yourselves."

I awoke in a very melancholy mood on Sunday. It was all I could do to hold back my tears when I saw Mickey. My sadness was compounded as I viewed, with the sharp eyes of the new day, the living conditions of the people. They, like Mickey, were sick and hungry. Mickey said that on the average we were losing a child a day.

We set up an open-air chapel, using a flat-topped tree trunk as an altar. Fortunato's red, white, and red Peruvian flag stood off to one side. Teodoro loaned me a light-colored *cushma* with vertical gray stripes. As I stepped to the altar, the Ashaninka gathered in front, standing reverently. Someone led the children in a song, and the lyrics floated into the sunshine and echoed off the canyon walls: "He told me Tasorensi would take care of us. The big God sent the son Jesus to us. . . ."

As I celebrated the mass, I offered a prayer of remembrance for Mario and Roy and so many others who had been killed in this horrific war. I could not hold back the tears. My voice cracked, and for several moments I could not continue. I was ashamed of myself, to be crying like an old lady in the midst of the mass. NBC had promised that they would not film the service, but they did anyway, and I found the cameras to be an intrusion as the Ashaninka walked quietly to our altar to dip communion wafers into a hollow gourd filled with the wine I had brought in.

Old Gregorio took communion with one hand as he held a shotgun in the other.

CHAPTER EIGHTEEN

*M*atías and Capitán helped me compile a new census. Our count showed eighty-four families. Since I was here last, twenty-five families had left, pleading scarce supplies of yucca. I knew that yucca was important to the Ashaninka, but I had not realized that they considered it so vital that they would risk their lives for it. My tuna fish, pasta, and bouillon did not compare.

In the interim, as some families left, another dozen had come in, most of them having escaped from the rebels. In all, we had twenty-nine families who had escaped from Sendero, and these were the most afraid.

Our problems were compounded as more and more natives brought in their new shotguns and threw them down in disgust. Of the total of twenty shotguns, only two were in working order. As soon as Armando came in with more supplies, I would have to send this batch of worthless junk to Father Ferrer at the Sinchi base.

Matías and I hiked across the plateau and through the surrounding mountainside jungle, seeking suitable spots for building. Several of the other natives came with us, bearing machetes and axes for use in clearing the brush. Over a period of days, we identified seven separate spots where we might establish a village. Each had an excellent water supply. The major problem appeared to be a lack of leaves suitable for thatching.

I was touched when the natives spent three days clearing land for a permanent home for me. They picked out a beautiful spot on the side of a mountain, near Nicolás's hut. The eastern view featured a spectacular, three-tiered waterfall on the far side of the Marioventi River. Many years ago, an American engineer named Drews, flying over the area, had dubbed the falls Las Tres Marías in honor of his three daughters, but the natives called the site Pearonchin, which, in Ashaninka, means "Where the People Disappear." It was said that sometime in the uncharted past a group of natives had gone to the area and never returned.

One night some of the natives killed a large *shushupi*, a bushmaster, that had got into Nicolás's hut. They skinned the snake and fried it. I had eaten and enjoyed *shushupi* several times before; the taste and consistency was similar to fish.

July 17. Our supplies were running low, and I received word that our benefactors in Lima were ready with more cash. Armando flew in to pick me up at Tzibokiroato for a supply run. Our first stop was in San Ramón, where Bishop Ojeda provided me with twelve hundred kilos of food for the Ashaninka, which greatly softened my disposition toward the Church hierarchy.

I spent several days shopping in Satipo and found that the prices on everything had skyrocketed. Inflation—already bad in Peru— was growing worse because of the rebel activity. I made surreptitious contact with a man who offered to sell me hand grenades at a price of about fifteen dollars apiece. Despite our limited resources, I struck a deal.

In Mazamari I was disappointed to learn that Father Ferrer had done nothing about getting our shotguns repaired. The Sinchi commander was apologetic and said that he would try to get them into working order as soon as possible, but it might take some time. Beyond that, he said, there was little he could do.

Oh yes there was, I told him. He could loan us Sinchi shotguns. Then, when the repairs were made, we could swap.

The *comandante* regarded me warily. We had always been on good terms. Now I was calling for a favor that could strain the friendship. Reluctantly, he agreed.

Now I had the shotguns, but the grenade deal fell through.

On July 27 a Wings of Hope plane flew me back to Tzibokiroato. Our pilot Hervé and copilot Enrique were nervous when they saw the tiny, treacherous airstrip. Hervé bounced the plane down hard on the ground but managed to retain control. I knew that they would want to avoid this trip in the future.

July 29. The gospel lesson for the mass was taken from Matthew, chapter thirteen:

> The kingdom of heaven is like treasure hidden in a field, which a man found and covered up; then in his joy he goes and sells all that he has and buys the field. Again, the kingdom of heaven is like a merchant in search of fine pearls, who on finding one pearl of great value, he went and sold all that he had and bought it.

I realized that this parable described my vocation with the Ashaninka. God had blessed me most richly. It was true that I had given up a few things in order to come here, but they were nothing compared to the richness that I found. I left behind crumbs and encountered a banquet. It seemed like such a contradiction: The circumstances I found myself in were not easy—they could hardly be any worse—yet I thought I was the happiest man alive. It is one thing to read the Scriptures; it is another to live them.

With a start, I realized that a tremendous change had taken place within me. Throughout my studies in the monastery and my years of parish and mission work, I had always believed in Christ, but my faith was in the Church. In the past, I had accepted the Church's teachings without question. Now, the situation was reversed. I believed in the Church, but my faith was in Christ. It was Christ, not the Church, who would see us to the end of this trouble.

Later in the day I watched the Ashaninka children at play. Their *cushmas* were ripped and soiled. They were scrawny and smelly. They were abandoned by the world, loved by very few. Yet as they scurried about, barefoot, they squealed and giggled, just like children everywhere. Their painted faces reflected Christ in all His splendor. These people are simple and noble, I thought. They are authentic. They are sublime. I wished that I could somehow put into words what I felt in my heart, but it was impossible. Tears rolled down my cheeks as I tried to thank my Creator for blessing me with this life. I knew, at this moment, that it would be impossible, throughout the entire universe, to find a more appropriate image of the Lord incarnate than one could see in the faces of these scruffy Ashaninka children.

Late that day, I spoke with the people regarding the need for security and vigilance. I stressed, "It is most important that if anything happens, we should keep very calm." Once more I went over the plan of defense: women and children to the inner circle, men to the perimeter.

We debated the advantages and disadvantages of Tzibokiroato. The consensus among the Ashaninka was voiced by one who shrugged and asked, "Why should we go far off to look for another place?" However, several of the Ashaninka men were interested in scouting the terrain across the Marioventi, near the three-tiered waterfall, Las Tres Marías. The area was even more remote than Tzibokiroato.

By radio, Armando reported that he was coming in on August 2 with more supplies, and he agreed to fly over the waterfall area and other nearby regions and give us a report on settlement possibilities. After that, Matías planned to send off small groups of men to explore further.

Since this entire area was known as Shirampari's hunting ground, I sent word to Parijaro, asking him to join us for the day. He made the trip up the sheer cliffs with ease.

When Armando arrived, he reported that the area around Las Tres Marías appeared inviting. There was a large plateau behind the waterfall and a convenient lake nearby. Matías, Shirampari, Nicolás, and I climbed into the plane to see for ourselves. From the air, the area at first seemed quite adequate for settlement, with plenty of available land for planting yucca, but there was also much swampland, and I had my doubts; I wanted to study the terrain from the ground. I also wondered if the climate was too severe; the altitude was much higher than at Tzibokiroato.

After Armando returned to Satipo, the three Ashaninka and I discussed what we had seen. The natives insisted upon sending out a foot patrol to inspect the ground and see if it would be good for yucca. They seemed unworried about my prediction that they would freeze.

Shirampari left to go back down the mountain to Parijaro, planning to return for the expedition. But he came back sooner than we expected.

About eleven o'clock that night Matías woke me with the grim news that a group of terrorists led by Moisés and Adrian had attacked Parijaro. Moisés and his men had murdered two Ashaninka men and captured a woman named Juana. The others wanted to kill her, too, but Moisés intervened, explaining that Juana was his sister-in-law. Thus, the other terrorists settled for beating her viciously. Pascual and Shirampari had managed to escape and had hurried up the mountain in the darkness to spread the news.

Everything went as we had rehearsed. The women and children took refuge in the inner huts. We men formed a defense perimeter, aiming our few shotguns and our arrows toward the only possible entry point.

We maintained our vigil throughout the night and into the following day. I was so distracted by the tension that I was not even aware of the noise of the arriving supply plane. When I was told about it, I went immediately to the airstrip and found a pilot there, growing more nervous by the moment as he realized that we were ready for an imminent attack. The plane was full of food supplies and a tiny but precious cargo of hand grenades supplied by the contacts of one of the Satipo bush pilots. There were six in all, but as I inspected them I realized that three were only practice grenades and of no use. I took careful custody of the three good grenades.

After the aircraft took off for its return flight to Satipo, we bolstered our defenses. We packed our powdered milk and beans, our firearms and the grenades, and moved them carefully past the huts near the airstrip, down to a small creek and then up several tiers of land to the highest point in Tzibokiroato, which we envisioned as our stronghold. A few houses were already set up nearby, just below us, and we could use them as a base. From here, we could also view the airstrip. Although it was not easily accessible from this vantage point, at least we could monitor activities there.

I hardly slept during the second night of alert. Periodically, one or another of the natives woke me, fearful and near panic.

In the morning, we continued the job of transferring our supplies to the highest elevation, but I told Matías that at least for the time being I would continue to live in the house they had built for me next to Nicolás.

Late in the evening Shirampari and three women arrived bearing a *paujil,* a turkeylike bird, and a *maquizapa,* a large, black monkey. Shirampari had shot both prizes on the way here. The women also had a little yucca and some bananas with them. We were all starved, and sat down to feast. Each person received a fair portion, which was delicious, but not enough to sate our hunger.

As we ate, we spoke about our precarious situation. One of the natives, only recently escaped from Sendero, reported that a settler named Mansília, who owned a boat, was ferrying guns and ammunition to the terrorists from Puerto Ocopa; other boats were plying the Ene also.

Lucio, a new arrival from the Cutivireni area, said he brought a message from Emilio in Cuti. I nodded in recognition. Emilio was one of the few Ashaninka to make his way in the outside world. He had served in the Peruvian Navy and used to visit us frequently at the monastery in Lima. His message to me was this: He had attended a meeting among the settlers and some of the natives. There, he said, the terrorists were spreading the word that if anyone finds the gringo priest, they are to kill him immediately.

Emilio's message pleaded with me: "You are to leave this place if you wish to live on."

August 5. I celebrated mass this Sunday, but few of the Ashaninka came. They were scattered throughout the area, nervously anticipating an attack. Today, biblical passages that I previously never gave much importance took on a new and deeper significance. One of the lessons was from Saint Paul's letter to the

Romans: "Who will separate us from the love of Christ, trial or distress or persecution or hunger or nakedness or danger or the sword?"

In the past, I tended to read Scripture as if it were a passage from a history book. Now it seemed that the message was timeless. The words written centuries ago had a very real application to the present.

August 6. We spent some time fixing up the house the Ashaninka had prepared for me. Dividing it into two portions with a wooden partition, we used the back as a storehouse for my personal belongings and supplies. For the front, we fashioned a handmade chair and a rustic table. I stashed my supply of instant coffee here, along with a bag of emergency equipment, including a flashlight, spare batteries and bulbs, a small piece of nylon rope, a change of clothes, a pair of sneakers, a small mosquito net, a couple of Band-Aids, a bottle of iodine, aspirin, a meager store of antibiotics, a notebook, two pens, a roll of toilet paper, and my pistol. That night I went to sleep early. Nicolás's son Jorge Luis and another boy named Piloto stayed in the house with me.

About nine o'clock, I was awakened by the sound of a grenade exploding. Immediately I scrambled from beneath my mosquito netting. I grabbed my bag of emergency supplies, and the boys and I ran for refuge at the high point of the camp. Several of the men joined me in standing guard, hiding behind trees. I was pleased to realize that the women and children had learned not to scream. For hours we waited in silence until Nicolás, his brother Juan, and another native called Rengifo straggled in with an account.

Nicolás's face was badly cut, and the flesh around one eye was split open. His face and chest were soaked with blood. Excitedly, he explained what had happened.

The three men were at the river fishing when they heard noise and spotted a group of terrorists, about thirty in all, approaching. Silently the three Ashaninka climbed to a hidden spot on a ledge and waited until the terrorists arrived below them, congregating in a clearing. Seizing the opportunity, Nicolás tossed a grenade into the midst of the terrorists. "There was a terrible explosion," he reported. Nicolás and Juan fired a few shotgun blasts into the group, but Rengifo was too scared to pull the trigger on his own gun. They fled before the enemy could regroup and counter. In his haste to scramble back up the mountain, Nicolás took a bad fall and split open his face.

The news that Rengifo had soiled his pants in fright brought much laughter and eased the tension.

I treated Nicolás's wounds as best I could while listening to his story. Other natives gathered around to hear the account, and they reacted with visible enjoyment.

Is this what my priesthood has come to? I wondered. I had no words to describe my sadness. I could only pray to God that we would soon find a place where we could get away from violence.

The next morning Nicolás led a group of men to the ambush site, approaching with great care to assure themselves that the enemy was not lying in wait for them. They found bloodstains all about, and could see where bodies had been dragged toward the river.

In the afternoon, a few more natives came into camp, reporting that they had seen two rafts going downriver, packed with bodies and injured men, but they were unable to give us an estimate on the number of Sendero casualties.

What a sad situation this is, I thought. I had absolutely no hate in my heart for our enemies; indeed, I felt sorry for them. What a shame that it had come to this. I vowed silently: We *must* find a place where we will be able to live in peace. It would be so sad if we become like the terrorists.

One of the Indians brought me a note that he had found in the jungle nearby. It read:

Miserable, naked slobs, don't you realize you stupid . . . that you are defending the imperialist priest? And don't you want to unite yourselves in our fighting in benefit of the poor? If you continue in this, you will all have to disappear from the face of the earth. The Maoist army will triumph. We will get the power. And we will possess this country. Hooray for the popular guerrilla army. Hooray for the force of Peru. Death to the slobs of Cuti.

The natives told me that one of the attacking forces was led by Taco Gonzalo, and I suspected that he was the author of this threat. I knew him and his brother Virgilio; Virgilio was one of the local arms traffickers now, shipping in guns and ammunition from Puerto Ocopa and selling them to Sendero. Taco used to come to the mission frequently in search of supplies. On a few occasions I had invited him to eat with me; we had shared a few beers.

"I should make some effort to talk things over with him," I suggested to Matías.

"It is foolish," Matías pronounced. "The only thing they want to do—the orders they have—is kill us unless we join them unconditionally. It is impossible to talk with them. It is better that you go to Satipo to see about supplies."

August 10. Armando flew me out to Satipo. I found the city all but closed. Sendero had called for a strike and threatened that any store owner who opened for business would be killed.

As I spent several days searching for supplies and information, I found my conscience bothering me very much. I had no idea of how to end this tragic warfare, and yet the Ashaninka were looking to me for the answers. I knew that the only way out was to negotiate some sort of compromise with Sendero, and as the days passed, I became more certain that I should have insisted on meeting with the terrorists. Somehow, this killing had to stop.

August 14. It was Saturday morning, and I had breakfast at Fortunato's café in Satipo. When I was about to leave, Fortunato warned, "Be very careful."

I did not know what to make of this, so I dismissed it and went about my business. I walked out to the airport to retrieve the motorbike that I kept at the Wings of Hope hangar. From there, I drove to visit one of my informants at his home. As I arrived, I spotted a man off to one side of the street, dressed in pants and a white T-shirt, crouched over. Our eyes met briefly, and a sudden, strange wave of suspicion washed over me.

My informant and I had a quiet conversation over coffee, but I did not learn anything significant. As I was leaving, my informant's wife walked me to where I had left my motorbike. This time we both saw the same man, still on his haunches.

I started my motorbike and sped away, trying to observe him out of the corner of my eye. He seemed to pay careful attention to me. There is nothing wrong, Mariano, I said to myself. You are letting your nerves get the best of you.

That evening, when I returned to Fortunato's place for a drink, he suggested that it would be best if I sat in the kitchen. I was in a chair in the back room of the café, sipping at my drink as a cook prepared sandwiches, when Fortunato reappeared and announced, "The captain from the Peruvian Army is looking for you." He need not have said this, for the captain had followed him right into the kitchen. I offered him a beer.

The captain reported that he and some of his men had seen two persons attempting to hide near the gate of the parish house. When the captain and his men had approached, the two bolted. The soldiers managed to catch up to them and discovered that they were only teenagers, a girl and a boy. The boy was carrying a package with a revolver in it.

Fortunato broke into the conversation. He told us that this morning, as I was having breakfast, he had noticed that someone was watching me from across the street. This is why he had insisted that I take care.

"Do you remember the color of the man's jacket?" the captain asked. Fortunato remembered that it was black. The captain said that this was the same color as the jacket on the young man with the revolver. The captain described the girl as being of medium height, somewhat plump, with her hair curled tightly. My eyes met Fortunato's—we both knew that this was one of the terrorists from the Ene River valley who, some time ago, claimed to have shot and killed two policemen near city hall.

The air of Satipo was laden with intrigue, and I was suddenly eager to have Armando fly me back to Tzibokiroato.

274

CHAPTER NINETEEN

August 14, 1990. One of Sendero's tactics was to place children in the vanguard of an attacking force. This way, if the terrorists encountered a booby trap, they would not lose soldiers. So the appearance of a group of children hustling up the pathway on the southern approach to Tzibokiroato was the first sign the people had of the assault. These were a mixture of Ashaninka and Quechua children forced to cooperate with Sendero.

There were women with the children, and the group stopped at the yucca fields below the western edge of the airstrip and immediately began uprooting what yucca was left here. Claudia—Cecilia's sister and the woman who had betrayed Mario—was with them.

The natives at Tzibokiroato reacted quickly. Matías helped to organize the women and children and sent them off to the northeast, away from the direction of attack and up to our small, high fortress point.

The men, more or less under the leadership of Nicolás, moved off in the same direction, but only for a short distance, taking up positions past a line of huts in the hilltop forests along and above the eastern edge of the airstrip. From here, they believed they could fend off anyone who ventured past the yucca fields and onto the area of the landing strip.

Too late, the natives realized that they had ignored my orders to store our supplies at the high point. Below them, in and around the quickly abandoned huts, were machetes, axes, long-handled knives, and our boxes of food.

Nicolás and the others watched in silence as the terrorist brigade of women and children tore apart the yucca fields. Then, through their midst, the main party of attackers emerged. There were no more than thirty men, a mixed force of Quechua and Ashaninka, but they were experienced fighters. Moisés was there to show the way. His fourteen-year-old son was with him; I had always liked the boy—someone had nicknamed him Gringo.

Unchallenged, the terrorists strode onto the airstrip. Some bent to the task of setting dynamite charges to blow craters into the runway while others moved to huts at the far edge and began to systematically loot the supplies. They threw tools into sacks and hoisted cardboard boxes full of food onto their shoulders. They laughed and joked and cursed loudly at the Ashaninka.

Suddenly a shotgun blast broke the relative quiet. The marauders instinctively ducked for cover, but the range was too far, the weapons too weak.

Undaunted, the terrorists returned to their plunder. They examined our wheelbarrow, decided that it was too cumbersome to carry, and smashed it to pieces. Then they began to torch the native huts.

A few more shotgun blasts disturbed their party, but again, no damage was done.

Some of the terrorists realized that Moisés was hanging back, and they chided him, "Why don't you come out and fight? Don't hide this way." The strident calls echoed off the mountain faces but brought no response from Moisés, who must have been overcome by a sudden dread of the consequences should he be captured by his betrayed friends from Cuti.

By the time the Sendero raiding party was ready to leave, its backpacks were stuffed with our supplies. All of the huts near the airstrip were ablaze, and the precious yucca fields were destroyed. The terrorists, moving slowly downslope toward the Cutivireni River, in the general direction of Parijaro, were in a jovial mood.

But down below the noise of the attack had galvanized Shirampari into action. He guessed correctly what was happening, and he knew that the terrorists would have to return down the steep path and pick up the Cuti at a point very near his settlement. He assembled a small group of men, including his brother-in-law Carlos, Timoteo, and Andrés. Moving swiftly and silently along the banks of the Cuti, hopping from rock to rock, they ran past Parijaro and on to the east, halfway to Sankatiaro. They took up posts behind a natural fortress of immense boulders and waited for the terrorists to appear as they moved downriver.

When the Sendero band appeared in the distance, Shirampari signaled caution. He waited patiently until the main group was directly below, trapped in a narrow canyon. Then, the Ashaninka ambushers heaved grenades down upon the unsuspecting terrorists.

The attack took only an instant. Amid the roar of gunpowder and flashes of light, Shirampari saw bodies flying about (as he described in his own words) "as though a deck of cards had been tossed into the air." Shotgun blasts followed from both sides.

At least twenty terrorists were killed. Although Moisés escaped, he suffered severely, for among the dead were his lover Claudia and his son Gringo.

Shirampari's group lost one man.

I was at the airport at Satipo, talking with Armando, when a radio message came in from Nicolás, reporting the news of the attack and counterattack.

I was sick with agony and angry that Sendero had once more found a moment to strike when I was away from my people. I was concerned about the damage to the airstrip, worried that I might once more be cut off from access.

At first, I felt a surge of pleasure over the news that a number of terrorists were killed. Then, from the dark recesses of my memory a passage from a book I had read years before flashed into my mind: "It is indispensable that one must live according to how he thinks or else he will end up thinking the way that he lives." Like a persistent melody that you cannot shake, the words haunted me, and I thought once more: What a shame that it has come to this.

I heard that Colonel Espinoza, General Delgado's aide, was in

Mazamari, so I went immediately to see him.

I told him the news of this latest attack and suggested that now was a good time to fly into the area in search of terrorists.

He responded coolly, "How do we know that we can trust what you say?"

I was extremely upset, tired of receiving the runaround from everyone, and I told him so. I sputtered, "You know what I'm fighting for. I'm trying to save the natives from the terrorists. I've given you lots of information about where the terrorist camps are. Why don't we take a helicopter, pick up a few of the natives, and they'll *show* you?"

My tirade made sense to the colonel. The atmosphere eased, and suddenly we were on friendly terms. I told him of my fears concerning the airstrip at Tzibokiroato, and he promised to fly me over by helicopter the next day to assess the damage.

August 15. Confusion reigned. As the helicopter prepared for its mission, one or another officer came by every few minutes to countermand a previous order. No one seemed to know what anyone else was doing.

Three hours late, we took off, under the personal command of General Delgado. The pilot stopped at Sonomoro and another place somewhere on the Anapati River. I found myself disoriented; for some reason, it seemed as if someone had redrawn the map, and nothing was familiar.

Finally we flew over the Ene River valley. Shortly before we reached Cutivireni, we spotted a *casco*, a large dugout canoe, close to the riverbank. The helicopter pilot made a sharp descent toward this target, and the occupants quickly took to their heels, abandoning their boat and running for the cover of the jungle. When the pilot landed his craft on the riverbank, Peruvian soldiers jumped out and immediately formed a perimeter, training their machine guns at the surrounding brush.

With the area secure, the rest of us climbed out and surveyed the prize. The canoe held several bags of cacao, salted meat, a supply of clothes, a few dishes, and three outboard motors.

"All of this has been stolen from our mission at Cuti," I declared.

General Delgado ordered the soldiers to salvage what they could, especially the food and clothes, which we would parcel out to the natives once we reached Tzibokiroato. Someone suggested that the soldiers riddle the boat with machine-gun fire to sink it, and I was quite upset when the general unaccountably vetoed this idea. We loaded the supplies, including the motors, and took off once more, but it made no sense to me to leave the canoe intact.

When we finally arrived at Tzibokiroato, I was the only one who got off the helicopter. Not a single Ashaninka was there to greet us. I trudged over to the side of the airstrip and called out. My voice echoed off the face of the cliff.

After a few minutes, one of the natives suddenly appeared, slipping out from the cover of the jungle. Soon, several others joined him. They were happy to see me and in surprisingly good spirits. Nicolás excitedly recounted the battle for me, and he was obviously pleased about the success of Shirampari's ambush.

A few of the Peruvian soldiers cautiously exited the helicopter and passed out the supplies they had salvaged from the canoe. Then they accompanied me as I inspected the airstrip. I was pleased to see that the damage was minimal. I was sure that we could fill in the dynamite craters with very little labor and make the landing area safe once more. However, I was dismayed to realize that the terrorists had stolen many of the axes and wheelbarrows that I had brought in from Satipo to help construct the airstrip.

"Why didn't you store these things at the top, as we planned?" I asked angrily.

Nicolás shrugged.

All the houses near the airstrip had been torched. What's more, the terrorists had journeyed into the woods to locate my house and burn it down, too. It had been pretty well hidden, and I wondered how they knew which house was *mine*.

I did not have the luxury of time to ponder this mystery, for the general was in a hurry to leave.

"What would you prefer?" I asked Nicolás. "Should I stay with

279

you now? Or should I go back with the helicopter and try to get some help?"

Nicolás replied as Matías had earlier. There was little I could accomplish in Tzibokiroato now. It would be better for me to fly out and see what kind of support I could muster.

In the helicopter, we continued south through the Ene River valley. We stopped at Luisiana, a large, upriver naval installation. I remained by the helicopter as the general and his aides went into an office to discuss business. One of the sailors disclosed that a large operation was imminent, and a loose-lipped Sinchi confided further details: It was to be a massive, coordinated, three-pronged assault, designed to squeeze Sendero. A naval force would move out from Luisiana, traveling north, downstream along the Ene. Concurrently, the army would launch a force by helicopter from Puerto Ocopa, moving south, and a Sinchi contingent would travel by convoy from Mazamari and close in by land from the northwest.

This was the same as Mickey's plan, except that it ignored the most important point! It would box in the terrorists from the north, the west, and the south, but it left an escape route to the east. The *only* refuge for Sendero would be to head up the Cutivireni River in the very direction of Tzibokiroato.

Discreetly, I detailed the fourth and vital aspect of Mickey's plan to Colonel Espinoza. For the attack to succeed, they had to prepare a back-door ambush at Camantavesti. Colonel Espinoza listened to me with a bored expression on his face, and then dismissed the idea. The Peruvian Army was not about to take tactical advice from a padre.

On the return flight, we stopped at several small army camps. Each time, I remained in the helicopter as the general and his men checked with the local officers. At one of these camps, I spotted a group of about fifty Ashaninka on the far side of the airstrip. They had obviously taken refuge with the soldiers. Some of them recognized me. They yelled, "Mariano! Mariano!" and tried to approach the open door of the helicopter, but they were held back by sentries with machine guns. Seeing this, I hopped out of the helicopter and ran to meet them.

The natives surrounded me and chattered questions:

"Where are the people of Cuti?"

"What are we going to do now?"

"Where can we live in peace?"

I had no answers.

Late that afternoon, the helicopter left me off in Satipo, where I heard from three separate sources—one of them Fortunato—the details of General Delgado's supposedly secret plan.

So much for security, I thought.

Weeks passed in utter frustration.

In a desperate series of attempts to get *someone* to do *something*, I traveled to Satipo, Mazamari, San Ramón, and Lima, talking to whoever would listen. Felix and Bishop Ojeda showed great interest in my welfare but expressed little consideration for the sad drama being played out in the world of the Ashaninka.

General Velarde, the head of the Peruvian Air Force, promised that an air force helicopter would fly me to Tzibokiroato, where we would pick up a few natives and make the short hop across the Cuti to Las Tres Marías so that we could begin work on a new settlement, even more remote than Tzibokiroato.

I received Ambassador Quainton's response to my earlier letter, refuting the charges that he had passed on to Washington about me. His words were conciliatory:

May I assure you that I have the highest regard and admiration for you and your work. . . . I have never at any time regretted our efforts to assist you, nor have I said that you were responsible for any costs to the United States Government. I do not believe that you are, nor would I ever express such a feeling publicly if I did.

He said that his decisions were made with regard to my "safety and well-being," based upon his belief that my parishioners and I were in "grave danger."

I thought: Who are you trying to kid? Is this why you blew up our airstrip?

I showed Quainton's letter to a journalist named Gustavo Gorriti, who was writing a book about Sendero. (At a social event where we met not long after I received the ambassador's response, Quainton publicly incriminated me, shouting how I had dared to show the document to a journalist.) Gorriti was sympathetic to the needs of the Ashaninka and asked if he could go in with me on the air force helicopter.

In anticipation of the upcoming flight, Anabeli and Carlos—the NBC reporter and her cameraman—took me shopping to buy supplies for the natives. We stocked up on machetes, axes, knives, forks, and various trinkets that the Ashaninka would appreciate. Anabeli and Carlos insisted on paying for everything.

Loaded with supplies, Gustavo and I journeyed to Mazamari for the helicopter flight, scheduled for Sunday, September 9.

September 8. This time, the terrorist raiding party was led by Gonzalo, Virgilio, Taco, and Máximo, also known as Ciro. A large force of renegade Ashaninka stormed Tzibokiroato and, when the natives ran for cover, pursued them beyond the airstrip into the high-altitude jungle. Fierce fighting ensued. Several of the natives were killed, and the remainder abandoned the settlement altogether.

As the attackers pillaged what remained of Tzibokiroato, Nicolás, watching from the forest, marshaled a small group for a counterattack. He led his party of men around the back of the camp, circling well behind the inner end of the airstrip and across to the west to one of the spots we had scouted as a possible village site. From there, they cut south and worked their way down to a point on the banks of the Cutivireni. They set their ambush and waited in silence.

When the victorious rebels trudged below them, following the watercourse, Nicolás and his band unleashed a storm of grenades and shotgun fire. They were certain that they killed many of the terrorists, but they did not remain on the scene to count. Slipping back into the jungle, they made their way upriver along the lower slopes of the mountains.

No one wished to return to Tzibokiroato. Nicolás and his group found a suitable crossing point, waded over to the south bank of the Cutivireni, and set up camp at a point on the mouth of the Marioventi River.

Not far from them in distance, but at considerably higher altitude, Matías relocated the remaining refugees. The site was on the second-highest tier of Las Tres Marías, below the first cascade, but above the other two. This was Pearonchin.

At noon, unable to reach anyone in Tzibokiroato, I persuaded Armando to fly Gustavo and me over Tzibokiroato for reconnaissance. Although we were unable to see any activity from the air, we could confirm that the landing strip was still unusable. In fact, it appeared to be in worse shape than before. But where were the people? Gustavo and I stayed in Satipo that night, and Armando agreed to fly us to Mazamari very early the next morning to rendezvous with the air force helicopter.

I spent a troubled night, sick with worry over the sudden loss of contact. When I rose at 4:30 A.M. to pack for the trip, I heard the rains outside, pouring down in torrents, and I worried that storms would prevent Armando from getting us to Mazamari on time. Nevertheless, I set out in the midst of this downpour to walk to the airport. I was drenched before a friend stopped to offer me a ride.

Gustavo and I shared breakfast. At 8:00 A.M. we tried to reach the natives by radio, but were still unsuccessful.

Finally, the news came in that the terrorists had once more attacked Tzibokiroato, this time with greater success.

Hearing this, Armando piled us into his plane and took off despite the treacherous conditions. He made it to Mazamari, but the trip was anticlimactic. We waited in frustration until 4:30 P.M., when we were informed that the weather had forced air force officials to postpone the helicopter flight for one or two days.

"The natives must be desperate," I said to Gustavo.

Late in this frustrating day, I managed to contact Matías by radio. He reported his new location on the second plateau of Las Tres Marías and implored me to come. I asked him to attempt to fashion some sort of clearing large enough for a helicopter to land, and told him that I hoped to be there tomorrow.

Then I prayed for a break in the weather.

September 11. The helicopter pilot's uniform was soon soaked with nervous perspiration. As we neared Las Tres Marías, his eyes darted about, wary and fearful. I spotted a high-altitude clearing near Pearonchin, pointed, and cried out, "There!"

But the pilot ignored me. Seeing a group of Ashaninka clustered on the banks of the Marioventi River far below, he swooped down and landed.

Nicolás, Capitán, and several others immediately surrounded the craft. "Are these settlers or natives?" the pilot asked in a shaky voice.

"Natives," I reassured him.

Gustavo and I hopped off. Gustavo proved to be a fearless reporter, for he ignored any consideration of danger and immediately began questioning Nicolás and Capitán about the latest attack, noting their answers on his pad.

Nicolás said that he would show us Pearonchin, where Matías was. He attempted to scramble into the helicopter, with Capitán and the others at his heels, but the pilot growled at them to get off, saying that he would take only me up to the top of Las Tres Marías.

"It is very urgent that Nicolás come with us," I argued. "Let at least one of the natives come to show us the clearing. The pilot relented and allowed Nicolás back on board. Within seconds, we were airborne.

It took us only about three minutes to find and land at the clearing at the top of the mountains.

"We do not have enough fuel to wait," the pilot said tersely. "I will come to pick you up one week from now." I knew that his excuse was phony, for he had refueled in Mazamari and flown for barely half an hour since then, but I had no opportunity to debate, for he was already gone. I thought: He is scared shitless.

We saw the helicopter retreat to the banks of the Marioventi, pick up Gustavo, and then head directly back in the direction of Mazamari.

My reunion with Matías was joyful but brief. We immediately turned our attention to the urgent matters at hand. Sendero's latest bloody attack had engendered a fresh wave of panic. When we had relocated to Tzibokiroato, the site had seemed remote and invulnerable, but the terrorists had demonstrated their tenacity and the intensity of their hatred. The survivors were more certain than ever that violent death was to be their fate if they remained anywhere in this area. The people believed that there was no choice now but to flee the valley forever.

Matías told me that a few families had set out to attempt the overland trek across the Vilcabamba Range to the Urubamba, but a combination of heavy rains and formidable terrain had forced them to turn back.

The situation was critical. There was no yucca. The natives were preoccupied with the terrorist threat. They were in such a state of shock that they were unable to construct even tiny, temporary huts—or even think about planting yucca.

Someone wailed, "There is nothing we can do except escape to the Urubamba."

"Why don't we sleep on it?" I suggested. "In the morning, we'll decide what to do." I asked Matías to send scouts down to the other camp, with instructions to bring the men here in the morning for a meeting.

We had little food. I had brought additional supplies of tuna fish, pasta, and bouillon with me, but that was already gone. Some of the men produced the catch of the day, a supply of snails, with shells as large as three inches in diameter. The women placed them on the ashes of a fire and roasted them until they popped. I dug the innards out of one of these and slipped it into my mouth whole. The meat was chewy and bitter. Olga saw me grimace at the taste. Laughing, she showed me how to eat this delicacy. She extracted the meat from a shell and, with her thumb, flicked aside a small, black, baglike appendage—filled with excrement. I tried this tactic and muttered, "It's much better without the crap."

We also ate some ground worms, called *majo*. These were similar to *imoqui*, a type of white worm found in the rotten wood of the palm. The outer skin of the *majo* was hard, and one had to chew thoroughly before swallowing. The fatty meat tasted like unsalted bacon.

September 12. Matías repeated his statement that escape to the Urubamba was the only hope. The journey was rigorous at the best of times, and everyone knew that it was suicide to attempt the trip through the Cuchiri canyon during the rainy season. Could we make yet another stand here?

"I don't think the terrorists are that many," I counseled. "And they are completely awkward in hiking through the jungle. You have a tremendous advantage over them."

My listeners conceded that this was true. But it was not the traditional Sendero warrior that concerned them. Rather, it was the increasing number of Ashaninka who had been recruited for, or coerced into, the cause. "There are many natives with them now," someone said. "Practically all of Cutivireni has been taken over by the terrorists." The speaker was referring not merely to the area surrounding our burned-out mission but to the entire Cutivireni River basin.

Matías was well informed via the mysterious Ashaninka news network. Altogether, he estimated that Sendero now had about five hundred Ashaninka families sufficiently indoctrinated and trained to fight for its cause. Soon, that number would swell to a thousand, and this estimate did not take into consideration settlements and families about which Matías was uninformed.

Matías and I lit cigarettes to calm our nerves as we made a careful list of our assets. We now numbered forty-four families. We had thirty-two children under the age of six; sixteen of them were breast-feeding. We had several 12-gauge shotguns, one pistol, and six hand grenades. Our ammunition was critically low. The shotguns were assigned to the most trusted, capable fighters: Nicolás, Juan, Pablo, Timoteo, Julio, Alberto, Luis, Siverio, Capitán, Lucio, Lorenzo, and Matías himself. We also had Mickey's shotgun.

Teodoro had a 12-gauge shotgun given to him by a Sinchi and

Perera carried a 16-gauge shotgun loaned to him by the Wings of Hope pilot Enrique.

Matías said that the terrorists had an adequate food supply. They had 16-gauge shotguns, some Korean-made machine guns, .44 automatics, A-1 rifles, pistols, dynamite, and plenty of black grenades—the good kind.

In a low, quiet tone, Matías said that everyone was so desperate that they were ready to attempt an overland crossing to the Urumbamba. There was no way the young children could survive the journey, he said, so . . .

Our eyes locked. The Ashaninka love their children as deeply as any parents in the world. But the ways of the rain forest are severe; there, survival of the fittest is a concrete concept. Matías fought valiantly to keep the pain from his eyes, and yet he knew that he had to deal with the horror that must have shown in mine. He snuffed out his cigarette and looked away toward the ground, silently communicating brutal reality: It is better for some to die, so that the majority may live.

"How is the airstrip at Tzibokiroato?" I asked suddenly.

"It is covered with weeds and grass," he said. "But we filled in some of the holes before the last attack."

I spoke rapidly, determined to divert his attention: "You don't have any yucca. . . . There is no food. . . . You say you want to leave, but you can't cross to the Urubamba because of the rains. . . . We don't have much of a choice but to return to Tzibokiroato and try to fix up the airstrip. . . . We can hide in the woods. . . . A group of us can stand watch while others fix up the airstrip."

Matías knew that this would entail great risk. Already, the terrorists had attacked Tzibokiroato twice. Patching the airstrip was the only chance we had to get everyone—including the small children—out of the area. The problem was, Sendero knew this also. The terrorists would surely learn of our activity, and their anger would drive them to a swift and obviously final assault.

I asked how long the repairs would take. Matías thought that if everyone worked—including the children—we could finish in a day.

I offered, "I don't know if Armando would be willing to fly us

287

out. But if you want me to, I will call him."

Matías lit a fresh cigarette. His eyes narrowed in thought. Finally he nodded.

I raised Armando on the radio and asked, "If we repair the field at Tzibokiroato, would you be willing to make an airlift, to take the natives from here to the mission at Kiriketi?"

"There are very large holes in the airstrip," Armando commented. But then he added quickly, "If you can repair those, I will support you in any way I can." He asked, "How many flights would you need?"

I calculated quickly, figuring that we could jam about a dozen natives into Armando's plane. "At least twenty-five," I answered.

Armando explained the practical considerations. Via the direct route, he could make it from Tzibokiroato to Kiriketi in twenty-seven minutes. But the Vilcabamba Range was fourteen thousand feet high, and even the lowest passes were at twelve thousand feet. That altitude would tax the sensible limits of his Cessna. Given the special circumstances, Armando was willing to accept the calculated risk, but there was another problem. The Vilcabamba Range is almost always covered with a thick blanket of clouds. A pilot could, perhaps, abandon caution and attempt a crossing through the obscurity— once. If he was lucky, he would make it. But to attempt twenty-five such flights was suicidal. The alternate route was much safer but far more time- and fuel-consuming. Armando would have to take a circular path, backtrack over Satipo, and then cut north, where he could follow the Tambo River to the Urubamba. While this northern route would bypass the higher elevations of the Vilcabamba Range, it would take at least forty-five minutes of flight time—each way. On top of this, Armando would have to make frequent refueling stops in Satipo, since there were no facilities at Kiriketi.

The thought of such an extended operation scared me.

"We have to do this in the shortest possible time," I said.

"Yes," Armando replied. He thought that he might be able to recruit some Wings of Hope pilots to ferry gasoline to Kiriketi so he would not have to make refueling stops at Satipo. Armando vowed, "I give you my word. You fix the airstrip, and I'll be there."

I thought: Armando, you are the son I never had.

CHAPTER TWENTY

September 13, 1990. We sent out scouts to make sure that Sendero was not waiting for us. The rest of us left at 7:45 A.M., with the men in the lead and the women and children following. Hiking in single file, our group of desperate refugees traveled in solemn silence.

We headed west from Las Tres Marías down the mountain toward the banks of the Marioventi River. Heavy rains during the night had made the route very slippery, and I spent much of the first part of the journey on my backside.

About eleven o'clock we reached the Marioventi and crossed easily. Soon we were at the larger obstacle of the Cutivireni, and the sight of its frothing rapids was alarming. The river was very high. "This is good," I told Matías. "If the terrorists come upriver looking for us, it will be quite difficult for them to cross."

Matías knew that I was putting the best face on the situation— for it would also be difficult for us to cross. In fact, we worried that the swift current might be an impossible obstacle for the mothers with small children. Someone suggested that it would be easier to backtrack across the Marioventi and cross the Cuti farther upstream, before the Marioventi emptied into it. Matías sent a couple of young men to check out this alternate approach.

Earlier, one of the men in our advance group had killed a monkey, so we dined on monkey soup, yucca, and *piarinsti* as we awaited a report from our scouts.

Soon they returned, and reported that the plan was a good one. We set off on our trek, recrossing the Marioventi and tracking upstream past the juncture of the two rivers until we found a suitable spot to ford the Cuti. Once on the northern shore, we again turned west.

That afternoon we encountered impassable terrain. The cliffs on this side of the Cuti jutted out into the river, and we had to choose between climbing these or crossing the water. As we debated our course, the heavens opened and a deluge fell. "We have no time to waste," I cautioned. "Rain or no rain, we have to go." A group of men constructed a makeshift bridge. Working deftly with their axes, they cut notches into the trunks of several medium-sized trees on the side facing the river. Then they moved inland to a very large tree. A team of two men attacked this with axes, standing on either side, swinging in rhythm. Others stood ready to spell them. After many minutes of labor, when the tall trunk was leaning toward the river, the green wood split and cracked. The tree toppled, crashed into the smaller, notched trees nearer to the bank, and snapped them. With a roar and a gigantic splash, the trees fell into and across the Cuti.

This helped, but it bridged only a portion of the gap. Clinging to vines and to one another, we pulled and pushed our way across the churning, treacherous river.

We had to repeat this process at several points where the trail crisscrossed the river. It was very difficult, but I again tried to make light of our travail and reminded Matías that it would be difficult for the terrorists to follow us.

The closer we remained to the riverbank, the more anxious the Ashaninka became. They wanted the safety of the jungle cover. By evening we had moved inland, north of the Cutivireni.

September 14. This morning we again faced a choice. We could return to the riverbank and continue to follow the easier path, or we could strike out overland, through the trackless jungle. Overnight, paranoia had festered, and few wished to risk the visibility of the riverbank. I dreaded the excruciating toll that their preferred route would take on my sixty-one-year-old body, but it was a decision that I left up to Matías and the others.

First, we had to climb about a thousand feet up from the river-bank. The land was laced with a network of small tributaries, which had etched a series of canyons into the mountain. Our only course was to work our way up and down the faces of these foothills. Some were relatively easy; others were treacherous.

Once, as my feet flew from beneath me, I grabbed onto a tree limb and swung, like a chimpanzee, clinging for dear life, lest I tumble down the steep slope. I was able to inch my way to the trunk of the tree and shimmy down to safety. Soon after that I again lost my footing, slipped on a large, exposed tree root, and fell, splitting my lip and cracking my cheekbone against a rock. My face swelled as if I had the mumps. I was tempted to feel sorry for myself, but I glanced at the women who were making the same arduous jour-ney, carrying small children on their hips—silently enduring—and I felt ashamed.

By evening, we reached Julio's house at a mountainous point between the Maisanteni ("Sleeping Beauty") and the Sariteto ("Where the Sun Shines") rivers. Over a period of more than an hour, the three hundred members of our group gathered, and we settled in for the night. There was very little food, but to me, it hardly mattered. I was too exhausted to eat.

From here, Tzibokiroato was in easy reach, and we could send a party of workers to the airstrip tomorrow.

September 15. I awoke very early in the morning, but I lingered under the mosquito netting. My body ached from the rigors of the previous two days. I was surprised to learn that two groups had gone out already: one to work on the airstrip, the other to stand guard.

Everyone who was strong enough, women and children in-cluded, labored at the task.

Shortly after noon, I reached Armando on the radio. "The air-strip is fixed," I said, "and the sun is bright."

"I should be there by two this afternoon," he assured me.

As I was talking to Armando, a few of the Ashaninka returned with a welcome surprise. They carried the carcass of a huge *sajino*, a wild boar weighing about 150 pounds. That afternoon we enjoyed a good feast.

Precisely at 2:00 P.M., Matías and I stood at the repaired airstrip, staring to the west. Across the chasm and above, Las Tres Marías continued to spew forth its alluring cascades of water. Far below was the Cuti, which, during unrecorded centuries, had gouged out the canyon that separated us from the rest of the world. That canyon cut north, past Tzibokiroato, and then turned nearly ninety degrees left, to the west. It was the airspace above this canyon that we watched for several minutes, until a speck appeared in the distant sky. We knew that this was Armando's Cessna, but it could have been Tasorensi, the white-tailed hummingbird.

With an agonizing slowness, the speck grew larger until it assumed the shape of an airplane. The sound of its engine was faint but comforting.

Matías and I stepped to the side.

The small aircraft hovered in the air, slowing its approach as Armando lowered the modified flaps. He banked right, then left, following the curves of the canyon.

Armando calculated precisely, and the plane touched down only a few feet beyond the edge of the precipice. The Cessna bounced along the patched runway and came to a sure, safe stop.

Armando emerged from the cockpit, and we quickly discussed our strategy. Several people were in need of medical attention, and they had to go first, not to the Urubamba but back to the hospital in Satipo. There would be time only for one flight today; the evacuation would begin in earnest at the first light of dawn.

We piled Olga, Lupe, Cecilia, Antonia and her baby, and Jorge Luis into the plane. Antonia's baby was very ill, and I feared for her survival. Jorge Luis was strong and able, and I thought it would be useful to have Nicolás's son with the group; like his father, he was a leader.

Matías and the others suggested that I also go out on this first flight to make contact with Father Adolfo, to inform him that the Ashaninka were ready to accept the offer of the Machiguenga tribe to take refuge in the Urubamba. The idea filled me with ambivalence. I hated the thought of leaving the people at this moment, but I could see the logic. Despite our initial warm reception by the Machiguenga tribe, everyone was apprehensive about the situation.

Armando sealed the decision when he surprised us with the news: "Father Adolfo is in Satipo now. I saw him there."

"This is great," I replied. "Now I will be able to talk with him in person. Then I will come back with you to help evacuate the people."

Before I climbed into the plane, I issued instructions to Matías regarding the upcoming flights. "The sick and the women with the smallest children are to go out first," I said. "The men will be the last to leave. You and Nicolás will be the very last."

Matías nodded.

Armando knew that weight tolerances were critical, but he could only guess at the size of this load. During the takeoff run, he realized that the plane was heavy, but it was too late to turn back. We plunged off the edge of the cliff, diving earthward until we picked up enough speed to achieve lift.

The remainder of the flight was uneventful, and I passed it by pondering a solution to the weight problem. I thought of Rosita, the proprietor of a stationery store in Satipo—who sold damn good liquor on the side. I remembered that she had a large scale in her shop, and I decided to see if she would loan it to us.

That evening in Satipo, I sat in Fortunato's café, trying to decide whether to sip my beer or cry into it.

I had arranged for medical attention for the natives. I had met with Father Adolfo and cleared the way; he would fly to Kiriketi the first thing in the morning to prepare for the arrival of three hundred Ashaninka refugees. I had spoken with Enrique, who pledged that he and other Wings of Hope pilots would help. I had borrowed Rosita's scale.

Suddenly, there was nothing left to do except wait for Armando's first flight in the morning, and I was assailed—and surprised—by a bout of loneliness.

Armando spoke with me and accentuated my mood. He suggested that I remain here to coordinate the movements of his own aircraft with those of the Wings of Hope pilots. In Tzibokiroato, he said, there was nothing I could do. Someone had to be on hand in Satipo, near the radio. Someone had to make sure the refueling process was coordinated. Someone had to be ready to deal with any unforeseen snag.

I knew that Armando was right, and I agreed to his suggestion. But I added in my mind: Someone has to sit here and do nothing, and you, Mariano, are not very good at that.

CHAPTER TWENTY-ONE

September 16, 1990. Thirty-five minutes after leaving the airport at Satipo, Armando guided his Cessna through a brilliant blue sky, sprinkled with cotton puffs of white clouds, into the canyon-walled approach to Tzibokiroato. It was still very early in the morning. Once more he focused on the perilous airstrip. Gritting his teeth, he zeroed in on the mountaintop. This time, he came in a bit too fast. Seeing that he was about to overshoot the threshold, he cut his engine speed severely. The airplane dropped sharply for the final few feet and bounced heavily; the landing-gear struts absorbed the impact and held together. As the plane rolled to a stop, Armando berated himself for an unusually hard landing.

Matías directed the first stage of the evacuation, loading the Cessna with women and children who had never flown before. They were obviously nervous. This first flight of the day would be another hop to Satipo, rather than Kiriketi, for these passengers, too, were ill and injured. One of the women had spilled boiling water on her legs this very morning.

Using Rosita's scale, Armando calculated the maximum safe load, accounting also for the weight of his remaining fuel. He reasoned that this would be a quiet trip, for none of these natives spoke Spanish, and Armando did not understand a word of the Ashaninka language.

The pilot aimed the nose of his airplane toward the edge of the airstrip. He gunned the engine, disengaged the brakes, and felt the takeoff roll begin. A cockpit indicator warned him that the nose was angled down. He thought that this was due to the weight distribution toward the tail, and concluded that he would have to compensate by pulling back on the stick more than usual.

As the craft careened off the edge of the abyss, it dipped quickly, eliciting gasps from those on board. Immediately Armando felt an extraordinary pressure on the stick, fighting him for control. Airspeed fell off quickly, and the aircraft plunged downward, threatening to spin. Armando battled the stick, trying to determine the cause of the problem. The resistance was worse than he had foreseen, and it could not be from an overload toward the tail. He thought that perhaps a small piece of wood or a branch had become lodged in the stabilizer.

Using all the strength in his arms, Armando pulled the stick back and leveled off the aircraft as it slid through the canyon. But he knew that this was a temporary solution, for he was straining every muscle and could not possibly maintain the necessary grip on the controls for very long.

Something is very wrong, he realized, *and I do not know what it is.*

He jammed his knees underneath the front of the stick and braced his feet against the floor. In this way, he was able to augment the visegrip of his fingers. But he did not know how long he could maintain this unnatural position. Already, his muscles were feeling excruciating spasms of pain.

Perspiration poured off of his brow, trickling into his eyes, but he could not wipe it away, could not remove a hand from the controls for an instant. Somehow, he managed to steer a path around the meandering walls of the canyons that flanked the Cutivireni.

He considered returning to Tzibokiroato, but he quickly discarded the plan. The airstrip was barely negotiable under the best of conditions, and he could not possibly land a stricken plane there.

With a sense of wonder, he realized that the terrain of the

mountaintop airstrip had saved their lives—at least initially. The plunge from the cliff had enabled the craft to maintain enough airspeed to avoid a stall.

What is wrong? he wondered. But there was no way to find out as long as he was in the air.

He looked at the terrain a few thousand feet below. The only flat land was near the riverbanks, and he considered an emergency landing. No, he thought, that would almost certainly be suicide; terrorists were all around. His only hope was to make it to the nearest airfield—and that was the military base at Mazamari, some thirty minutes distant.

Armando risked freeing one hand. He grabbed for the radio microphone and contacted his brother in Satipo. He explained what he could about the problem and reported, "I will try to get to Mazamari. Tell them to please clear the runway."

The passengers realized that the airplane was in trouble, but Armando had neither the time nor the language skills to explain the situation. He wished that the passenger sitting to his right was a man, who could perhaps help to apply the strength needed to keep the plane level. But there were no men aboard. Armando was on his own. His only hope was to attempt the nearly impossible feat of making it to Mazamari.

Within minutes Armando's arms and legs were numb. Within a few more minutes he *knew* that the pain was more than he would be able to bear. But somehow he held on. There was simply no alternative. By the time he approached Mazamari, his entire body was without feeling.

Up ahead, soldiers and airmen awaited, ready to run to the rescue.

As Armando eased back on the throttle, slowing the airspeed prior to landing, the controls became easier to manage. But by now his feet were too weak to work the rudder pedals properly.

The airstrip came up to meet him. He bounced the Cessna onto the landing field. It swerved back and forth as it journeyed down the runway—and finally it came to a stop.

Armando opened the door, tumbled out, and collapsed onto the ground, sobbing in pain. His body was twisted from stomach cramps. Tears poured down his cheeks.

"His pulse is very, very low," a military doctor warned.

Armando realized that he was in the first-aid station at the Mazamari base. The doctor massaged his sore limbs; others poured liquids into him.

Armando's brother, nicknamed Pollo ("Baby Chick"), flew the natives from Mazamari to Satipo in his own plane. He was especially concerned about getting proper medical attention for the woman who was suffering from scald burns.

Meanwhile, Armando slowly gathered his strength, and by afternoon he was able to return to the aircraft. He examined the stabilizer assembly, but could find nothing wrong there. Finally he determined that the problem was in the equalizer. He disassembled this, found a broken pin, and assumed that the force of his landing at Tzibokiroato must have shattered it. It was only a tiny fracture in a small part, but it had nearly caused a tragedy. Armando inserted a nail in the place of the pin, tested his plane, and found that it functioned normally. Although he was exhausted and aching from the aftereffects of his painful ordeal, he climbed back into the cockpit and flew on to Satipo.

I had spent a frustrating, seemingly endless day in Satipo, assuming that the evacuation was proceeding as planned. In the morning, I moped about the mission house, trying not to think about my personal dilemma, berating myself for selfish concerns. What was to become of me? I wondered. The Ashaninka were on their way to a Dominican mission. My life's work—my passion—was flying away from me.

To soothe my mind, I stepped outside into the central plaza of Satipo. The peacefulness of the day belied the clandestine nature of this troubled town on the border between civilization and savagery. Which direction, I wondered, was civilization? Did it lie to the west, in Lima, with its skyscrapers, banks, politicians, and late-twentieth-century luxuries? Or did it lie to the east, where the dream of the Ashaninka was to live in simplicity?

298

I walked diagonally across the plaza to Fortunato's café. My good friend and I shared a couple of beers and spoke, not of my future, but of that of the Ashaninka. Would the people of Cuti be happy in the Urubamba? Or would they pine for their own lands? Would they be safe from Sendero, or would the authorities push the devil across the Vilcabamba Range? Was the past behind us, or was it merely prologue?

And what about the rest of the Ashaninka? Even after the Cuti refugees evacuated, another twenty thousand natives—no one could know the precise number—would remain in the valley. Many were already victims of Sendero, and others stood directly in the way.

"I have never felt so helpless," I confided to Fortunato.

My giant friend smiled sympathetically. Fortunato was more of a listener than a talker, but he ventured the comment, "You did the right thing."

Late in the afternoon I made my way to the Satipo airport, knowing that Armando would arrive before nightfall, after his day of work. I was surprised to find him already there, along with Pollo, and listened intently to the story of his brush with death.

"I am going to buy dinner for both of you," I said.

At the restaurant Armando said that he would be ready to resume the evacuation flights the next day. "If you are too tired, you can wait," I suggested politely, hoping that he would not agree. "If you don't feel better tomorrow—"

"I am ready," Armando interrupted.

Coincidence?

Dumb luck?

Divine intervention?

Call it what you will. The Vilcabamba Range between Tzibokiroato and Kiriketi is almost *always* obscured by clouds; a clear day is an aberration. But as Armando's Cessna took off the next morning, Sunday, the clouds dispersed and the skies opened wide. Armando could now fly the direct route, cutting an hour-and-a-half trip to twenty-seven minutes.

Tasorensi is taking care of us, the natives proclaimed.

Armando flew steadily for the next two days, from 6:00 A.M. to 6:00 P.M., with little time for rest. He was impressed with the manner in which Matías, Nicolás, and some of the others organized the evacuation. Each time, the plane was loaded with fearful men and women who had never flown before. They carried what few belongings they could, a pot or a pan, a machete, a bit of cloth, a bunch of green bananas. Their faces showed tension as the Cessna plunged off the edge of the cliff, and they remained in a state of shock throughout the flight, their anxiety compounded by the journey to a new and unknown destination.

During each short hop, Armando's passengers did not show any effects from the scarcity of oxygen at high altitude, but Armando suffered from the accumulated lack of adequate air. The long hours of concentrated attention drained his mental energies. Exhaustion swept over him.

At the end of each flight, when Armando delivered his charges to the Dominican mission at Kiriketi, Father Adolfo and several Machiguenga greeted them warmly. Lucas, upon learning of the evacuation, had chartered a plane from Mazamari to Kiriketi and was on hand, offering his help wherever it was needed.

During each turnaround, Armando climbed on top of the wings of his plane, accepted buckets of gasoline hoisted up to him, and filled the tanks. Then he was off on another trip, wasting no time.

September 18. If the weather held, Armando could complete the evacuation today. He estimated that seven more flights would accomplish the task. Then he would return to Satipo and make a final trip to Kiriketi, taking me along.

This morning, by radio, Matías informed me of a complication. Lucio had decided to disarm a booby trap along the trail in order to salvage an old shotgun. As he attempted to disengage the trip wire, he was distracted by a girl and began to flirt. The shotgun roared and the pellets tore into his right hand and arm. Lucio had lost a great deal of blood.

"Get him out on the first flight," I instructed. "There are doctors waiting at Kiriketi."

300

Armando set about his work, thankful that the sky remained clear over the Vilcabamba Range. He got one load of passengers out and hurried back for more.

After the sixth flight of the day, only five Ashaninka remained at Tzibokiroato. Matías and Nicolás stared out over the gorge, waiting anxiously for Armando to return one last time. Matías shifted his gaze across and down and suddenly saw a party of terrorists watching from the other side of the canyon. As we had feared, Sendero had noted the comings and goings of Armando's Cessna.

Matías was convinced that Moisés was over there, glaring in frustration. He estimated that it would take the terrorists little more than an hour to reach them. "If the plane doesn't come in time, do we run away?" he asked Nicolás.

"What if they grab the pilot?" Nicolás asked in response.

When Matías reached me by radio and asked me these same questions, I could hear panic in his normally calm voice. I instructed, "Leave the supplies. When Armando arrives, get on the plane and get out!"

Soon Armando's plane bounced to its final heavy landing. Matías, Nicolás, and the others scrambled aboard, leaving behind a few machetes, axes, pots, and pans—and Rosita's scale. Armando revved his engine and took off for Kiriketi.

As the Cessna cleared the Vilcabamba Range, the clouds, which had parted two days earlier, closed in behind them.

301

PART FOUR

The Parting

CHAPTER TWENTY-TWO

September 19. At Kiriketi, I celebrated a mass of thanksgiving, attended by all the Ashaninka who had come from Tzibokiroato, as well as by many of their Machiguenga hosts. So many came that we could not pack them all into into the wooden pews of Father Adolfo's chapel. As I conducted the service, wearing a *cushma* and a white stole, natives pressed close to the doorway, peering inside. In my sermon, I thanked the mission, the Dominican bishop, the authorities of the town, and all of the Machiguenga for their warm reception. "We had to leave everything behind," I said, "but we have a lot to be thankful for in finding such true friendship among our paisanos. You can buy pots and pans. You can plant yucca. But one thing you cannot buy is true friendship. The outside world could learn a lot from you people."

After the service, we gathered in a meetinghouse directly across from the chapel. Matías, as representative of the Ashaninka, spoke for quite some time, recounting the tribulations of his people. He stressed that it was not their intention to be *una carga* ("a burden") upon the Machiguenga.

When Matías was finished, Flavio, the teacher from Cuchiri, delivered the admonition: "We have to help one another." He said that it was not necessary for the Ashaninka to move far from the Machiguenga settlements, "where there is no yucca. We will welcome you next door, and help until you can grow your own yucca."

305

Later, I met with Ciro Miranda, a representative of the Center for the Development of the Amazonian Indian, based in Lima, who showed me on a map several sites where the Ashaninka might relocate. He said that he would see to it that they received title to the lands in question.

September 22. Groups of Ashaninka, in boats provided by Father Adolfo, began making their way up the Pavoreni River in search of new homelands. Each boat was equipped with a small Briggs & Stratton engine, a type that the natives called *pecca-pecca* because of the distinctive woodpeckerlike noise that it made.

Father Adolfo recorded the exodus on videotape.

Finally the last boat was ready, and I watched them board: Matías and Olga, Carlos and his family, and a few others. One of the women carried a huge supply of bananas on her back. They stepped over smooth stones, waded into quiet waters, and positioned themselves in the slim, elongated boat. I laughed as a little boy hiked his *cushma* up over his round, bare bottom in order to scramble aboard. The solitary figure of Capitán straddled the prow so that he could watch for low areas and advise which way to steer. The boat moved toward the center of the river, under the side of a striated cliff guarding the far bank.

I felt an immense sadness, even though I knew that the Ashaninka would be safe and well here in the Urubamba and that Father Adolfo would nurture them.

As I lit what I vowed would be my last cigarette ever, I prayed, Dear God, I'm sure there is a reason for this. I don't understand it at all. But never have I believed so much in Thee.

Matías turned and waved at me from the retreating boat, and over the purr of the *pecca-pecca*, he called out softly, *"Jatajana"* ("Good-bye").

I returned his wave and stood watching until the boat moved out of view, around a bend in the river.

I found a clearing nearby and sat alone on top of an immense rock, put my head into my hands, and cried like a baby.

EPILOGUE

*T**he three hundred* Ashaninka who migrated to Cuchiri are doing well there, although they someday hope to return to the Cutivireni area.

Meanwhile, the Peruvian Army has moved into Cuti and utilized some of the foundations of the mission's burned-out buildings to construct a jungle base of operations against Sendero. The new base has become a sanctuary for many of the Ashaninka seeking refuge from the horror that pervades the Ene River valley.

Michel Saenz solved his visa problem and returned to Peru where he is once again working on the proposal to have Cutivireni designated as a national park. Beyond this, Mickey has also made a significant contribution to the Ashaninka by founding a house in Satipo where visiting natives can stay; there is even a private yucca field.

Armando Velarde Torres continues to operate his flying service out of the Satipo airport.

I have little doubt that Lucas Adins was with the CIA from the very beginning, planted by the Americans in our mission at Cuti with orders to somehow penetrate the top echelons of the drug traffickers, with no consideration for the effects of his presence upon the Ashaninka and the mission. But I have no proof.

September 12, 1992. At 9:00 P.M., a Peruvian antiterrorist unit raided a house in the middle-class Lima neighborhood of Surco and captured eight Sendero leaders, including the notorious Abimael Guzmán himself. After a dozen years of insurrection, Guzmán's war was estimated to have cost Peru twenty-five thousand deaths and twenty-two billion dollars in damages.

Guzmán was taken quietly, and reportedly said, "My turn to lose."

My provincial, Felix, strongly suggested that I go "back to the States for a time." Bishop Ojeda made it clear that my services were no longer required in the vicariate, adding a threatening note that should I persist, he would withdraw my priestly faculties.

Why? I wondered. Did Bishop Ojeda fear Sendero's threat to wreak vengeance upon anyone helping the Ashaninka? Was he still concerned about the press coverage that depicted me as a "Pistol Packin' Padre"? Had he succumbed to unfathomable pressure from the American embassy? I did not know, and no one would tell me.

Eventually I learned, from sources whom I consider highly reliable, that U.S. ambassador Anthony Quainton had contacted the papal nuncio, the Vatican's representative to Peru. Apparently the nuncio then contacted Bishop Ojeda, whereupon I was "encouraged" to leave.

Felix advised me to think about taking a course, perhaps at Catholic University in Washington. He noted that there had been many changes in theological outlook and Church practice since Vatican II.

I thought ruefully: Felix, you should practice what you preach.

I did return to the United States, primarily to tell the Ashaninka's story to the world. Upon the completion of this project, I hope to resume my work in Peru and perhaps rebuild the mission of San José de Cutivireni yet again.

I pray that I can do this with the blessing of my superiors.

INDEX

Montaro, Martín, 133
Moya (Gagnon's friend), 91

Natasha (Ashaninka), 28, 41
National Geographic Society, 93
native populations, Spanish
  subjugation of, 12–13, 18,
  201–214
  see also specific groups
NBC, 254, 255, 256, 259, 264, 282
New Testament, Ashaninka
  translation of, 27
Nicolás (Ashaninka), 36, 39, 41, 53,
  80, 88, 174, 268
  at Cubeja, 155–156, 157, 159, 167,
    168, 169, 172
  education of, 37, 235
  personality of, 37, 42, 60, 74
  terrorist actions and, 170, 172,
    173, 235, 250, 271–272, 275,
    276, 277, 279–280, 282–283,
    284, 286
  at Tzibokiroato, 235, 236, 250,
    266, 270
  Urubamba move and, 292, 293,
    300, 301
  weapons supplies and, 177, 260
Nóbrega, Manuel de, 202

obedience, vow of, 198, 216
Obenteni, Franciscan mission at, 35
Ojeda, Julio, 67, 90–91, 156, 218,
  221–223, 239, 266, 281, 308
Olarte, Father, 214
Ortiz, Father, 83
ownership, Ashaninka concept of,
  40–41, 45, 52, 138

Pablo (Ashaninka), 36, 174, 258, 286
Paino, Alfredo, 93, 252
Pan American Union, 29
Paniso, Admiral, 251, 252
parachute jumping, 22–23, 31,
  227–228
Paraguay, Catholic Church in, 248
Pardo, Anna, 220
Pardo, Christina, 199, 219–220
Pardo, Francisco, 189

Pardo, Jamie, 156, 189–190, 192,
  220, 221
Pardo, Javier, 96, 156, 199, 220
Pardo, Juan, 30, 39, 189
Pardo, Mari, 30, 39
Pardo family, 30, 129
Parijaro, Ashaninka settlement near,
  93, 139–140, 141–148, 186, 269,
  276–277
Parque Nacional de Cutivireni, 29
Paul, Saint, 270–271
Paulino (Ashaninka), 259
Paul VI, Pope, 26, 215
Pedro (Quechua), 37–39
Pereira (drug trafficker), 75–76
Pérez, General, 91, 121
Peru:
  climate of, 11
  coca usage in, 54–55; *see also*
    cocaine trade
  communist intelligentsia of, 12
  earthquake relief program in, 42
  economic distribution in, 54, 94
  first missionaries in, 211–212
  Franciscans in, 18, 20, 211–212; *see
    also* Franciscans, Franciscan
    missions
  government corruption in, 76, 77,
    80
  history of elitism in, 12–13, 30
  Indian groups of, 11, 18, 19, 41,
    51–52, 53; *see also* Ashaninka;
    Machiguenga; Quechua
  land distribution in, 51, 52–53, 54
  national elections in, 64, 112
  rain forests destroyed in, 54, 61
  school curriculum in, 41
  secret police of, 70, 71–72
  Spanish control of, 12–13, 18
  upper class families of, 30
Peruvian Air Force, 91, 92, 93, 94,
  121, 126, 187, 216
Peruvian military forces:
  in assault plans against Sendero,
    13, 192–193, 197, 280, 281
  cocaine trade and, 56–57, 75, 76
  conscription in, 65, 243
  at Cuti, 67–72, 96, 307

317

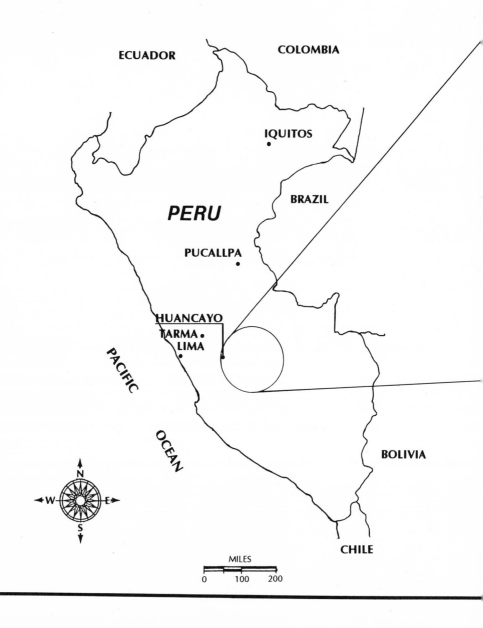

ECUADOR

COLOMBIA

IQUITOS

PERU

BRAZIL

PUCALLPA

HUANCAYO
TARMA
LIMA

PACIFIC

OCEAN

BOLIVIA

N
W E
S

CHILE

MILES
0   100   200